# GUNS, SAILS, AND EMPIRES:

Technological Innovation and the Early Phases
of European Expansion 1400-1700

# GUNS, SAILS

# AND

# EMPIRES:

Technological Innovation and the Early Phases
of European Expansion 1400-1700

# CARLO M. CIPOLLA

MINERVA PRESS

© 1965, by Carlo M. Cipolla

Published by arrangement with Pantheon Books.

Library of Congress Catalog Card Number: 66–13017

Funk & Wagnalls Publishing Company, Inc.

5—73

ISBN 0-308-60014-2

# PREFACE

I am an inveterate pacifist since while I recognize that wars and revolutions are one way of settling human affairs I am inclined to believe that they are neither a rational nor a polite one. I am also a poor sailor, and as soon as I set foot on board a ship, I am apt, after a few minutes, to feel more sickly dead than deadly sick. The first person to be utterly surprised at having written a book entitled " Guns and sails " is most definitely the author, and readers may feel confident that the book is neither magnetized by some Freudian attraction for weapons nor biased by an ancestral love for salt water. The book has been written simply because, in studying the history of the early modern period the author was forced, by over-whelming evidence, to recognize, against his tastes and inclinations, the importance of guns and sails.

As Professor Panikkar wrote, " the 450 years which began with the arrival of Vasco da Gama in Calicut (in 1498) and ended with the withdrawal of British forces from India in 1947 and of the European navies from China in 1949 presents a singular unity in its fundamental aspects. These may be briefly stated as the dominance of maritime power over the land masses of Asia and the domination of the peoples of Europe who held the mastery of the seas ". The " Vasco da Gama era " is now over. Our generation is witnessing the end of it and the beginning of another age. We do not know what lies ahead. But we are in a good position to look back and try to understand what the " Vasco da Gama era " has been and what it has meant in the history of mankind. This book is devoted to the study of what made it possible.

The research work took in most of the inhabited areas of the globe and covered more than three centuries. The abundance of the historical material would be overwhelming for a single historian. I have had to call on many distinguished colleagues and friends for help. This has been so generous and so important that the book is in many respects more the product of a joint effort than the fruit of the labours of one person only. If only one name appears on the cover, the justification is that there is only one person who is responsible for the mistakes the book contains, and that is the person who had decided to put them into printed form.

The Italian Ministry of Education and the Department of Economics of the University of Turin were good enough to give me leave of absence for preparing this book. The Universities of Lund and Göteborg obligingly invited me for a semester in Sweden. Many things impressed me during my visit to Sweden, most of all the kindness and generosity of my colleagues and friends at the Institutes of Economic History in Göteborg, Lund, Stockholm and Uppsala. I am much indebted to Prof. A. Attman, O. Bjurling, E. F. Söderlund and Dr. G. Utterström. I have especially great obligations to my good friends Dr. L. Jörberg and K. Olsson at Lund who gave me a hand while I was struggling with Swedish texts and documents. My thanks are also due to R. Adamson, I. Nygren, I. Svensson, K. Bengmark, O. Cederlöf, Mrs. I. Schiller. Mr. G. Fredin in Uppsala brought to my attention the documents of the Cronberg's administration on which he was working. From Belgium I received the help of F. L. Ganshof, A. Arnould, J. Bovesse and E. Helin. Prof. Virginia Rau of Lisbon and Dr. Jordi Nadal of Barcelona supplied me with Portuguese and Spanish materials. Miss A. M. Millard investigated for me some of the Port Books at the Public Record Office in London. At the University of California I thoroughly exploited all those who had the misadventure of either being my friends or inadvertently falling into the radius of my action. I was helped by my learned friend

Gregory Grossman, by Dr. T. A. Hsia, Mr. R. G. Irwin, Prof. E. Sluiter, Prof. D. M. Brown, and Dr. M. Desai. Extremely efficient in my parasitic endeavour, I also exploited some of my graduate students: I. Sengün from Turkey, M. A. Loufti from Egypt, S. Y. Kwack from Korea, Miss P. H. Cottingham, R. A. Pollmann, R. W. Roehl, J. R. Schauer, S. L. Lanfranco and W. H. Sewell.

Among those who helped me in the research were also Dr. F. Dahl of the University Library at Lund (Sweden), Miss Raquel Pousão Lopes, director of the Arquivo Historico Ultramarino of Lisbon, Dr. Vogal-Nato and Dr. Alberto Iria of the Centro de Estudos Historicos Ultramarinos in Lisbon, and Dr. Yurii Klokman of the Academy of Sciences of the U.S.S.R. in Moscow.

J. Guthrie was good and patient enough to read the two main chapters of the book and improve upon my poor and broken English. Ph. Grierson, R. Ollard, C. Poni and A. Pepelasis gave me all kind of help and information. My secretary Franca Zennaro has acquired new titles for a prominent place in the history of martyrdom. To all of them I wish to extend the expression of my gratitude.

# CONTENTS

# ILLUSTRATIONS

*following page* 96

PAX MULTA IN CELLA,
FORIS AUTEM PLURIMA BELLA

# PROLOGUE

On the 28th day of May 1453 the Turks entered Constantinople. All Europe trembled overwhelmed by amazement and dismay. "A thing terrible to relate, and to be deplored by all who have in them any spark of humanity, and especially by Christians" —wrote Cardinal Bessarion to Francesco Foscari, Doge of Venice—"A city which was so flourishing, with such a great empire, such illustrious men, such very famous and ancient families, so prosperous, the head of all Greece, the splendour and glory of the East, the school of the best arts, the refuge of all good things, has been captured, despoiled, ravaged, and completely sacked by the most inhuman barbarians and the most savage enemies of the Christian faith, by the fiercest of wild beasts . . . Much danger threatens Italy not to mention other lands, if the violent assaults of the most ferocious barbarians are not checked".

One can easily understand the shock experienced by contemporary Europeans and the wave of fear that the event spread throughout Europe [1]. Yet, there was nothing essentially new. Europe had lived a chronically precarious life throughout the centuries of the Middle Ages always at the mercy of potential invaders. Granted, things were not so bad in the later as they had been in the early Middle Ages. The Moslems had been completely expelled from the Iberian Peninsula as well as from Southern France and Southern Italy. The

[1] The Turkish menace was the thing about which fifteenth- and sixteenth-century Europeans were most deeply concerned. Among the books printed in France between 1480 and 1609 the titles relating to the Turks and the Turkish Empire were twice as many as the titles relating to the Americas. Cf. Atkinson, *Horizons*, p. 10. Shortened versions of the titles of works cited are used throughout this book. Full titles appear in the bibliography.

Vikings and the Hungarians had been assimilated. Large territories had been acquired east of the Elbe river. However, the general balance of power had not turned in favour of Europe, and in the long run the Europeans remained on the defensive.

The Crusades should not mislead us. The success that characterized the first phases of the European attack was largely due to surprise and to the temporary weakness and disorganization of the Arab world. As Grousset once said it was the victory of "French monarchy over Moslem anarchy", but the Moslem forces were soon reorganized and the Europeans had quickly to retreat[1]. Echoing a speech by Urban II and summing up the experience of the First Crusade, William of Malmesbury wrote: "This little portion of the world which is ours is pressed upon by warlike Turks and Saracens: for three hundred years they have held Spain and the Balearic Islands and they live in hope of devouring the rest".

The aggressiveness and success in expansion that the West showed after the eleventh century on the commercial plane, did not have a counterpart in the military and political field. The disaster of Wahlstatt in 1241 dramatically proved that Europe was militarily incapable of coping with the Mongol menace[2]. If Europe was not invaded, it was because of the timely death of the Mongolian chief (death of Ögödäi, December 1241) and because, in the long run the Khans were more attracted by the South and the East than by the West[3]. In the following century, the defeat of the Christians at Nicopolis (1396) showed once again the military weakness of the Europeans in face of Eastern invaders. Again Europe was saved by purely fortuitous circumstances: Bāyāzed, the conqueror, got involved with the Mongols of Timur Leuk (Tamerlane) and one potential danger luckily and unexpectedly

[1] Among many cf. Lewis, *Arabs*, pp. 150-2.
[2] On the military superiority of the Mongols cf. Sinor, *Mongols*, pp. 45-6.
[3] Cf. Sinor, *Mongols*, pp. 46 and 59-61.

eliminated the other. In the fifteenth century Europe was still under the pressure of Turkish attack, and although at times capable of slowing down the advance of the enemy, she never succeeded in stopping it altogether.

The reasons for the chronic weakness of medieval Europe are clear enough. To begin with, the Europeans were not very numerous (never more than 100 million people). More important than that, they were divided and constantly busy in " waging wars against each other, staining their hands with the blood of their own people, defiling their arms with the blood of Christians ". When composite armies were put together the main result was general confusion. Last but not least, the military organization of the European potentates was far from being efficient. Europe and more especially Eastern Europe relied on heavily armoured cavalry which was colourful but unwieldy. As has been said, " European nobility sacrificed tactics and strategy for the impossible dream of striking heavily at the enemy while remaining invulnerable "[1]. For one reason or another, throughout the Middle Ages, Europe's main hope of survival continued to be placed in large measure in the hands of God.

After the fall of Constantinople things became progressively worse. The Turkish advance continued powerful and seemingly irresistible. Northern Serbia was invaded in 1459. Bosnia-Herzegovina in 1463-6. The Negroponte was taken from the Venetians in 1470. Albania was invaded after 1468. " I cannot persuade myself that there is anything good in prospect "—wrote Pope Pius II—" Who will make the English love the French? who will unite the Genoese and the Aragonese? who will reconcile the Germans with the Hungarians and Bohemians? If you lead a small army against the Turks

[1] Lot, *Art militaire*, p. 429. On the inferiority of the heavily armoured western cavalry in comparison with the light eastern cavalry cf. Sinor, *Mongols*, pp. 45-6. This author stresses the fact that the brave, colourful but highly individualistic western knight was a poor opponent to the strictly disciplined and highly obedient eastern horsemen. Cf. also the remarks by Moryson, reproduced below in chapt. 2, footnote 1, p. 91.

you will easily be overcome; if a large one, it will soon fall into confusion".

Yet, at the moment when the enemies of Christendom seemed to be striking at the very heart of Europe, a sudden and revolutionary change occurred. Outflanking the Turkish blockade, some European nations launched successive waves of attack over the oceans. Their advance was as rapid as it was unexpected. In little more than a century, the Portuguese and the Spaniards first, the Dutch and the English later, laid the basis of world-wide European predominance.

Some decades ago it was fashionable to argue that the oceanic exploration and expansion of Europe in the second half of the fifteenth century were the direct consequence of the advance of the Turks who had interrupted the flow of spices to Europe via the Near East. This view was an excellent piece of historical naiveté and it actually proved to be totally incorrect [1], however, as it often happens, mixed with the error, one may possibly find also a grain of truth. One way to look at the European quest for the direct routes to the Spice Islands and the coasts of West Africa is to consider these phenomena as an aspect of the tension between the economic expansion of Europe and the military and political blockade that was imposed upon her.

However, no matter how strong the tension, the motive is one thing and the instrument by which the motive can be transformed into effective and successful action is quite another. The need to outflank the Moslem blockade and reach the Spice Islands was already felt in the thirteenth and four-teenth centuries. But the fact that the Atlantic expeditions of the brothers Vivaldi and of Jaime Ferrer failed, is a proof—if a proof is needed—that although there were " motives ", the necessary " means " were not available [2]. It has also been

[1] Cf. Godinho, *Expansão*, pp. 27-40 and Godinho, *Economia*, pp. 51-68. For a recent defence of the old theory cf. Colenbrander, *Coen*, vol. 6, pp. 10-17.

[2] Cf. Godinho, *Découvertes*, pp. 15-20.

written that the Europeans "went into Asia in a spirit of determination to succeed which was stronger than the will of the Asiatic people to resist" and that this mainly accounted for European success[1]. But no spirit of determination, strong as it may be, is enough to win a battle if the necessary means are not available. The brothers Vivaldi certainly did not lack the "spirit of determination", but their galley was not fitted to brave the oceans. Why did Renaissance Europe succeed where the Europeans of the thirteenth and fourteenth centuries failed? Why, after the end of the fifteenth century were the Europeans able not only to force their way through to the distant Spice Islands but also to gain control of all the major sea-routes and to establish overseas empires? What allowed the Europeans to accomplish the dramatic and sudden transition from a state of insecure defence to that of bold and aggressive expansion? Why did the "Vasco da Gama era" come into being?

[1] Sansom, *Western World*, pp. 68-9 whose views are shared by Boxer, *Portuguese*, pp. 196-7.

CHAPTER I

# THE EUROPEAN SCENE

1—As early as the first decades of the fourteenth century
Europeans began to use cannon in warfare. Florentine official
documents refer to the acquisition of "*pilas seu palloctas
ferreas et canones de mettallo*" in 1326 (see p. 32) thus
indicating that by that date bronze guns shooting iron balls
were already in use. In 1327 an illuminated manuscript was
produced in England containing the picture of what is undoubtedly a very primitive gun (see p. 32). Unfortunately
the text makes no reference to the illustration, but at the
Statens Historiska Museum of Stockholm there is a rare piece
which corresponds to the gun of the Millimete manuscript[1].
This is the earliest evidence of European artillery in the
modern sense of the word[2]. After 1330 guns were commonly

---

[1] On the Millimete ms. and the gun there depicted cf. White, *Medieval
Technology*, p. 163. On the piece preserved at Stockholm's Museum cf.
Jakobsson, *Vapenhistorisk dyrgrip*, pp. 20-6. Rathgen, *Geschütz*, tafel 4 abb.
13 reproduces from a fifteenth-century German manuscript the picture of
a gun very similar to that of the Millimete manuscript.

[2] On the origins and early developments of European artillery, cf.
Bonaparte-Favé, *Études*, book 1, vol. 3; Montù, *Artiglieria*, vol. 1, pp.
83-183; Köhler, *Kriegswesens*, vol. 3, part. 1, pp. 225-337; Carman,
*Firearms*, pp. 15-21; White, *Medieval Technology*, pp. 96-100. Much effort
has been spent and many pages have been written about the " when, where,
and by whom " artillery was " first " used. The general results have been
rather elusive, for the simple reason that the problem has been stated in an
inappropriate form. Between the invention of gunpowder and the
appearance of cannon *in the modern sense of the word*, weapons of every type
and description have been tried that in one way or another shot " something " with " fire " and " thunder ". To determine " when artillery was
first used " largely depends on the definition of cannon that one assumes; to

used in warfare and in the 1350's Petrarch (*De Remediis*, lib. 1, dialog. 99) wrote that "these instruments which discharge balls of metal with most tremendous noise and flashes of fire ... were a few years ago very rare and were viewed with greatest astonishment and admiration, but now they are become as common and familiar as any other kind of arms. So quick and ingenious are the minds of men in learning the most pernicious arts".

Early artillery was conspicuous for its inefficiency. No verbal description can convey the awkwardness of the first European fire-arms more vividly than the artistic impressionism facing p. 32. But in the second half of the fourteenth century, normal cannon was well established in warfare, and European metal workers were striving for super-weapons. Huge guns of the bombard type were then developed and became very popular. As has been written, "the most striking occurrence in the early history of cannon is perhaps the great size which they soon attained"[1]. In 1382 at the siege of Oudenarde the army of Philip van Artevelde "made a marveylous great bombard shotyng stone of marveylous weyght and when this bombarde shot it made suche a noyse in the goynge as though all the dyvels of hell had been in the way"[2]. In the British Isles, huge 'Mons Meg' appeared sometime during the

---

put down a definite date is equivalent to ignoring the graduality of technological progress. As pointed out in the text, by the third decade of the fourteenth century, cannon *in the modern sense of the word* had been fully developed in Western Europe, but long before that date the Europeans as well as the Indians and the Chinese had played with "naphtha", "Greek fire", "gun powder", rockets, etc.

The references to the use of cannon at Brescia (Italy) in 1311 and at Metz in 1324, are not conclusive. The claim that under the date 1313 the Memorial Books of the town of Ghent contain a reference to guns made in Germany has been proved incorrect by Sir Charles Oman. As to the claim that there was a bombard aboard a Genoese vessel in 1319, cf. below note 1. p. 75.

[1] Russell, *Introduction*, pp. xv-xvi.

[2] Froissart, *Chronicle* ad datam. On Artevelde's huge bombard see Rathgen, *Feuer und Fernwaffen*, pp. 299-300.

fifteenth century weighing 14,560 pounds and with a calibre
of 20 inches (see p. 33). These weapons were scarcely mur-
derous but were effective in battering down fortresses and
city walls [1]. At the siege of Calais (1346) when " gunnes gret
and other gret ordinance " were used,

> gonners to schew ther arte
> in to the town in many a parte
> schote many a fulle gret stone.
> Thankyd be God and Mary myld
> the hurt nothir man, woman ne child.
> To the housis thow they did harm.
> Sent Babara! then was the cry
> when the stone in the stone did fly [2].

Guns could be made either of iron or bronze. Iron guns were
built by the smith from bars of wrought iron welded into
crude tubes which were further strengthened by thick iron
hoops shrunk over the tubes. The idea of casting guns must
have been there from the very beginning, but iron is very
difficult to cast effectively and cast iron is dangerously liable to
fractures [3]. Bronze, on the other hand, is technically much
easier to cast and all over Europe there were craftsmen well
acquainted with the process because of the early and widespread demand for church bells. It is indeed one of the ironies
of history that a technique developed in the making of such
essentially civilized objects eventually fostered the progress of
deadly weapons. Cast bronze ordnance in fact appeared at an
early date [4] and met with great favour not only because bronze

---

[1] Cf. *Chronica Trevisana* (Muratori, *Rerum Italicarum Scriptores*, vol. 19,
col. 754): " *Est bombarda instrumentum ferreum fortissimum . . . vi pulveris
accensi magno cum impetu lapis emittitur, nec obstant muri aliqui, quantucumque
grossi; quod tandem experientia compertum est in guerris que sequuntur* ".

[2] From a contemporary poem edited by Wright and Halliwell, *Reliquae*,
vol. 2, p. 23. Edward III had at least twenty guns at the siege of Calais:
cf. Carman, *Firearms*, p. 23.

[3] For a historical perspective of the problems involved in the casting of
iron cf. Wertime, *Steel* especially chapt. 6.

[4] Brunet's statement that bronze cannon did not appear until 1370
(Brunet, *Artillerie*, vol. 1, p. 120) does not seem to be correct. The Floren-

is less subject to corrosion, but also because the process of casting made the manufacture of muzzle-loaders possible and therefore the avoidance of all the dangers and problems connected with breech-blocks and obturation[1]. In regard to the economic aspect of the alternative, there is no doubt that as raw material iron was much less expensive than bronze. However, until a satisfactory process for casting iron had been discovered, the alternative was between cast bronze and wrought iron. Now the process of forging guns absorbed more labour and consequently cost more than that of casting. Therefore the final price differential was noticeably reduced[2]. Wrought-iron guns continued to be made well into the sixteenth century, but were considered an inferior type of artillery.

Copper, the basic raw material for the making of bronze ordnance came mainly from Hungary, Tyrol, Saxony and Bohemia[3]. Tin, the metal to be mixed with copper, came

---

tine document reproduced facing p. 32 proves that bronze cannon was made as early as 1326.

[1] Wrought-iron cannon had to be open at either end because it was impossible for the smith to make the barrel properly without a mandrel. The breech-loader was impractical for powerful weapons until the nineteenth century when adequate obturation solved the problem. The difficulties of the detachable breech-block proved insurmountable in big guns. Making the breech-block screw into the breech was not a very satisfactory solution because the heat of each explosion expanded the thread, and for several hours, until it cooled, the breech could not be unscrewed for reloading.

[2] Cf. Henrard, *Documents*, p. 243.

[3] On the production and trade of copper in the late Middle Ages cf. Schick, *Fugger* passim but especially pp. 54-5 and 275-90. Sweden produced and possibly exported copper in the late Middle Ages, but only in negligible quantities. Still around 1500 England was importing copper from Saxony (Mansfeld), Bohemia, Hungary and Tyrol (cf. Schulte, *Ravensburger Handelsgesellschaft*, vol. 2, p. 196). Swedish copper production and exports rapidly grew after 1570 and remained on a very high level throughout the seventeenth century (Heckscher, *Ekonomiska Historia*, part. 1, vol. 1, p. 169 and part 1, vol. 2, p. 444). Norwegian copper mines were not exploited to any important extent before the 1640's (Christensen, *Danmark*, pp. 23-5).

mainly from England, Spain and Germany. Although the raw materials were produced in only a few areas, the casting of bronze guns was carried on almost everywhere by artisans who had no difficulty in shifting from producing bells to producing guns and *vice versa*. These artisans worked to specific orders or were hired for definite periods of time. Later on, more or less permanent governmental arsenals were also established [1] in which guns were produced by a permanent staff or by experts temporarily hired. It should be added that in those days the division of labour between gunners and gun-founders was not always clear-cut and much casting was actually done by gunners who were serving in the armies.

From the mid-fifteenth century the demand for guns entered

---

Spain got her supply of copper mostly from Hungary until the middle of the sixteenth century when she began to import copper in increasing quantities from Mexico, Peru and Cuba. In 1646 the Marquis de Loriana complained that the quality of the American copper had deteriorated "while at the beginning it was as good as that of Hungary". In 1578 it was said that copper from Hungary cost in Spain five times as much as copper from Cuba (Carrasco, *Artilleria de bronce*, p. 45).

The Dutch exported much copper from Japan in the course of the sixteenth and seventeenth centuries but they mostly sold it in other parts of Asia and only occasionally brought it to Europe (cf. Glamann, *Trade*, pp. 175-6).

[1] I say "more or less" because in some cases—e.g. the Venetian governmental cannon foundry in Brescia—the arsenal was opened only when some work had to be done. Once the work was completed, the arsenal was closed and served as storage house for artillery and utensils. Cf. Quarenghi, *Fonderie*, p. 21. As to "permanent" arsenals one of the most famous in southern Europe was that of Venice where cannon were cast on a large scale from the beginning of the fifteenth century (cf. Nani Mocenigo, *L'arsenale* and Lane, *Venetian Ships*, pp. 129-216). In England the main arsenal was in the Tower of London (cf. Tout, *Firearms* and Ffoulkes, *Gun-Founders*, passim). Maximilian I had an arsenal in Innsbruck which acquired a very good name for the bronze guns it produced (cf. Schick, *Fugger*, p. 271, *n*. 3). On Spanish arsenals see below, footnote [2], p. 33. In the first part of the seventeenth century Botero (*Aggiunte*, p. 52) wrote that the two most remarkable arsenals in the West were those of Venice and of the Duke of Saxony in Dresden. On the arsenal in Dresden at the very beginning of the seventeenth century cf. also Moryson, *Itinerary*, vol. 4, p. 344.

a secular phase of rapid growth. The establishment of the great national states with big armies and navies and their incessant wars, together with geographical exploration and overseas expansion, all added to the demand for cannon. The sovereigns themselves became personally interested in the matter of ordnance, and as in the case of Duke Alfonso d'Este, King John II of Portugal, King James IV of Scotland, and the Emperor Maximilian, they developed not only enthusiasm but real, technical expertise in the "art of gunnery". They patronised gunners and gun-founders and devoted a good deal of their resources to the building and the improvement of arsenals and artillery trains. The trade in raw copper and in bronze ordnance became one of the flourishing and profitable activities of the day moving mainly around the markets of Nuremberg, the main centre of German metallurgy; Lyon, through which France bought her provisions; Bolzano, on the way from the Tyrol to Northern Italy; and Antwerp where the flow of commodities from West Africa and later the Spice Islands met the flow of metallurgical products from Germany and Flanders[1]. Much of the European " *Früh-*

---

[1] Schick, *Fugger*, pp. 277–80. For Antwerp in particular cf. Van Houtte, *Anvers*, pp. 254 and 256 and Van der Wee, *Antwerp*, vol. 2, pp. 126, 130. The following table is derived from Van der Wee, *Antwerp*, vol. 1, pp. 522–3, and shows the copper exported from Hungary by the Fuggers.

| | Total export | Export to Antwerp via Danzig and Stettin | Export to Venice and Trieste |
|---|---|---|---|
| | *yearly average (tons)* | % of the total | % of the total |
| 1497–1503 | *c.* 1390 | — | 32 |
| 1507–9 | 1476 | 49 | 13 |
| 1510–12 | 2253 | 55 | 3 |
| 1513–15 | 1263 | 63 | 4 |
| 1516–18 | 1358 | 50 | 0 |
| 1519–22 | 1434 | 34 | 5 |
| 1526 | 893 | 48 | 3 |
| 1527–32 | 1105 | 61 | 6 |
| 1533–5 | 944 | 48 | 15 |
| 1536–9 | 1207 | 49 | 12 |

*Kapitalismus*" had its origins firmly rooted in this very fertile trade: the Fugger, to quote the most conspicuous example, were great merchants of copper and had a prosperous gun foundry at Fuggerau, near Willbach (Carinthia) [1].

The rapid growth of cannon production was accompanied by technological progress. Advances had been made in the previous hundred and fifty odd years; however, until the middle of the fifteenth century European gun-founders spent most of their efforts in merely increasing the size of guns which in a few instances acquired monstrous proportions. By the middle of the fifteenth century the core of the European artillery was represented by huge bombards of wrought iron which could be moved only with great difficulty, aimed only with rough approximation, and reloaded only with great loss of time. Guns were effective only in siege operations [2]. In the open field they had only a psychological effect, and even that could not be guaranteed. At the battle of Aljubarrota (1385) the Castilians had sixteen great bombards which hurled huge balls of stone, but the battle was won by the Portuguese who had no artillery. However, if it is true that Europeans did not have effective field ordnance, it is also true that they never discarded the almost useless small pieces they possessed. In the course of time, realizing the limitations of the huge bombards, they actually devoted more attention to the guns of lesser calibre. The new trend was advanced by French artillerymen in the course of the fifteenth century [3].

---

On the exports of copper from Antwerp to Portugal cf. below, footnote [3], p. 31. France received copper from the Tyrol at Lyon (Schick, *Fugger*, pp. 277-80) but occasionally also via Antwerp (Coornaert, *Les Français*, vol. 2, p. 117). On the trade of the Tyrol's copper, routes and freight rates at the very beginning of the sixteenth century cf. also Paumgartner, *Welthandelsbräuche*, pp. 72, 73 and 90.

[1] Schick, *Fugger*, pp. 52, 84, 271. See also previous footnote.

[2] Field mitrailleuses, called *ribaulds* or *ribauldequins* were produced but their performance was not satisfactory. Oman, *Sixteenth Century*, vol. 2, pp. 222 and 227-8.

[3] The manufacture of cannon made noticeable progress in France during

When the army of Charles VIII invaded Italy in 1494 the Italians, then unanimously considered masters in matters of war and artillery, were surprised by the new features of the French ordnance: the huge clumsy proportions of the traditional bombards—as Guicciardini noticed—had been abandoned, the pieces were " lighter and all cast in bronze . . . were drawn by horses with such dexterity that they could keep up with the marching speed of the army . . . shot at very short intervals . . . and could be used as usefully in the field as in battering walls " [1]. The statement by Guicciardini should be taken with a grain of salt. The new French gun seemed highly " mobile " in comparison to the old clumsy bombards, but by modern standards they were certainly not conspicuous for mobility. It is generally admitted that at Ravenna in 1512 and at Marignano in 1515 field battles were won by artillery for the first time in history[2], but it has also to be admitted that other circumstances heavily influenced the result of these battles. European field artillery remained characterized by a low degree of mobility and poor rate of fire until the middle of the seventeenth century. However, by the end of the sixteenth century the distinction between siege artillery and field artillery was recognised [3] and European gunners started devoting their

---

the time of Charles VII and in this regard special mention should be made of the brothers Jean and Gaspard Bureau: cf. Oman, *Sixteenth Century*, vol. 2, pp. 226 and 404.

[1] Guicciardini, *Storia*, vol. 1, chapt. 2. Cf. also the more detailed passage by Iovius, *Historiae*, vol. 1, pp. 24-5. On the technical characteristics of the guns of Charles VIII cf. Bonaparte and Favé, *Études*, book 1. vol. 3, pp. 206-8.

[2] Oman, *Sixteenth Century*, pp. 50, 130-50, 160-71; Hardy, *Tactique Française*, vol. 2, p. 240; Lot, *Armées Françaises*, p. 36; Lot, *L'art militaire*, p. 439.

[3] In 1592 Colliado (*Platica*, p. 11 v.) wrote that: " three are the types of artillery . . . because three are its main tasks; to hurt the enemy as rapidly as possible; to destroy the walls of towns and fortresses; to sink the ships and galleys of the enemy ". Similar remarks were made by Ufano, *Artillerie*, pp. 33 ff. early in the seventeenth century. In 1641 Chincherni, (*Bombardiere*, p. 897) wrote that " two are the tasks of artillery: one is to hurt the enemy

[28]

ingenuity to the problem of further improving upon the mobility of guns without affecting their striking power[1].

Guns were individuals; not only had they individual names like ships, they were actually different one from another. Colliado tells us that in the Castle of Milan more than two hundred different types of charging instruments were needed when 11 would have been sufficient had the guns been properly standardized[2]. The first efforts to remedy this state of affairs go back to the sixteenth century and were continued in the seventeenth century, although satisfactory results were not attained before the eighteenth century[3].

Another problem which became very pressing in the course of the sixteenth century was essentially an economic one, although it had technological implications. We have seen that during the course of the fifteenth century preference was given to cast bronze guns. Wrought-iron guns continued to be made but were rightly considered poor artillery; cast-iron guns were often tried in the fifteenth century[4], but not

---

in the field and the other is to destroy the walls of those places that one wants to conquer. One has therefore to use different types of artillery: for the first purpose it is sufficient to use small ordnance of 12 or less calibre; for the second, one needs large ordnance of 12 calibre or more ".

[1] Among many cf. the documents collected by Angelucci, *Documenti*, vol. 1, pp. 386, 387, 396, 398, 400, 405 and by Doorman, *Patents*, pp. 143, 178, 182.

[2] Colliado, *Platica*, p. 9 r, who adds: " *el primero inconveniente es que las balas de las pieças de un presidio no pueden servir a aquellas del otro antes cada suerte de balas han de menester sus particulares pieças* ".

[3] In 1549 Charles V issued a provision in order to standardize the calibres of cannon but he did not attain appreciable results (cf. Henrard, *Documents*, pp. 254-5 and 283-4). In France Henry II introduced " the six calibres of France " about 1550 but only the Ordonnance Vallière of 1732 succeeded in establishing " *l'exactitude des formes et des dimensions* " (cf. Basset, *Historique*, pp. 928-30 and 947).

[4] Mention of guns (or parts of guns) cast in iron can be found in documents of the late fourteenth century and more frequently in the documents of the fifteenth century, especially in Germany (Johannsen, *Quellen*, pp. 365-94). The casting of iron guns was introduced from Germany into

very successfully. The trouble with bronze artillery was that it cost too much. Copper and tin were very expensive, and as the need for artillery grew larger, the less bearable became the high cost of bronze[1]. It has also to be remembered that, owing to imperfect technology, the life expectancy of the pieces was very low[2], and this provided another reason for trying less expensive artillery.

2—Before the middle of the sixteenth century, the most relevant part of European production, quantitatively as well as qualitatively, came from the Southern Provinces of the Low Countries (Malines, Dinant, Namur, Antwerp, Tournai, Mons, etc.), Germany (Nuremberg, Augsburg, Marienburg, Frankfurt, etc.) and Italy (Venice, Bergamo and Brescia, Genoa, Milan, Naples, etc.). As to quality, Colliado says: " there is no doubt among experts that the castings of the Flemish and of the Germans are the best available, and this for various reasons : . . . the Germans are phlegmatic people and do things more

---

France early in the fifteenth century and iron guns were later cast in Burgundy (Sprandel, *Ausbreitung*, p. 89).

[1] A clear indication of such a state of affairs is colourfully given by the appearance of the " right to the bells ". In an English sixteenth-century manuscript laying down the duties of the Provost Marshal it is stated that " the master gunners and their companie shall have the best bell within the place soe wonne ". As late as 1807 Major-General Blomfield stated that it has been " an invariable custom in our service whenever a place capitulated to allow the officer commanding the Royal Artillery a claim of the bells in the town and its dependencies ". In the French army, the " *Grand Maitre des Arbaletriers* " could claim cannon, bells and utensils of copper or brass of any captured town and Spanish troops practised the same custom (cf. Ffoulkes, *Gun-Founders*, p. 26 and Vigon, *Artilleria*, vol. 1, p. 103). At the time of the dissolution, many bells were confiscated in England from the monasteries and became a primary source of gun metal (cf. among others Walters, *Bells*, p. 350, and Tawney and Power, *Tudor Economic Documents*, vol. 1, p. 262). According to Colliado (*Platica*, p. 10 v.) " the metal of the bells is not suitable by itself for gun founding; it contains too much tin namely 25 per cent, and the pieces made out of it are too brittle ".

[2] Conturies, *Fonderie Nationale*, p. 93.

accurately and more patiently than the Spaniards or the Italians who are choleric people, especially the Spaniards who are the most choleric of all; the Germans enjoy a greater and better supply of copper and tin, with which metals they produce excellent bronze; most important of all the Germans do not use but very dry moulds which they age for years in the sun . . . After the castings of Germany, the castings of Venice, where the German style and rules are strictly followed, are considered very good " [1].

While it seems that at least until the beginning of the sixteenth century, Italian production mainly served to satisfy the large local demand for cannon, a good part of the Flemish and German production was exported. In the last decades of the fifteenth and the first decades of the sixteenth century one reads of Flemish artillery sold to England but most of all of German and Flemish artillery sold to Portugal and Spain.

During the last quarter of the fifteenth century Portugal had become an excellent market for cannon merchants. With her involvement in overseas trade and expansion, Portugal's needs for artillery grew vastly beyond her inadequate home resources, while the large profits from overseas commercial ventures translated needs into effective demand. Portuguese kings imported Flemish and German gunners and gun-founders as well as guns [2]; the large imports of copper from Antwerp [3], even when allowance is made for the metal used in ship-building, may indicate that a local industry had been started [4],

[1] Colliado, *Platica*, p. 8 r.

[2] Cordeiro, *Apontamentos*, p. 49; Teixeira Bothelo, *Novos subsidios*, vol. 1, pp. 12, 289 and vol. 2, pp. 10, 55, 56; Pieris and Fitzler, *Ceylon*, part 1, pp. 290-6. Most of the gunners aboard Portuguese ships in the fifteenth, sixteenth and seventeenth centuries were Flemish or Germans.

[3] During the reign of Manoel the Great (1495-1521) Portugal imported from Antwerp more than 5200 tons of copper in addition to guns and ammunition of all kinds (cf. Van Houtte, *Anvers*, pp. 254-6).

[4] Cordeiro, *Apontamentos*, pp. 59-60; Pieris and Fitzler, *Ceylon*, part 1, pp. 291ff. The main centre of cannon production was of course Lisbon, but the productive capacity of that place was always rather limited because of shortage of skilled labour. In 1616 the *Conselho de Guerra* pointed out

but it was of modest proportions and it never grew enough to satisfy the demand. The gold, ivory, and black pepper of West Africa and the spices of the Far East were easily exchangeable in Antwerp for Flemish and German guns. Imports of all kind of weapons were declared duty free[1] and Portugal remained largely dependent on foreign guns as well as on foreign gunners. The inherent weakness of the situation became obvious in the course of the second half of the sixteenth century, when a severe and prolonged crisis affected the productive potential of the Southern Low Countries[2]. The annexation to Spain in 1580 did not help in solving the problem. Throughout the seventeenth century, Portugal suffered from a chronic shortage of artillery that became dramatically acute in moments of crisis when it endangered the safety both of the country and of the empire overseas[3].

Spain's story is more complicated but substantially not very different. When the country became suddenly and almost

---

that " there are in Lisbon three royal gun-foundries and two private ones, but three of the gun-founders are inept " (Teixeira Bothelo, *Novos subsidios*, vol. 2, p. 56).

[1] Paumgartner, *Welthandelsbräuche*, p. 280: " all weapons which enter the Kingdom of Portugal are duty free and are not subject to *disma* (decima) nor to *zisa* (assize)". From 1515 copper imports were free from *zisa* but had to pay *disma*.

[2] Pirenne, *Histoire*, vol. 4, pp. 407-33.

[3] In the 1620's and 1630's, the Crown Council in Lisbon repeatedly wrote to the Viceroy in India that the mother-country could not send to the colonies guns or gun-founders in sufficient quantities. The Council strongly advised the Viceroy to develop local manufactures. Most of the artillery available in the Portuguese colonies was in fact cast in Macao, with Chinese labour (cf. Boxer, *Expedições Militares*, pp. 7-9). When Portugal severed the connections with Spain in 1640, she was forced to turn to Holland, her traditional foe, for guns and ammunition: cf. Rau, *Embaixada*, pp. 95 ff. (imports from Holland in 1645 and 1648 are also mentioned in Teixeira Bothelo, *Novos subsidios*, vol. 2, p. 58 *n.*). When the war broke out between Portugal and Holland in 1656, Portugal had to import ammunition from Hamburg: cf. Baash, *Verkehr*, p. 543. Occasionally, Portugal imported cannon directly from Sweden: cf. below, footnote 1, p. 56.

unexpectedly engaged in overseas expansion and in European grand politics, its productive capacity in matter of artillery was exiguous. Guns were made in many places by artisans who shifted from the casting of bells to the casting of bronze guns or from the forging of iron utensils to the production of wrought-iron ordnance[1]. This arrangement had been satisfactory in medieval times but it was patently inadequate under the new circumstances. The Crown took steps to face the new situation and built arsenals and gun foundries in Medina del Campo, Malaga and Barcelona[2]. The main problem however was the shortage of skilled labour. " I do not think "—wrote the Venetian Ambassador Badoer in 1557—" I do not think there is another country less provided with skilled workers than Spain ". The Spanish administration never managed to break down this formidable handicap. Its action in regard to the manufacture of artillery as in regard to the establishment of a navy[3] remained in general at the level of occasional, short-sighted measures. Mental attitudes of monarchs and officials carried their share of responsibility, but there was more in it than that. The Empire of Charles V had one great asset beside the never-setting sun: it had absorbed within its boundaries most of the European areas

[1] Cf. the remarks by Carrasco, *Artilleria de bronce*, pp. 32ff.

[2] In 1495 arsenals were established in Medina del Campo and in Baza but in 1497 after the conquest of Malaga the arsenal and the gun-foundries of Baza were transferred to Malaga for fear of French attacks (Vigon, *Artilleria*, vol. 1, pp. 53-4). Early in the sixteenth century the gun-foundries of Medina del Campo entered a period of decline while those of Malaga flourished for a good part of the century, but by 1590 also the gun-foundries at Malaga were in poor condition and the gun-founders " *se iban acabando, pues no tenian generalmente donde trabajar* " (Carrasco, *Artilleria de bronce*, p. 185; Vigon, *Artilleria*, vol. 1, p. 309).

In 1611 royal gun-foundries were established in Seville to serve the " *Armadas y flotas de Indias* " (Fernandez Duro, *Disquisiciones*, vol. 5, p. 55). Throughout the seventeenth century Seville was one of the main centres of artillery production in Spain (cf. Carrasco, *Artilleria de bronce*, pp. 168ff.), but its productive potential was rather limited.

[3] On the ineffective policy of the Crown in regard to the navy cf. below footnote 3, p. 85.

with the greatest potential in artillery production. It seemed natural to Spain's rulers that if and when artillery was needed either the orders should be placed to the famous centres of production in Flanders, Italy and Germany, or Flemish, German and Italian founders should be invited to Spain[1]. The second alternative was frequently adopted and if consistently pursued would have undoubtedly helped to solve Spain's problem. But after the emergency needs were satisfied, the foreign gunners were sent back to their homes for economic reasons and the few Spanish workers were left without jobs or money[2]. In the short run the action of the Crown could hardly be condemned[3]. Its failure was in the long run and, contrary to the famous Keynesian dictum, nations live in the long run.

During the second half of the sixteenth century, wars, religious intolerance and misgovernment disrupted the economy of the Southern Low Countries[4]. Skilled labour emigrated in mass[5]. Italy did not keep up with contemporary technological developments[6] and proved unable to fill the gap

[1] On Spanish orders placed to Flemish and German foundries cf. Vigon, *Artilleria*, vol. I, pp. 124, 220, 247, 311, 313, 314, 345 *n*.86 and Yernaux, *Métallurgie*, p. 157. In 1520 Charles V established a royal gun-foundry in Malines, in the Southern Low Countries. On Flemish and German founders invited to Spain cf. Carrasco, *Artilleria de bronce* passim and Vigon, *Artilleria*, vol. I, p. 220 and 311. In 1547 Philip II instructed his ambassador in Germany to look for gun-founders " *de los de Nuremberg que fusen catolicos* " to bring to Spain (Vigon, *Artilleria*, vol. I, p. 345, n.82). On gun-founders brought to Spain from Liége cf. Yernaux, *Métallurgie*, p. 162.

[2] Cf. Carrasco, *Artilleria de bronce*, p. 184*ff*.

[3] The decision to obtain cannon from Flanders or Germany or Italy rather than from Spanish foundries was generally reached after careful analysis of comparative costs. Cf. Carrasco, *Artilleria de bronce*, pp. 53, 184 and passim.

[4] Pirenne, *Histoire*, vol. 4, pp. 407-33.

[5] As will be seen below, the development of the Swedish and Russian iron industries was made possible by a massive migration of " Walloons " (as they were called in Sweden) or " French " (as they were called in Russia). This loss of " human capital " weighed heavily in the decline of the Southern Low Countries.

[6] Cf. Cipolla, *Decline*, pp. 182-5.

left by the Flemish crisis. With the collapse of two of its main suppliers, Spain underwent an acute armament crisis. The crisis is already apparent in the 1570's and it grew alarmingly worse in the following decades[1].

A few initiatives did result in substantial and durable achievements, such as the establishment of the royal gun foundries in Seville in 1611 and the establishment of cast-iron manufactures in Biscay in the 1620's, but on the whole Spain's armament industry lagged behind the needs of Spain's grand imperial politics[2]. The country had often to depend on the enemy's manufactures[3]. For this, the Crown and its

[1] From the 1570's onward one frequently hears of frantic efforts on the part of Spaniards to secure imports of English cannon. In 1578 " a person " offered to get 150 guns out of England and deliver them to Spain. The whole transaction had to be made in great secrecy " *para que no se sepa en Inglaterra donde hai tanto recato en la saca de artilleria* ". In 1583 twenty-three guns were imported from England for a total weight of 13.5 tons of iron besides 1.5 tons of ammunition (Carrasco, *Artilleria de hierro*, p. 66). In 1588 two Spaniards attempted to induce an Englishman, Richard Thomson, " to undertake the delyverie of a great quantitie of yron ordnance, either in Hamborghe, Rotterdam in Holland or Callis, profferinge to deposit in any of these places twentie thousand crownes to receave the valiewe in cast ordnance " (*Calendar State Papers*, Domestic, Elizabeth, 244 *n.* 16, April 3, 1593). So urgent was the demand that the Spaniards offered him a pension of forty ducats for life. In 1591 the Spaniards tried again to import iron cannon from England (Cunningham, *English Industry*, vol. 1 p. 57). In 1619 " great quantity " of English ordnance was imported into Spain, this time through legal channels (see below footnote [2] p. 45).

[2] One of the main centres of cannon production in seventeenth-century Spain, Seville, could not produce more than 36 guns of average calibre per year (Carrasco, *Artilleria de bronce*, pp. 53-4). This at a time when in England and Sweden many factories could produce 100 to 200 guns of all calibres per year (cf. appendix 1).

What is stated in the text about cannon production is also valid for the production of gunpowder. In 1592 Colliado, *Platica*, p. 76 v. complained that despite " the great abundance of saltpetre " the Spaniards did not develop a local industry and " always have to beg for gun-powder abroad ".

[3] As indicated above in footnote [1], the Spaniards imported iron cannon from England during the last decades of the sixteenth century and the first decades of the seventeenth century. In the course of the seventeenth century they started the manufacture of iron artillery in the region of Santander (see below footnote [5], p. 50). The products were very good

bureaucracy were not the only ones to be blamed. In contrast to English, Dutch and Swedish developments, private enterprise in Spain was conspicuous for its inaction and not only in the armament industry. " Spain supplies itself from other countries with almost all things which are manufactured for common use and which consist in the industry and toil of man " wrote a well-informed contemporary observer; and the Venetian Ambassador Vendramin, commenting on the effects of this situation on Spain's balance of payments, added: " This gold that comes from the Indies does on Spain as rain does on a roof—it poures on her and it flows away ".

3—Across the Channel, in the early years of the sixteenth century England looked almost insignificant. There were less than 4 million people living in England and Wales, while France certainly numbered more than 10 million and Spain about 7 million in addition to another 4 million in its newly conquered Italian territories [1]. The small size of the English population was not offset by greater *per capita* incomes or productivity. On the contrary, to any continental observer England looked most certainly an underdeveloped country. The English cannon industry and English armament were no exception. The fact that the bow was not finally and officially discarded as an English weapon until 1595 [2] belongs more to the history of English folklore than to a serious history of English technology. But even when due allowance is made for folklore and tradition, it remains substantially true that during the fourteenth and fifteenth centuries the English armament industry did not keep pace with that of the continent. One reason was that the English had a good supply of

but the output was very limited and iron ordnance had to be imported from the Netherlands throughout the second half of the century (Janiçon, *Provinces-Unies*, vol. 1, p. 498).

[1] Urlanis, *Naselenija*, pp. 137-58 and 164-9.

[2] Fuller, *Armament*, pp. 88 and 102 *n.* 28. As late as 1625 there were still people in England recommending the reintroduction of the long-bow.

easily found iron ore in the proximity of well-forested lands. This made them stick mostly to iron in their metallurgical endeavours, and put them at a disadvantage as long as the technique of working iron remained less developed than that of working cupreous alloys.

One of the main areas of the English iron industry was in the Weald of Sussex, in Ashdown Forest. Here in the last decades of the fifteenth century, under the impulse given by Henry VII, the production of artillery expanded. Much effort was devoted to improving current techniques, and technological progress was undoubtedly achieved[1]. From available records it seems that many of the founders who worked in Ashdown Forest were gunners of French origins[2] which proves that even in the field of iron work the need was felt to import technicians and "know-how" from the more developed continent. Between 1490 and 1510, side by side with the casting of gun-shot, the casting of iron guns was tried and by 1509-13 we know that guns made of cast iron were manufactured[3]. We have no way of telling how good such artillery was, but it is unlikely to have been very satisfactory.

When Henry VIII (1509-47) came to the throne, he was quick to realize his weakness in the matter of artillery. The majority of the English naval and land guns were of the old outdated type, constructed by welding together longitudinally a number of wrought-iron bars[4]. There was only one bronze gun foundry in England, the one at the Tower, and this could not possibly cope with the King's vast needs[5]. The

[1] Schubert, *Iron Industry*, pp. 162-70.
[2] Schubert, *Cannon*, pp. 132 P.-135 P.
[3] Schubert, *Iron Industry*, p. 167.
[4] Clowes, *Sailing Ships*, vol. 1, p. 62.
[5] King Henry packed a great number of guns into the hulls of his ships, provided his land forces with good artillery trains and established a long chain of well-gunned forts for the protection of vulnerable points on the seaboard facing France. The fortification of the coast especially turned out to be enormously expensive; cf. Oman, *Sixteenth Century*, vol. 2, pp. 352-5. For Henry's naval artillery cf. Clowes, *Sailing Ships*, vol. 1, pp. 62-4 and Lewis, *Armada*, p. 65.

cast-iron guns made in Weald apparently did not inspire him with much confidence. Full of admiration for continental bronze guns, Henry, like the Spanish monarchs, turned to the famous gun foundries of the Southern Low Countries, and placed large orders to the great master Hans Poppenruyter of Malines. In less than two decades he received from Poppenruyter at least 140 bronze guns of all calibres including the twelve great bombards named "the twelve Apostles"[1].

At the beginning of his reign, King Henry was able to keep pace with his extravagant expenditure thanks to the treasure that his father had carefully collected, but before long this was exhausted and Henry did not have at his disposal the American resources that the Spanish monarchs had. As early as 1523 Master Poppenruyter was—to use his own words—" in great dispair and danger " for the money due to him by the King, and after several vain attempts to obtain payment he declared himself ready " to make finance with artillery ", which possibly meant that he was ready to reach a settlement[2].

When war with France became imminent in 1543 and armaments had to be increased, Henry was practically bankrupt and the need to resort to native industry and local raw materials[3] became dramatically obvious. It was Henry's good luck that in Ashdown Forest, iron-founding had never ceased completely although much neglected. Only two years

[1] Ffoulkes, Gun-Founders, pp. 4, 29, 41-2, 106, 107. On Hans Poppenruyter cf. Henrard, Documents, pp. 250-1. In those days the Southern Provinces of the Low Countries were not yet a dominion of Spain. They belonged to Maximilian I of Austria, (1493-1519), a good friend of Henry and the grandfather of Charles V.

[2] Ffoulkes, Gun-Founders, pp. 29 and 109.

[3] The English were handicapped by the lack of copper ore in the British Islands. Still during the reign of Elizabeth, when cast-iron cannon was largely produced, a patent was granted by the Queen for a "notable invention ... very profitable for the making of our ordnance ". The authors of the "notable invention " claimed that they could change iron into copper by heating it with blue vitriol. Cf. Cunningham, English Industry, vol. 1, p. 58.

before, in 1541, Henry had appointed William Levett sub-tenant of the royal iron works at Newbridge. William Levett was the rector of the parish of Buxted and although he had distinguished himself as a deputy for the receiver of the King's revenues in Sussex, the King's choice might look rather odd. But it turned out to be an excellent one. In 1543, when the King needed cannon, the enterprising parson secured the services of a large number of French founders who were working in the vicinity, obtained from London Peter Baude, the best founder of bronze guns in the King's service, and completed the group with a skilful iron-master Ralph Hogge who knew how to operate a furnace and was able to furnish the liquid iron for the castings. Having thus collected the best experts available, the energetic parson set them to work and somewhere in his parish a number of good cast-iron guns were successfully produced [1]. The event marked the beginning of a prosperous era for the iron industry in Sussex and opened a new chapter in the history of artillery [2].

The new guns gave such good results that in 1545 Levett was ordered to cast no fewer than 120 iron guns which he managed to produce in nearly two years [3]. The further request for large siege guns led to the building of a double furnace in the Forest of Worth, west of Ashdown Forest, which was the first furnace of that kind in England known to us [4]. By 1573 there were eight furnaces in Sussex and one in Kent casting guns and shot for a total annual output of 500-600

[1] Schubert, *Iron Industry*, pp. 171-2.
[2] It is generally conceded that in 1543 " the first iron cannon was cast in England ". As it has been pointed out in the text, iron guns were cast in England as early as 1509-13 (Schubert, *Iron Industry*, pp. 164 and 167), but there were noticeable differences between the early specimens of 1509-13 and those cast after 1543. The first ones were of the mortar type, of short length and large calibre. The second ones were longer, heavier, and of smaller calibre. Furthermore, the first ones were equipped with detachable chambers while the second ones were cast in one piece. For all this cf. Schubert, *First cannon*, and Schubert, *Iron Industry*, pp. 249-50 and 255.
[3] Schubert, *Iron Industry*, p. 247.  [4] Schubert, *Iron Industry*, p. 247.

tons of iron. Around 1600 annual production had increased to about 800-1000 tons[1].

The particular reason why the English should have almost suddenly succeeded in the production of relatively safe cast-iron guns is not completely clear. Writing some decades ago, Jenkins admitted that Sussex iron was a good foundry ore but allowed that such was to be found in a good many places on the Continent. The explanation which he proposed was that " the Sussex men had invented some better and cheaper mode of making the moulds " and possibly devised good proportion for their guns[2]. Dr. Schubert essentially adheres to Jenkins's point of view, but he adds that the guns cast in Sussex after 1543 " were longer and of smaller calibres " than those cast before. In his opinion " this ensured a much greater propelling power " and " was a tremendous advance "[3], but it still remains to be explained why they did not blow up as frequently as cast iron guns of earlier vintages. In his book on the origin of the steel industry, Wertime emphasizes the importance of the presence of phosphorus in the Sussex ore. To him, the " *thoughness and validitie* " of Sussex guns " were due in some important degree to the presence of phosphorous in the ore . . . It seems reasonable to believe that masters in the Sussex tradition came to grasp in a limited practical way the majority of basic rules still applicable in iron founding. These related to the positive role of certain phosphorus-bearing limonite ores; the negative role of sulphur; the central importance of gray iron; and the importance of proper pouring and molding practice, including slow cooling without quenching "[4].

Whatever the reasons for the technological success, we know that it turned into an economic one. As has been rightly pointed out, " the manufacture of guns was the most profit-

[1] Schubert, *Iron Industry*, p. 250.    [2] Jenkins, *Sussex*, pp. 22-3.
[3] Schubert, *Iron Industry*, p. 255.
[4] Wertime, *Steel*, pp. 168 and 175. The microspecimens of cast iron firebacks of the same period show that cast iron produced in Sussex was preponderantly grey cast iron. (Cf. Schubert, *Iron Industry*, p. 255).

able proposition in the sixteenth century iron trade." [1] The production of cast iron guns grew very rapidly while the fame of English products and skill quickly spread throughout Europe. Before the century was over, an expert like Gentilini, a Venetian gun-founder of good repute, although strongly biased in favour of Continental artillery, wrote that " English people, to say the truth, are judicious people and of great intelligence . . . and are very ingenious in their inventions " [2]. By then, English technicians as well as English guns were eagerly sought after throughout the Continent [3]. To use Toynbeean phraseology, it was a typical case of challenge met with bold and successful response.

4—Actually cast iron guns were in many respects still inferior to bronze artillery. This was certainly by far the most prevalent opinion among military experts, especially on the Continent, where cast bronze artillery had reached a high state of perfection [4]. " Brass ordnance does not become rusted "—wrote Gentilini—" and therefore can be fired without danger for the gunner, while this is not the case with iron ordnance because shots become rusted when they have been inside the gun for a while " [5]. But there was more to it than

---

[1] Schubert, *Iron Industry*, p. 253: " From the very beginning guns were priced much higher than anything else produced at iron-works. In 1546-8 e.g. ordnance from Worth, in Sussex, sold at £10 per ton but bar iron mostly at £8 or 9."

[2] Gentilini, *Bombardiere*, p. 55.

[3] Between 1570 and 1650 English iron workers were highly coveted on the Continent. Cf. the examples quoted by Straker, *Wealden*, pp. 151-4, and Schubert, *Iron Industry*, p. 253 *n*.4 and p. 254 *n*.1. For English iron-founders invited to Spain cf. Carrasco, *Artilleria de hierro*, p. 66.

[4] Cf. Wertime, *Steel*, pp. 168-9. Very few held the opposite view. Among these few one may mention the English gunner Eldred who maintained " that brass the hotter it is the weaker it is; and iron ordnance the heat doth not hurt it anything at all; also your brass ordnance is compounded of divers other metals as copper, latten and tinne, and iron of one only metal and therefore the stronger, for unity is more forcible than plurality ". Cf. Ffoulkes, *Gun-Founders*, pp. 24-5.

[5] Gentilini, *Bombardiere*, p. 55.

that. Despite the enormous progress accomplished by English founders, cast iron guns were still more brittle than bronze ones. In the Ordnance Minute Books in the London Record Office one reads over and over again notes of cast-iron guns that missed proof, and the records of accident in action abundantly testify that cast iron guns were less reliable than cast bronze artillery [1]. Furthermore, because of the lower resistance of the metal, iron guns had to be made noticeably thicker than bronze ordnance. As a result, cast iron guns were much heavier than corresponding bronze guns [2].

However, cast iron guns had one great advantage over cast bronze ordnance: that of costing much less. The price of bronze artillery seems to have averaged normally three or four times that of cast iron guns [3]. Essentially, therefore, the English had come out with a product whose deficiencies in

[1] Ffoulkes, *Gun-Founders*, pp. 12, 23.

[2] For the weights of different types of guns see below footnote [1], p. 65. Iron guns were heavier than the bronze ones. The Dutch had aboard their vessels many 36 pounders made of bronze. As to iron artillery they limited themselves to 18 pounders " *parce qu'ils sont extremement pesans et qu'ils font autant d'effet que s'ils estoient plus gros* " (Bibl. Nat. Paris, Dept. mss. Colbert 4219, *Addition au memoire concernant la fonderie des canons*, July 1671, f.4).

[3] Since iron guns had to be made much heavier than the bronze ones for safety reasons, the differential cost between similar pieces was somewhat reduced. However, in England around 1632, John Browne presented a plan for the substitution of cast iron ordnance for bronze ordnance on all the smaller ships of the Navy. Browne stated that ninety tons of bronze ordnance would cost £14,332 5s. but if made of iron would cost only £3,600. Around 1636 it was estimated, always in England, that the cost of casting culverins and demi-culverins weighing 33 tons 12 cwts. would have been £5,355 2s. in bronze but only £1,176 in iron (*Calendar of State Papers*, Domestic, 1631-3, vol. 230, *n*. 36 and 1636-1637 vol. 340. *n*. 48). In 1578 in Spain " *el Capitan General del Arma* " Don Francis de Alava emphasized " the great utility of introducing into the Kingdom " the production of cast iron cannon and pointed out that while bronze cannon cost 16 ducats per hundred kilos weight, cast iron cannon cost only 5½ (Carrasco, *Artilleria de hierro*, p. 66). In 1644 Louis de Geer told the Swedish Privy Council that cast iron cannon cost one third the price of copper cannon (Heckscher, *Ekonomiska Historia*, part 1, vol. 2, p. 454). As to the price of the raw materials see below appendix 1.

quality were more than compensated by advantages in price. In their contemporary struggle to outsell foreign competitors in the textile sector, the English showed exactly the same attitude and followed the same line of action[1]. Their national genius for practicality becomes lucidly obvious in matters of decoration. " Through the whole series of English guns "— wrote Mr. Ffoulkes, Master of the Armouries at the Tower of London—" from the reign of Henry VIII to the middle of the nineteenth century one of the noticeable features is the simplicity of form and subordination of decoration to practical needs. . . . The same realization of technical and practical needs is to be found in English armour throughout the ages. We were never caught up in the maelstrom of magnificent incoherence which marks the designs for armour by Cellini, Campi, Giulio Romano and the Louvre School "[2]. What mostly mattered to the English was that their products would perform the task and cost as little as possible. No more striking contrast can be found to this attitude than the extravagance of some contemporary Italians who for the sake of beauty were engraving and decorating not only the guns but even the gun-shots, knowing perfectly well that this was detrimental to the efficiency of their artillery.

English cast iron guns soon became very popular throughout Europe. Many expert continental gunners fought a noisy opposition against them, but the economic advantages were too conspicuous for the governments to dismiss the new weapon lightheartedly and excellent export opportunities immediately arose for the English industry. By 1567 Queen Elizabeth granted Ralph Hogge the monopoly of exporting " cast iron ordnance with gunstone ", but already by 1573 Hogge was complaining that his privilege was constantly being infringed and that other gun-founders were exporting to Sweden, Denmark, France, Spain, Holland and even Flanders[3]. The structure of the demand for English cannon

[1] Cipolla, *Decline*, pp. 182-3.     [2] Ffoulkes, *Gun-Founders*, p. 28.
[3] Tawney-Power, *Documents*, vol. 1, pp. 262-3. The report by Mr.

underwent remarkable changes. Because of the increase of English privateering and seaborne trade, private internal demand grew very rapidly, and in time of peace it was much more substantial than public demand: in 1621 John Browne declared that the King's service would have only taken up ten days a year of his furnace's activity[1]. Foreign demand also became increasingly relevant, and around 1573, according to Master Hogge, the greater part of the cannon cast in England " was not to be sold nor bought to remain within the Realme "[2]. This aroused suspicion and anxiety among politicians. English guns were, in the words of Sir Walter Raleigh, " a jewel of great value "; why, argued the politicians, should the English place such " a jewel " in the hands

---

Hogge gives a colourful account of the way in which guns were smuggled out of the country. For exports to Denmark cf. Christensen, *Historia*, pp. 24-5.

[1] *Calendar State Papers*, Domestic, Addenda 1580-1625, vol. 42, no. 66, dec. (?) 1621.

[2] According to Mr. Hogge's report " there is above 400 tonnes cast yearly and all this will not be sold nor bought to remain within the Realme" (Tawney-Power, *Documents*, vol. 1, pp. 262-3). Some calculations preserved in *Calendar of State Papers* 14, vol. 26 no. 52, February 17, 1607 seem to suggest that between 1596 and 1603 about 2270 tons of cast-iron ordnance were exported from England under licence (about 58 tons by English merchants and 2212 tons by aliens), at an average of about 325 tons per year. The figure sounds reasonable, although the text of the document is obscure and its interpretation open to dispute.

In 1601 a certain Edward Peake made an appeal to the House of Commons to forbid any export of ordnance. He maintained that the Queen might make £3,000 a year out of a custom of £4 a ton on exported ordnance. He therefore implied a volume of exports as high as 750 tons per year (Taylor, *Camden's England*, p. 357). However, in the *Calendar of State Papers* 14/8/132 (July 1604) one reads that " the impost of ordnance ... may be valued at about £1,200 a year ". At the rate of £4 per ton, this would bring us back again to about 300 tons per year.

These were legal exports. To them one should add the illegal ones, whose amount is of course totally unknown. As indicated in the previous footnotes, during the last decades of the sixteenth and the early decades of the seventeenth centuries, English iron cannon was largely exported to Holland, Spain, France, Sweden and Denmark. It was also exported to Hamburg: for this cf. Ehrenberg, *Hamburg und England*, p. 296.

of potential enemies? This point of view was largely shared in political circles, and as a result Queen Elizabeth issued an order in 1574 restricting the number of guns to be cast in England to those " for the only use of the Realm ". From that time onward the export of guns was a point of contention between gun-founders anxious to sell as large a number of guns as possible whether at home or abroad and politicians no less eager to prohibit this export altogether. The natural result was a succession of petitions, proposals, arguments and counter-arguments, Acts of Parliament and regulations of licences on a scale sufficient to delight the heart of any Dr. Parkinson of those days[1].

Licences could be obtained to export ordnance, especially (although not exclusively)[2] to friendly Protestant powers. In 1619 Thomas Browne, who owned probably the largest gun foundry in England, admitted that half of his production was exported under licence to Holland[3], " the Dutch havinge bargained with him to take of all that the English doe not buy "[4]. When licence could not be obtained evasion was

[1] Cf. Straker, *Wealden*, p. 152; Hall, *Ballistics*, pp. 23-7; Taylor, *Camden's England*, p. 357.

[2] In 1619 there was " much murmuring " in England over the King's allowing the Spanish Ambassador to export a great quantity of powder and ordnance (*Calendar of State Papers*, Domestic, 1619-23, vol. 105, no. 103, Febr. 13, 1619). In 1621 Sir Richard Bendloss was reported having said that the King was mad to allow the Spanish Ambassador to export ordnance from England (*Calendar of State Papers*, Domestic, 1619-23, vol. 122, no. 71, August 12, 1621). In 1625, the King of France obtained permission to export from England 40 demiculverins (*Calendar of State Papers*, Domestic, 1625-6, vol. 2, no. 47, May 11, 1625).

[3] *Calendar of State Papers*, Domestic, 1619-23, vol. 105, no. 92, February 11, 1619).

[4] Schubert, *Iron Industry*, p. 249. Not many years before, in 1612, Thomas Browne was in trouble for having " transported much iron ordnance from that furnace (at Brenchley) against the law restricting the export of such ". The justices of the peace were ordered to seize all the iron ordnance stored at furnace (Schubert, *Extension*, p. 246). On Thomas Browne and his furnace at Brenchley as well as on his father John and the furnace at Ashworth cf. Schubert, *Extension* and here below appendix 1.

tried[1]. In 1583, twenty-three pieces *"de la fundicion nueva de Inglaterra"* were received in Spain with all their ammunition, certainly not through official and legal channels[2]. In 1589 Lord Buckhurst complained to the justices of the Rape of Lewes that as a result of their neglect, the surreptitious export of ordnance was going on. At the beginning of the seventeenth century, Edmund Mathew of Radyr was accused of having sent ordnance to Amsterdam, Danzig and Denmark without a licence, although he admitted to exporting only to Holland. In 1623 there were complaints that many Dutch ships were being furnished with English ordnance under the pretence of their belonging to Englishmen[3]. However, despite licences and surreptitious sales, there is no doubt that exports were hampered by the very existence of the general prohibition.

The views of the politicians sounded sensible as far as they went, but in fact they did not go very far. It was totally unrealistic to believe that the Continent, with an abundant supply of entrepreneurial ingenuity, and manufacturing skills, would easily submit to English superiority, especially in such a vital matter as the armament industry.

5—In 1574 there was a state of chronic war in the Low Countries between the Spanish-Catholic forces on one side and the Protestant dissidents on the other. Don Luis de Requesens, the new Spanish governor, was in principle favourable to the idea of peace negotiations but faced with a rapidly deteriorating military situation he had first to try to reorganize his forces and strengthen their armament. He

[1] On the methods used for exporting guns illegally from England see the Hogge's report reproduced by Tawney-Power, *Documents*, vol. 1, pp. 262-3.

[2] See above footnote [1], p. 35.

[3] Robertson, *Naval armament*, p. 79; Straker, *Wealden*, pp. 162-4; Taylor, *Camden's England*, p. 357; Schubert, *Cannon*, p. 139P; *Calendar of State Papers*, Domestic, 1619-23 (June 25, 1623).

revitalized the royal gun foundries at Malines by sending there about 35,000 lbs. of copper from Hungary and about 2,000 lbs. of English tin to be made into 38 guns [1]. But copper and tin were expensive. Requesens's financial situation was at the point of bankruptcy [2] and he needed more than 38 new guns. It is, therefore, not at all surprising if in the midst of his financial troubles the governor thought of English iron ordnance as a workable solution and placed a large order for cannon directly in England. Those, however, were the days when Queen Elizabeth had prohibited the export of English guns especially to Catholic powers, and no licence was issued in favour of Don Luis's request. Faced with the English refusal, the governor turned to continental foundries. Liége, then the capital of an independent and uncommitted principality, could boast of a great tradition in iron works since the Middle Ages. Guns had never been made there, but iron gun shot was currently cast and light arms were also produced. Requesens contacted a local prominent manufacturer, Wathier Godefrin, and placed an order for 46,000 cannon balls and 300 guns to him: a grand total of 620,000 lbs. of cast iron. Time and place of delivery: within six months in Antwerp. Despite the relatively short time allowed, guns and ammunitions were cast and delivered on time, but, alas, at the testing, the guns failed. The disappointed Spaniards got hold of M. Godefrin and clapped him for a while in the jails of Antwerp [3].

The list of continental failures in the race with English technology did not end with the misfortunes of M. Godefrin. A Spanish project to introduce the new technology in Biscay in 1574 failed because the available founders from England of Liége were not willing to move to Spain for fear of the Inquisition "*en que todos estaban harto danados*". In 1603 Flemish masters were again taken to Spain in order to set going the production of cast-iron guns, but again the project

---

[1] Henrard, *Documents*, p. 258.    [2] Pirenne, *Histoire*, vol. 4, p. 51.
[3] For all that precedes cf. Lejeune, *Capitalisme*, p. 185 and Evrard and Descy, *Vennes*, pp. 41-2.

had to be abandoned with a heavy financial loss for the admin-istration[1]. However, in the course of time, it was English politicians and not English gun-founders who were proved to be wrong.

6—The effective catalyst for continental developments was Holland. The Dutch needed cannon in ever-increasing quan-tity for their incessant wars against the Spaniards, for their huge navy[2] and for their overseas expansion. Their rapidly increasing wealth transformed need into effective demand. On the other hand, the conflict with Spain cut off Holland from the centres of cannon production in the Southern Low Countries. The Dutch had to find new solutions for their new problems. English cast-iron guns seemed at one point to offer a practical solution. Between 1560 and 1600 the Dutch imported large quantities of them[3] and looking back over the last decades of the sixteenth century a Venetian Ambassador wrote in 1603 that the Dutch " had been able to supply them-selves from England with all necessities and especially with artil-lery "[4]. But in 1574 under the pressure of English politicians,

[1] On the 1574 project cf. Carrasco, *Artilleria de hierro*, p. 66. On the 1603 affair which was rather poorly conducted see Carrasco, *Artilleria de bronce*, p. 187. It was calculated that it was more expensive to cast iron artillery in Spain than to import it, but we have no way of ascertaining the reliability of such calculations.

[2] Impressed by Dutch naval power, contemporaries generally over-estimated the size of the Dutch navy in the seventeenth century. Sir Walter Raleigh claimed that the Hollanders built one thousand ships a year and had 20,000 ships and vessels. The Jesuit Father Antonio Vieira gives the figure of 14,000 ships. Colbert in 1669 estimated that " the trade of all Europe is carried by 20,000 vessels of any size, and out of these 20,000 vessels, 15,000 to 16,000 belong to the Dutch 3,000 to 4,000 to the English and 500 to 600 to the French " (Clément, *Lettres*, vol. 6, p. 264). For a critical evaluation of all these more or less fantastic estimates and a more realistic appraisal of the size of the Dutch fleet in the seventeenth century cf. Vogel, *Handelsflotten*, pp. 268-334; Blok, *Geschiedenis*, vol. 2, p. 370; Boxer, *The Dutch*, pp. 204-5; Christensen, *Dutch Trade*, pp. 91-4.

[3] Elias, *Zeewezen*, vol. 1, p. 56; Baasch, *Wirtschaftsgeschichte*, p. 270*n*.; and here above paragraph 4.

[4] Barbour, *Amsterdam*, p. 36, *n*.93.

Elizabeth had established a control on the ordnance trade. Licences were more freely issued for exports to Holland than to the other countries[1]. Moreover, surreptitious exports to Holland were so frequent and easy[2] that they caused much loud complaint in England[3]. But the arrangement was not very satisfactory for the Dutch. Furthermore, with the beginning of the seventeenth century English industry ran into a serious bottleneck. As we will see later this must have affected English exports negatively and the first to suffer the consequences were obviously the Dutch. Guns were always in short supply in the United Provinces, and when the navy needed to equip the larger ships of the fleet for an action, guns had to be taken from the battlements of towns[4].

Under the pressure of the circumstances the Dutch set on foot a local cannon industry. Gun foundries, private as well as public sprang up like mushrooms in Maestricht, Utrecht, Amsterdam, Rotterdam, The Hague[5] and by the early seventeenth century the Dutch looked to Fynes Moryson " no less

[1] John Browne, who owned probably the largest gun foundry in England at Brenchley, declared in 1619 that half of the ordnance that he manufactured was bought and exported by the Dutch under licence (*Calendar of State Papers*, Domestic, 1619-23, vol. 105, no. 92, February 11, 1619). In 1625 Elias Trip of Amsterdam obtained licence to export 328 pieces of iron ordnance provided he marked each piece with its weight and quality (*Calendar of State Papers*, Domestic, 1623-5, vol. 182, no. 75, January 31, 1625; on the exports of English cannon by Elias Trip, cf. also Unger, *Middelburg*, doc. 1060 and Baasch, *Wirtschaftsgeschichte*, p. 270n.). Frequently Dutch merchants acted in England as special agents for their government. In 1594 and 1596 for instance Ludolph Engelstedt and Giles de Vischer were in London to buy cast-iron cannon and to procure export licences. Cf. Schubert, *Iron Industry*, p. 249.

[2] *Calendar of State Papers*, Domestic, 1619-23, vol. 147, no. 53, June 25, 1623.

[3] See above footnote [3] p. 46 and also Barbour, *Amsterdam*, p. 36, n.93.

[4] Elias, *Zeewezen*, vol. 1, p. 57.

[5] Cf. among many Elias, *Zeewezen*, vol. 1, p. 56; Van Dillen, *Amsterdam*, doc. 839 and 947; Van Dillen, *Amsterdam*, doc. 1408 and 1414; Unger, *Middelburg* doc. 1060. In 1601 mention is made of a patent given to a gunsmith in The Hague to manufacture wrought-iron cannon (cf. Japikse, *Resolutien*, p. 705).

witty than industrious so particularly they have great skill in casting great ordinance "[1]. In an early phase they kept to bronze artillery but they did not spare efforts to emulate the English in casting the cheaper iron guns. In 1601 and 1619 patents were granted to residents in Holland for the casting of iron guns in the English way[2]. In 1604 a double furnace was operating at Asslar west of Wetzlar in Germany, where iron ordnance was cast mainly for the Dutch[3]. In the 1620's iron guns were cast by the Dutch at Marsberg in Westphalia[4]. By then the new techniques were spreading throughout Europe, including areas that were not under direct Dutch influence[5].

---

[1] Moryson, *Itinerary*, vol. 4, p. 474. On the technical characteristics of the Dutch artillery, cf. Bonaparte-Favé, *Études*, book 1, vol. 3, pp. 314-22.

[2] Doorman, *Patents*, pp. 101 and 118.    [3] Schubert, *Cannon*, p. 138 p. ,

[4] Van Dillen, *Amsterdam*, doc. 537 and doc. 539; Doorman, *Patents* p. 118.

[5] At Letterewe in Scotland, where bog-ore and timber were locally available, Sir George Hay established a colony of Englishmen skilled in making iron and casting guns in the early 1600's (Lyth, *Scotland*, pp. 44-5).

In 1620, Henri de Harscamp and Guillaume Moniot " *maitres de forges et bourgeois de Namur* " having come to know " in their travels as well as in talks with other merchants that in England a method for casting iron cannon had been developed ", declared their intention to establish an iron-gun foundry and asked the government for monopoly privileges (Borgnet, *Chartes namuroises*, p. 155, doc. 505). Their enterprise was successful, which is proven by the fact that late in the 1630's the King of Spain was heavily indebted to the families Harscamp and Moniot for artillery sold to him (cf. Del Marmol, *Industries*, p. 251). For iron cannon cast in Liége, cf. the text by Firrufino quoted by Carrasco, *Artilleria de hierro*, p. 68. Significantly enough in 1622 when the Spanish officials planned to establish manufactures of cast-iron cannon in Spain, they asked the famous merchant John Curtius of Liége to take over the project. In Italy the main centres for the production of iron fire-arms were Bergamo and Brescia. In the case of Liége as in that of Bergamo and Brescia however, it was mainly a question of hand-guns. For France we know that in 1627 a Frenchman, acting on behalf of the Duc de Bouillon tried to persuade Sussex iron-founders to go to France and disclosed that an English iron-founder had already settled there (Schubert, *Iron Industry*, p. 254, *n.1*).

In Spain, after the abortive efforts of 1574 and 1603 (see above footnote [1] p. 48), the Crown tried to establish iron-gun foundries again in 1622. This time the enterprise met with success and a manufacture was set up at

In the course of time the Dutch arranged their armament production on a double basis. They retained the production of bronze guns in the Netherlands, where through their commercial network, they could amass copper from Sweden and Japan and tin from England and Germany. They organized the casting of iron guns abroad where suitable iron ore and charcoal were available[1].

---

Liérganes, near Santander. By the early 1630's good ordnance was cast there. The founders were allegedly Germans. (Carrasco, *Artilleria de hierro*, p. 67ff.). In 1666 Colbert wrote to his cousin Colbert de Terron: " *l'on me donne avis qu'il se fond en Biscaye de canons de fer fort bons* " (Clément, *Lettres*, vol. 3, part 1, p. 85. Biscay and especially the town of Bilbao had a tradition in iron manufactures and throughout the later Middle Ages wrought-iron cannon was produced in Bilbao: Guiard y Larrauri, *Industria naval*, p. 12n. and 56n.). On the iron industry and trade in Biscay and Guipuzcoa cf. also Lapeyre, *Ruiz*, pp. 586-9. Beck, (*Geschichte*, vol. 2, p. 991) gives references to iron cannon cast in Prussia in 1667 and (*ibid*, vol. 2, p. 992) in Bohemia.

[1] According to Janiçon, *Provinces-Unies*, vol. 2, the " red copper " of Japan was considered superior to the " copper of Rosetta " (the best available in Europe) and the Dutch used it also in the production of bronze ordnance. On the Dutch imports of copper from Japan and Sweden and the price of copper in Amsterdam cf. Glamann, *Trade*, passim. For the relative prices of iron and copper in Amsterdam cf. below appendix 1. For the price of English and German tin in Amsterdam in the early 1670's (respectively 52 and 45 *livres* per hundred pounds weight) cf. the report by Seignelay in Clément, *Lettres*, vol. 3, part 2, p. 311.

Occasionally some bronze guns were imported into the Low Countries in the course of the seventeenth century (cf. Bang, *Tabeller*, under the years 1630, 1636 and 1639) and some cast iron guns were manufactured there at the beginning of the same century (see above footnote [2] p. 50). By 1671 the Marquis de Seignelay wrote in his *Addition au memoire concernant la fonderie des canons* (Bibl. Nat. Paris, Dept. mss. Colbert 4219, *f.* 10) in regard to cast iron cannon that " *il ne s'en fond pointe en aucun endroit de Holande et il vient tout fondu de Suede et de Moscovie quoy qu'il en vien assez peu de Moscovie* ".

But one should not take this statement too literally: there were Dutch imports of cast iron cannon also from Western Germany (see below, footnote [3], p. 59) and a patent was granted in Amsterdam in 1677 for the casting of " iron cannon that cannot burst " (Doorman, *Patents*, p. 185, July 1677).

The production of both iron and bronze artillery in the Netherlands

7—Sweden is naturally endowed with abundant and excellent copper, tin and iron ores, with vast charcoal-producing forests and enough streams for water power and transportation. Since the days of Gustav Vasa (1523-60) manufactures for the production of fire-arms had been set on foot especially in the mining districts of Central Sweden. A very active role in these developments was played by the Crown, which owned many of the factories and tried to improve the standard of production by employing foreign technicians [1].

Three phases seem to stand out: a first between 1530 and 1560 in which a number of factories were opened for the production of wrought-iron guns; a second between 1560 and 1580 in which foundries appeared mostly for the production of cast-bronze ordnance; and a third after 1580, which saw the appearance and growth of the furnaces for the production of cast iron guns [2]. In catching up with the rest of Europe, Sweden was concentrating into a few decades the evolutionary process that the Continent had taken centuries to accomplish.

Cast iron guns in Sweden are first heard of in 1560, but it seems that this was only a matter of more or less experimental activity. The effort was evidently continued and after 1568

was accompanied by technological progress documented, among other things, by a series of patents for new types of guns with a high rate of fire: cf. Doorman, *Patents*, p. 143 (29th April 1645) p. 178 ( July 1645) and p. 182 (August 1666).

[1] Guns are first mentioned in Swedish sources in the fifteenth century, but were not currently used till the time of Gustav I Vasa. This enterprising and ruthless innovator not only imported guns from Lübeck and other Hansa towns but also initiated the manufacture of fire-arms in Sweden. On this and the royal policies regarding the development of arms manufactures cf. Jakobsson, *Beväpning*, pp. 25-48 and Heijkenskjöld, *Styckegjutning*, pp. 57-85.

[2] Jakobsson, *Beväpning*, pp. 44-6, gives a list of gun factories that operated in Sweden in the sixteenth century. For each factory he gives either the date when gun production was started or the date when the first mention of arm production is encountered in the extant documents. I have arranged the data in the following table. Jakobsson, does not make reference in his list to the gun factory at Åkers: I have therefore integrated his information with the data that I derived from Hahr, *Åkers*, p. 6. There are

there are no further references to wrought-iron guns, while there is clear evidence of castings of iron artillery[1]. How satisfactory such cast iron guns were, it is difficult to say, but it seems that they were not very good[2]. Production seems to have been very limited also from a quantitative point of view[3]. The fact of the matter was that the growth of Swedish manufacture was severely hampered on the one hand by shortages of capital, entrepreneurship and skilled labour and on the other by the lack of financial and commercial organization to help in the marketing of the product abroad.

Knowing how desperately the Dutch were looking around for ordnance, it cannot be surprising if they soon became

---

some other gaps in Jakobsson's list that I could not fill, however I do not think that the picture could be substantially changed.

| year in which the factory began to operate or first mention is made of its cannon production | number of factories producing | | |
|---|---|---|---|
| | wrought iron cannon | cast bronze cannon | cast iron cannon |
| 1530 to 1540 | 2 | | |
| 1541 to 1550 | 5 | | |
| 1551 to 1560 | 2 | 2 | |
| 1561 to 1570 | 2 | 2 | |
| 1571 to 1580 | | | 1 |
| 1581 to 1590 | | 1 | 3 |
| 1591 to 1600 | | 1 | 4 |
| 1601 to 1610 | | | 3 |

[1] Jakobsson, *Beväpning*, p. 42.

[2] On the fact that before the 1620's Swedish cast iron cannon were not very dependable weapons cf. below footnote [1], p. 61. One scarcely hears of Swedish exports of ordnance before 1615 (cf. Heijkenskjöld, *Styckegjutning*, p. 72). In 1618 Louis de Geer was still importing war material from Holland into Sweden (Christensen, *Dutch Trade*, p. 164). Considering how much in demand cannon was on the Continent, the absence of Swedish exports is further proof of the poor quality of early Swedish products. For an occasional export of bronze cannon from Sweden in 1562 cf. Odén, *Netherland merchant*, pp. 20-1.

[3] Heijkenskjöld, *Styckegjutning*, p. 58 *n*.2 quotes a few figures whose real meaning is not very clear, but seem to indicate that until 1600 production of cast iron cannon was very limited.

interested in the Swedish developments. The growth of their trade and activities in the North and the fact that some technicians from the Low Countries were working in Swedish factories, undoubtedly helped to the establishment of the contacts. The arrival of the Dutch brought to Sweden the human element[1] and the capital necessary to activate Swedish wealth fully. At the same time the Dutch commercial organization transmitted to the Scandinavian manufactures the stimuli of the large demand for cannon connected with the Dutch and English overseas expansion, the Dutch-Spanish wars and the Thirty Years War. Within the three first decades of the seventeenth century, Swedish industry underwent a revolutionary change and Sweden took its place in the front rank of the European armament industry[2].

---

[1] Many skilled workers emigrated to Sweden from the Low Countries during the first half of the seventeenth century. The majority of them came from the Southern Low Countries and were generally referred to as " Walloons ". On this emigration one may consult Wiberg, *De Geer et la colonisation*. Catholics and Calvinists alike enjoyed in Sweden complete religious freedom at least until 1654 (cf. Pehrsson, *Invandrade Vallonernas*). The tolerant attitude of the Swedes toward Catholic technicians vividly contrasts with the intolerant attitude of the Spaniards toward Protestant workers (cf. above footnote [1], p. 34). In fact, non-Catholic technicians did not go to Spain for fear of the Inquisition (cf. above p. 47).

[2] For a broader view of the change with reference not only to cannon manufacture but to the whole iron industry cf. Hildebrand, *Historia*, pp. 3-84. A short English summary of this important work is given by Boëthius, *Swedish iron*, pp. 144-75. It should be emphasized that the development of the Swedish iron industry was largely dependent on the exports of a semi-finished product, namely bar-iron whose exports grew from less than 6·5 thousand metric tons around 1620 to about 11 thousand tons around 1640, about 17 thousand tons around 1650, about 30 thousand tons around 1700. Cannon was the only finished product which was manufactured and exported on a large scale by the Swedish iron industry. Comparing the figures of bar-iron exports with the figures of cannon exports reproduced in Tab. 1 one must consider that cannon was valued more than bar-iron per unit of weight. In the 1670's the price of cannon was about 30% higher than that of bar-iron (cf. the report by De Seignelay about Holland: " *le fer dont ils se servent pour leur menus ouvrages est du fer en verge qui leur vient de Suède et qui couste 6 à 7 livres le*

The key-men in this phase of our history were Guillaume de Beche, Elias and Jacob Trip and their sons and especially Louis de Geer, the fabulous founder of a huge industrial empire[1]. The Dutch were essentially interested in getting cast iron guns from Sweden and the nature and weight of their demand strongly influenced the patterns of Swedish developments. The production of cast iron guns expanded very rapidly and so did exports. We first hear of exports of some size in 1615 when a letter of Gustavus Adolphus discloses that the States General of Holland had requested 400 Swedish iron guns[2]. In 1620 an unknown quantity of guns was purchased by Elias Trip and shipped to Holland[3]. In the same year it was noticed in Amsterdam that Swedish cannon were finding an easy outlet there[4]. Six years later exports of cast iron guns from Sweden amounted to nearly 22 metric tons[5]. From then onward, they increased at a great speed. Over the period 1637-40 they reached the level of *c.* 780 metric tons per year, between 1641 and 1644 *c.* 940 tons and in the three years period 1645-7 *c.* 1,100 tons per year. Between

---

cent. *Leur fer en barre leur vient du mesme lieu et le meilleur ne leur couste que 6 ou 7 livres.* (Clément, *Lettres*, vol. 3, part. 2, p. 311.)

The export of cannon contributed also to the development of Swedish shipping industry. According to the Sund's statistics until 1628 Swedish iron cannon were brought westward on Dutch vessels. Between 1629 and 1635 Swedish vessels carried part of the exports. After 1635 the greatest share was shipped under the Swedish flag. Cf. Bang, *Tabeller*, ad annos.

[1] On De Beche, De Geer and the Trips cf. appendix 1.

[2] Heijkenskjöld, *Styckegjutning*, pp. 72-3.  [3] *Ibid.*, p. 75, *n.*1.

[4] Dahlgren, *De Geer*, vol. 1, p. 115.

[5] Cf. table 1. It does not seem that 1626 was a year of exceptionally low exports. By that time the Swedish cannon industry was not yet fully developed. In a letter written in 1626 from Lübeck, Conrad von Falkenberg noticed: " Swedish iron cannon and ammunition are much in demand and I could do good business if only I had enough to sell ". Two years later von Falkenberg wrote from Amsterdam that " the guns that come from Sweden are considered very good. The people here use them to arm their vessels and do not go very much after other artillery. There is no evidence that many iron-guns are now imported from England." (cf. Heijkenskjöld, *Styckegjutning*, p. 73).

1655 and 1662 the yearly average was again around the 1,100 tons, with a peak in the years 1661 and 1662 when exports reached respectively 1,459 and 2,556 tons (see table 1) mostly shipped to Holland [1]. As to the numbers of guns involved, it may be calculated that the average weight of the pieces exported varied in different years, ranging generally between *c*. 610 kg. (in 1660) and 1,810 kg. (in 1662). The number of pieces exported in selected years was as follows: [2]

| | |
|---|---|
| 1655 | 367 |
| 1656 | 1,048 |
| 1657 | 698 |
| 1658 | 1,191 |
| 1660 | 1,150 |
| 1661 | 2,440 |
| 1662 | 1,412 |

[1] Not all cannon exported to Amsterdam was necessarily retained in Holland, some being re-exported to England, Portugal and other places.

Direct exports of cast iron cannon from Sweden to England are first mentioned in 1632. Records of direct exports to Lübeck and Hamburg are preserved for the following years, namely:

| | |
|---|---|
| 1656: | 233 metric tons |
| 1657: | 95 |
| 1658: | 111 |
| 1660: | 58 |
| 1661: | 55 |

Portugal turned to Holland and Sweden for her cannon supply after the revolution of 1640 against Spain. There were direct shipments of cast iron cannon from Sweden to Portugal in 1661 (127 metric tons) and in 1694 (114 metric tons).

In 1694 iron cannon was exported from Sweden to the following places:

| | | | |
|---|---|---|---|
| England: | 10 metric tons | Wismar: | 1 metric tons |
| Holland: | 8 | Danzig: | 52 |
| Portugal: | 114 | Riga: | 14 |
| Denmark: | 36 | Reval: | 2 |
| Hamburg: | 65 | Rostock | 28 |
| Lübeck: | 48 | Nyenskans: | 12 |
| | | Narva: | 41 |

All data are derived from Heijkenskjöld, *Styckegjutning*, pp. 75-6. As to the metrological problems involved cf. here in the text note to table 1.

[2] Heijkenskjöld, *Styckegjutning*, pp. 75-6.

To give a meaning to these figures, one can say that the guns exported in one year from Sweden, were enough to equip a small fleet[1], or at least half a dozen powerful squadrons[2].

TABLE I

## EXPORTS OF CAST IRON CANNON FROM SWEDEN
(metric tons)

| year | total | of which to Holland |
|------|-------|---------------------|
| 1626 | 22 | |
| 1637 | 576 | |
| 1638 | 467 | |
| 1639 | 1,047 | |
| 1640 | 1,044 | 1,044 |
| 1641 | 1,202 | 1,202 |
| 1642 | 1,156 | |
| 1643 | 654 | |
| 1644 | 761 | |
| 1645 | 1,498 | |
| 1646 | 1,084 | |
| 1647 | 728 | |
| 1650 | 1,210 | |
| 1655 | 364 | 364 |
| 1656 | 1,234 | 1,000 |

[1] The guns in the rival fleets in the Armada campaign (1588) including 4-pounders but not smaller ones, numbered 1124 for the Spanish and 1972 for the English (Lewis, *Armada*, p. 78). In 1618 all the warships of the Mediterranean navies carried no more than 5,000 guns altogether (cf. below footnote [3], p. 79). In 1661 the armament of the whole French navy (counting not only guns on board the ships but also guns temporarily deposited in the arsenals) amounted to 1,045 guns. (Clément, *Lettres*, vol. 3, part 2, pp. 699-700). Admittedly the French fleet was then in poor shape. By 1677 as a result of Colbert's efforts, its armament (always including cannon in the arsenals) had increased to nearly 12,000 guns out of which about 9,000 were of iron (Basset, *Historique*, p. 1004).

[2] The squadron sent by the French to the East Indies in 1670 under Admiral De la Haye, had aboard 238 guns. The squadron was considered strong enough to impress all Asian potentates and to challenge the Dutch and the English power in Asian waters (Kaeppelin, *Compagnie*, p. 29).

| year | total | of which to Holland |
|---|---|---|
| 1657 | 778 | 683 |
| 1658 | 1,242 | 1,131 |
| 1659 | 243 | |
| 1660 | 931 | 873 |
| 1661 | 1,459 | 1,277 |
| 1662 | 2,556 | 2,394 |
| 1664 | 1,274 | |
| 1668 | 1,346 | |
| 1685 | 259 | |
| 1694 | 432 | 8 |

Source: Heijkenskjöld, *Styckegjutning*, pp. 73-4. The figures are originally given in *skeppund*. The value of this unit of measure varied from place to place, from about 195·4 kg. in some districts to 136 kg. in most "staple districts" (cf. Jansson, *Måttordbok*, pp. 72-3). According to the indications given by Hildebrand, *Historia*, p. 457 I have adopted the equivalence of 136 kg. (1 metric ton=1,000 kilos =0·9842 English tons=7,353 skeppund).

The figures given by Heijkenskjöld correspond to the figures derived from different sources and published by Boëthius-Heckscher, *Handelstatistik*, pp. 102-3 for some years (1637, 1638, 1639, 1640, 1641, 1645 and 1650). Only for the year 1641 does one notice a small difference between the two sources (8,840 skeppund according to Heijkenskjöld and 9,293 according to Boëthius-Heckscher). For a number of years no data are given in Table 1. This is imputable to the state of the available Swedish records and it does not imply that in the corresponding years there were no exports of cannon from Sweden. The documents relating to the passages at the Sund (Bang, *Tabeller* ad annum) prove that iron cannon was brought "westward" also in the years 1622, 1623, 1624, 1625, 1627, 1628, 1629, 1630, 1631, 1633, 1635, 1636, 1648, 1649, 1651, 1652, 1653, 1654, etc. The absence of any figure in the column *Holland* means that indications are not given about the destination of Swedish exports for the corresponding years.

8—Germany was another area where Dutch demand for cannon gave impetus to the manufacture of iron artillery. Mention has been made of the iron works at Asslar which were operating as early as 1604. In 1612 the Dutch controlled two of the six blast furnaces at Marsberg in Eastern Westphalia, where in the 1620's they set on foot iron cannon production[1]. The Dutch were also the main customers of Jean Mariotte, a native of Liége, who between 1630 and 1650 established successful manufactures of iron ordnance at Weinhär in the domains of the Abbey of Amstein and at Stromberg, north of Koblenz[2].

The Thirty Years War, while stimulating local demand for artillery, caused widespread destruction of plants and loss of skilled labour. Developments were therefore erratic. But after the middle of the seventeenth century, the production of Western Germany grew very rapidly and by the 1660's Swedish industry was feeling its competition. It seems that the main centre of trading in German iron ordnance was Cologne where the Dutch were active buyers still at the end of the century[3].

The Dutch were also instrumental in developing gun foundries in Russia. In the 1630's a Dutch group established iron works near Tula, about 120 miles south of Moscow[4] and allegedly was the first to bring to Russia western and modern methods of casting iron[5]. Skilled labour was not available in Russia, and technicians had to be imported from abroad. This was not easy[6]. On the other hand, with serfdom still

[1] Schubert, *Superiority*, p. 86, and above footnote [4], p. 50.

[2] Yernaux, *Métallurgie*, pp. 79 and 172-5.

[3] For the impact of German competition on Swedish production cf. Barbour, *Amsterdam*, p. 41, *n*.114. On Dutch purchases of German iron cannon in Cologne cf. Janiçon, *Provinces-Unies*, vol. 1, p. 473.

[4] For the complicated story of the enterprise cf. Strumilin, *Istoriia*, pp. 102*ff*. and Amburger, *Marselis*, pp. 92-130, 150-4 and 168-74. A. Winius, Peter Marselis and Ph. Akema played the main roles in the whole story but for a short period also Elias Trip, J.Willekens and Th. de Swaen had interests in the business. The project was officially started in 1632 but the factory was not in full operation until 1639-40. Internal struggles and other difficulties caused two big crises and interruptions in the works in 1647 and in 1662.

[5] Portal, *L'Oural*, p. 188.

[6] Cf. Amburger, *Marselis*, pp. 104-5. Most of the skilled workers were brought from the Southern Low Countries and were generally referred to

prevailing in the country, unskilled labour was plentiful and could be secured at very low cost[1]. It was largely employed in cutting trees and in providing fuel. The government looked very favourably upon the Dutch initiatives and supported them with annual subsidies as well as with grants of rights on serf-labour[2]. But the result of all these efforts was not very satisfactory. The products of the Russian foundries could be offered at a very low price in Amsterdam, but their quality was extremely poor, and still at the end of the seventeenth century Russian production was not considered very important[3]. Anyhow a nucleus had been established and its significance was to become clear in the following century[4].

---

as " French ". Also Swedish iron-workers were induced to go to Russia. This caused concern in Sweden and in 1647 the Swedish resident in Moscow endeavoured to have some of the Swedish workers repatriated (cf. Amburger, *Marselis*, pp. 104 and 109). Actually it was not easy to attract skilled workers to Russia (Amburger, *Marselis*, pp. 104*ff.* and Strumilin, *Istoriia*, pp. 103*ff.*) and this bottleneck caused serious difficulties to the entrepreneurs.

[1] According to Strumilin, *Istoriia*, pp. 105*ff.* the average wage of the Russian workers was one fourth of the average wage of foreign workers.

[2] Strumilin, *Istoriia*, pp. 106*ff.* and Mavor, *Russia*, vol. I, pp. 434-5.

[3] The Marquis de Seignelay wrote in 1671 to his father Colbert that the Dutch were importing " a few cast-iron guns from Moscovia which however are not very good and are sold at very low price" (Clément, *Lettres*, vol. 3, part 2, p. 311). In his *Addition au memoire concernant la fonderie des canons* dated July 1671 (Bibl. Nat. Paris, Dept. mss., Colbert 4219, *f.* 11) the Marquis added: " *a les gard des canons de fer il ne s'en fond point en aucun endroit de Holande et il vient tout fondu de Suede et de Moscovie quoy qu'il en vien assez peu de Moscovie ... Le fer de Suede est le meilleur et le plus estimé. Il en vien peu de Moscovie qui mesme n'est pas bon* ". In 1674 Kilburger (*Handel*, p. 324) wrote that the cannon produced at the Russian factories (only up to 24-pounders) " were exported via Archangel to Holland where they generally blew up at their testing ". According to Amburger (*Marselis*, p. 105) the poor quality of the Russian products was mainly due to shortage of skilled labour. On the report by Kilburger and its information on Russian cannon cf. also Kurts, *Socinenie Kilburgera*, pp. 451-69. On the report by Kilburger in general cf. Nyström, *Mercatura*, pp. 239-96. According to Strumilin (*loc. cit.*) 600 cannon were exported to Holland in 1646 and 360 cannon in 1647.

[4] Cf. below Epilogue, p. 144.

9—The early imitations of English cast iron guns were far from satisfactory: "Att first"—said an English Report dated 1623 about Swedish products—"theis peeces in the proovinge brake most of them"[1] and in 1627, out of eleven cast-iron guns that the Dutch obtained from France, six exploded during "reasonable testing" and one lost its rear[2]. But soon substantial improvements were accomplished and by 1623, according to the English Report, Swedish guns were "so amended that they are scarce to be knowne from English peeces and now keepe good proofe"[3]. That they had been "amended" and that they kept "good proofe" was certainly true, but to say that "they are scarce to be knowne from English peeces" was possibly an exaggeration in which the author of the Report indulged in order to get help from the Crown for the local industry. The son of Colbert, the Marquis de Seignelay, reported to his father in 1671 that "there

[1] Public Record Office, London, State Papers 14/155 no. 11 (f.840) December 3, 1623: "Relation of Iron Ordenance made beyond the Seas. Sir, there hath bene cast about the space of 4 yeres since many iron ordenance in Soreland (Södermanland) brought by the way of Breame to Amsterdam and there sould. Much is now suppressed by reason of the trobles where the merchantes of Amsterdam had 4 furnaces to cast and have still 2 furnaces now casting. Likewise there are iron peeces cast in Lukeland (?) and brought from thence into Holland and there sould. And there are merchantes of Amsterdam, Lewes de Geere and his companie which have in Sweden fowor furnaces to cast iron ordenance and have done theis 4 yeres, which peeces they bringe to Amsterdam and there is now to sell at Amsterdam about 3 or 400 peeces which they doe sell for 15 or 16 gilders per centum. If any man please to have anie of them brought at theire charge to London and that they may bee carried backe againe in some reasonable tyme, they shalbee brought to proove my words true. Att the first, theis peeces in the proovinge brake most of them and now they are so amended that they are scarce to be knowne from English peeces and now keepe good proofe. The workemen that cast them are dutch-men and wallons. Nevertheles I take it if English peeces weare suffred to be carried over all theis furnaces would be suppressed in short tyme. If not, peeces they must have whatsoever they cost and daily they will be more and more experienced in casting of peeces".

[2] Van Dillen, *Amsterdam*, doc. 1108.

[3] See above footnote [1].

is a great difference between the Swedish and the English guns, those cast in England being far superior " [1]. This also was possibly an exaggeration in which the Marquis indulged under the influence of English current opinion but it is not improbable that he was nearer to the truth than the author of the English Report of 1623. The Dutch were not so concerned with quality as they were with costs and in their trades they were always ready to sacrifice the first to the latter. They did so also in the cloth trade and in the wine trade [2]. If they did not produce iron guns as good as those produced in England, they certainly succeeded in underselling English iron ordnance and in making Amsterdam the main munition market of Europe [3]. Their task was made easier by England's increasing difficulties with her local supply of timber. Since the accession of Elizabeth complaints about deforestation were frequently heard and in the course of time became more alarmingly frequent in one county after the other [4]. In table II, I have compared a general price index with an index for the price of charcoal in England during the period 1560 to 1670 [5]. The results of a comparison

[1] Clément, Lettres, vol. 3, part 2, p. 332.

[2] For the cloth trade cf. Hyma, The Dutch, p. 19; for the wine trade cf. Dion, Histoire, pp. 426-7.

[3] On the role of Amsterdam as the main European market for arms and munitions during the seventeenth century and the first decades of the eighteenth century, cf. Barbour, Amsterdam, pp. 40-2.

[4] Nef, Coal, vol. I, pp. 158-61. The casting of iron cannon was one of the reasons for the shortage of timber in many areas of England. As early as 1548-9 the English Government had ordered an inquiry on the wastage of timber caused by iron-works in Sussex (cf. Tawney-Power, Documents, vol. I, pp. 231-8). In 1637 the clothmakers of the town of Cranbrook in Kent complained to the Privy Council against John Browne on the ground that he had raised the price they paid for wood by burning large quantities in his furnace (Nef, Coal, vol. I, p. 214). However, another important reason for deforestation was the claim of timber for shipbuilding: cf. Albion, Forests and Sea Power.

[5] The general price index has been calculated by Phelps Brown and Hopkins and represents the aggregate price for a composite commodity unit made up of some given amounts of farinaceous, meat and fish, drinks, textiles, light and fuel including charcoal. The other index is based on the prices paid by Eton College for charcoal. Cf. note to table II.

between the two series should be accepted with reserve. General price indexes look attractive when neatly printed but their real meaning is always obscure. The series of charcoal refers to one limited area only and other instances should be considered before drawing general conclusions. Tentatively however one may say that according to available figures the fuel crisis seems to have exploded in all its gravity during the 1630's [1]. English iron guns were still exported in the second and third decades of the seventeenth century but, notwithstanding the vociferous allegations of patriots, it does not seem that the trade was very prosperous [2]. In the 1630's when the fuel

---

[1] According to Albion, *Sea Power*, chapt. 3, the timber problem became acute " during the Restoration ". According to Nef, *Coal*, vol. 1, pp. 158-61 the " crisis " was more acute " in the century and a half preceding 1660 than in the century and a half following ". Some of the figures on which Professor Nef bases his assertion were derived from Wiebe's work and do not inspire much confidence. The figures and the facts quoted above in the text seem to indicate that the crisis exploded before 1660 but after 1600.

[2] In 1610 the House of Lords passed a bill forbidding the " transportation of Ordnance, gun metal, iron ore, iron mine and iron shot " to places outside the Realm, except such as were directed for defence or by persons holding letters patent from the Crown. Those who did this were " taken for felons " and were submitted to heavy penalties (*Calendar of State Papers*, 14/58/12, November, 1610 and *Journal of the House of Lords*, 6th, 10th, 13th, 20th and 23rd November, 1610). A bill prohibiting the export of ordnance was again introduced in the House of Commons in 1614 on the grounds that " the Hollanders are nowe so stronge by reason of our English ordinance that they beginne to outbrave the Englishe " (Barbour, *Amsterdam*, p. 36).
Iron ordnance was in fact still exported from England in the 1610's and in the 1620's (Tawney, *Business*, pp. 70-1 and here above footnotes [1] and [2] p. 45), but despite the assertions of patriotic speakers at the House of Commons, it does not seem that after 1610 English exports of iron cannon amounted to any considerable volume. Prof. Friis noted (*Kobbermarked*, p. 175, *n*. 3) that " the English tollbooks for the first quarter of the seventeenth century do not show exports of cannon of any importance ". This does not prove much, first because " the impost of ordinance was always paid into the Receipte and was not charged in the customes Bookes " (*Calendar of State Papers*, 14/8/132), and secondly because much ordnance was exported illegally. However, it is true that in 1628 a Swedish observer in Amsterdam wrote that " there is no evidence that many iron-guns are now imported from England " (Heijkenskjöld, *Styckegjutning*, p. 73).

crisis became acute England began to import iron cannon. The first mention one encounters of Swedish iron guns shipped directly from Sweden to England is in 1632 [1] and from 1638 we know of many shipments of Swedish guns from Amsterdam to England [2]. In the early 1670's the Marquis de Seignelay wrote that the English " not having enough timber for casting all the ordnance they need, get cannon from Sweden although they esteem that the Swedish iron is not as good as that of England." [3]

TABLE II

INDEXES OF PRICES IN ENGLAND
1560–1670
(1630=100)

| year | price-indexes | |
|------|---------|----------|
|      | general | charcoal |
| 1560 | 46 | 60 |
| 1610 | 90 | 95 |
| 1620 | 87 | 100 |
| 1630 | 100 | 100 |
| 1640 | 106 | 135 |
| 1650 | 133 | 225 |
| 1660 | 121 | 220 |
| 1670 | 102 | 250 |

Sources: Phelps Brown and Hopkins, *Prices*, pp. 194-5 and Beveridge, *Prices*, pp. 144-5. In order to avoid the effects of the short run fluctuations of food prices, the figures for the general price index have been calculated on the basis of a five years' average about the corresponding year.

[1] See above footnote [1], p. 56. In the Sund's statistics one also notices iron cannon being brought " westward " on English vessels in 1647 and 1648 (see Bang, *Tabeller*, ad annum).

[2] Barbour, *Amsterdam*, p. 38, n.98.

[3] Clément, *Lettres*, vol. 3, part 2, p. 322.

10—Iron guns in general, even those of the best quality, continued to be considered an inferior substitute for bronze ordnance. For reasons of safety iron guns had to be heavier than bronze ones[1]. This caused a series of inconveniences because the greater weight reduced the mobility of the pieces on land and on the sea it endangered the seaworthiness of the vessels in rough weather. Furthermore, despite their greater thickness, iron guns did not reach the same degree of reliability of bronze ordnance. In 1621 the Dutch Government requested the Admiralty to cast new bronze artillery each year in order to replace the cast iron that they still considered too dangerous for both ships and crews[2]. In England Lord Carew declared in 1626 that during and since Elizabeth's time it had been thought fit, when possible, to furnish forts with iron ordnance and to reserve bronze ordnance for ships[3]. However, the high cost of bronze, and the growing need for artillery never allowed such perfectionist plans to be fully carried out. Moreover, in the course of time, progress was made in the casting of iron. By 1626 the Officers of the English Navy Board, after having been directed to see what could be done towards "reforming the abuse of overweight" of iron ordnance, pointed out that John Browne at his famous gun foundry had succeeded in casting six iron guns which had endured the King's double proof and yet were lighter than bronze ordnance[4].

[1] For instance in the 1620's and 1630's a Swedish 6-pounder had an average weight of about 500 kg. if cast in bronze and of 800 to 1000 kg. if cast in iron. A 3-pounder averaged normally around 400 kg. if cast in bronze and 500 to 550 kg. if cast in iron. Cf. Jakobsson, *Beväpning*, pp. 213-4, 231 and 248-9.

[2] Elias, *Zeewezen*, vol. 1, p. 88.

[3] *Calendar of State Papers*, Domestic, 1625-6, vol. 19, no. 2 (Jan. 21, 1626).

[4] *Calendar of State Papers*, Domestic, 1625-6, vol. 25, no. 79 (April 28, 1626). The Venetian ambassador Alvise Contarini was probably referring to the "invention" of John Browne, when he wrote to the Doge in 1629 that "two sorts of guns may be had here [in England]. The light one invented lately, which does not weigh one half of the usual artillery, and will cost about $5\frac{1}{2}$ ducats the quintal that is 112 pound weight. The heavy

The use of cast iron guns became progressively more common in the course of the seventeenth century especially on the seas, and by the end of the century cast iron guns were the predominant artillery aboard European vessels [1].

It was mainly in connection with the needs of the navy that Colbert took action to remedy the weakness of France in the armament industry and to develop the manufacture of cast-iron guns. After the exploits of French artillerymen during the period 1450 to 1550, the French cannon industry entered a period of disruption and decline. The civil wars and the political confusion that followed were mainly responsible for this state of affairs. A chaotic administration, weakened by antagonistic factions could not lend any organized support to the armament industry while this one could not live without some kind of government assistance. Many skilled workers left the country for religious reasons or in search of better pay

---

guns of the old sort will cost about 3 ducats *di banco* the quintal " (*Calendar of State Papers*, Venetian, vol. 21, p. 572, no. 780).

[1] In Sweden in 1658 fifty per cent of the cannon of the navy were made of cast iron. In 1677 the proportion had increased to about 66 per cent (Heckscher, *Ekonomiska Historia*, part 1, vol. 2, p. 454). Similarly in France the proportion was 45% in 1661 and 70% in 1667 (Clément, *Lettres*, vol. 3, part 2, pp. 699-700). In England, according to a report by the Marquis de Seignelay, dated 1671: " the large first class warships are ordinarily gunned with brass ordnance . . . On the second and third class warships they have one third brass ordnance and the rest is iron artillery. On the other vessels they place artillery according to what is available " (Clément, *Lettres*, vol. 3 part 2, pp. 312 and 332). As to the Dutch, a Swedish observer in Amsterdam noticed in 1633 that less than one out of fifty ships had bronze cannon aboard (Heckscher, *Ekonomiska Historia*, part 1, vol. 2, p. 454). In 1671 the Marquis de Seignelay reported that the proportion of brass and iron artillery aboard Dutch vessels " depended upon the will of the superintendent of the armament. However, one may say that the admirals have always the inferior artillery on the lower decks . . . The warship of Ruyter is armed only with brass ordnance " (cf. Clément, *Lettres*, vol. 3, part 2, pp. 312 and 332). In Denmark an inventory of the arsenal in Copenhagen in 1593 shows 158 bronze cannon, 344 wrought-iron cannon and 426 cast-iron cannon (Christensen, *Historie*, p. 25). English privateers, according to the Venetian ambassadors, used mostly iron artillery.

and more security[1]. Amid troubles and wars, paradoxically enough, the cannon industry collapsed. A few manufactures survived here and there but on the whole they were of no importance. For armaments France became largely dependent on foreign supply.

The reconstruction ruthlessly and skilfully accomplished by Richelieu was not only limited to the political and administrative sectors. The energetic Cardinal-Duke rebuilt the French army and remade the French navy practically from scratch. But he did not rebuild the French armament industry. A few timid attempts to develop cannon manufactures at Brouage and Le Havre were of no great consequence[2]. Richelieu remained essentially dependent on foreign supply. His market was Amsterdam and there he had permanent agents who bought large quantities of bronze and iron ordnance, muskets, anchors, and gunpowder[3].

After the tight-budget years of Mazarin, the rearmament policy was vigorously revived by Colbert. French productive capacity however was still almost non-existent in the early 1660's. In regard to the iron industry there had been some modest developments in Anjou, Normandy and Brittany during the 1630's, but the Thirty Years War had ruined the manufactures in Lorraine and Champagne while the civil war at the time of the minority of Louis XIV had provoked new waves of emigration of skilled workers and the closing of many foundries all over the country[4]. The small isolated furnaces with very low capacity were the typical production units of the French iron industry[5]. The dearth of capital was sorely felt. Saving was not lacking but the nobility and

[1] De Montchrétien, *Traicté*, p. 49: " *l'Angleterre depuis nos guerres civilles faisant profit des confusions de ce Royaume, s'est si bien instruite par l'adresse de nos hommes qui s'estoient jettez chez elle comme en un port de repos, que maintenant elle pratique avec gloire et profit ces mesmes arts que nous avions long temps gardez comme en proprieté* ".

[2] Basset, *Historique*, p. 989.

[3] Basset, *Historique*, pp. 988-9 and Barbour, *Amsterdam*, p. 38.

[4] Gille, *Origines*, p. 12.          [5] Gille, *Origines*, p. 47.

the Church were not interested in industry and the "Third Estate" liked to invest in "*les charges et les offices*"[1]. In striking contrast with Dutch and English developments, private enterprise was conspicuous for its inertia. The propensity of the government to buy cannon abroad did not help to change this state of affairs. On the other hand, since local production was inadequate, the government was obliged to turn to foreign producers. It was a vicious circle. From 1661 to about 1666 Colbert was forced to follow the traditional patterns. He had permanent commercial agents at The Hague and Amsterdam and he bought large amounts of cannon in Holland as well as in Sweden, Denmark, Hamburg and Biscay[2].

Of all people however, Colbert was the one who found this arrangement least satisfactory. In a letter dated 1666 he wrote unambiguously that "it is highly necessary to be careful in purchases. It is better to buy French rather than foreign products even if the French ones are a little less good and a little more expensive. There is a double advantage in doing so: the state does not lose liquid assets and is not impoverished and on the other hand the subjects of His Majesty make a living and develop their skills"[3]. In accordance with these principles, just about 1665 Colbert started a general plan for the development of the French armament industry. He had two reasons for being in favour of iron guns: (1) iron guns were less expensive than bronze ordnance and (2) France had plenty of iron ore while she had to depend on imports for copper and tin. This second reason would not have necessarily appealed to a free-trade zealot. Colbert was a zealot, but not a free-trader. Furthermore, the deterioration of France's relations with Holland gave him other reasons to carry on his plan. This was conceived as an organic whole for the entire

[1] Gille, *Origines*, pp. 30 and 46.

[2] Basset, *Historique*, p. 990. Cf. also Heijkenskjöld, *Styckegjutning*, p. 76 for 100 iron cannon (162 tons) purchased in Sweden by the French ambassador in 1662 and Boissonade-Charliat, *Colbert*, pp. 41-2 for cannon purchased by French agents in Denmark in 1665-6.

[3] Clément, *Lettres*, vol. 3, part 1, p. 76.

country[1]. The location of the iron ores and the availability of water routes for the transportation of the finished products dictated the choice of the areas: Angoumois, Périgord and Nivernais to serve the arsenals of the western coast; Burgundy, Lyonnais and Dauphiné to serve the arsenals of the northern and southern coasts. A most serious bottleneck was that of the shortage of technicians and Colbert had to get them from abroad[2]. Distrusting small enterprise, he promoted the formation of large private concerns which he favoured through large orders, preferential treatment in the supplying of iron ore, and help in the recruitment of labour[3]. As usual with him, he carried out his plan with meticulous care[4],

[1] In June 1671 a royal letter informed Admiral De La Haye that the war with Holland was imminent (Kaeppelin, *Compagnie*, p. 53) and war was actually declared in 1672.

As to Colbert's plan for the armament industry, cf. Basset, *Historique*, pp. 995-6.

[2] By that time Swedish technicians were deservedly famous and Colbert invited to France Abraham and Hubert Jr. De Beche, nephews to the famous Wilhelm De Beche (see appendix I). Swedish workers were also brought to France. This emigration was a source of preoccupation for the Swedish government which asked the "*Bergskollegium*" to investigate. The results of the inquiry were presented to the government in 1669. It appeared that a number of Swedish workers sailed from Nyköping believing that they were being brought to some other part of Sweden. But they were brought to Lübeck and from there to Hamburg and finally to France. A few escaped and one of them, Anders Sigfersson returned to Sweden in 1675 (cf. for all this *Svenskt Biografiskt Lexicon*, under De Besche). In regard to the esteem in which Swedish technicians were held in the seventeenth century one may quote the episode of the Swedish iron-founder who was invited to India and taught the Indian blacksmiths a quick method of manufacturing nails and cannon balls which would have quadrupled the rate of production. But the local authorities disallowed the introduction of the new methods as they might eventually deprive many blacksmiths of their livelihood (cf. Raychaudhuri, *Coromandel*, p. 174).

[3] Gille, *Origines*, pp. 50-1.

[4] One can get an idea of how meticulous he was by reading the instructions that he sent to his son, the Marquis de Seignelay. Especially pertinent to the subject of this book is the letter that Colbert sent to the Marquis on the 10th of July 1671 asking him to inquire about the various technical and economic aspects of the Dutch and English cannon industry (cf. Clément, *Lettres*, vol. 3, part 2, p. 35).

indefatigable energy and stubborn willpower. While strenuously pursuing the general lines, he kept a watchful eye on details. In 1670 he wrote to his son that " the iron guns are damaged by useless ornaments which furthermore cannot be graceful when made in iron. Iron guns must be compact and one has to worry only about the purity of the metal "[1]. He was determined to the borders of blind obstinacy. When many of the newly produced cannon blew up at a test, he wrote to the navy commissioner in Dunkerque: " I do not know anything about the quality or the provenance of the iron [guns] that blew up at Boulogne. But I know that whenever naval equipment is manufactured in this Kingdom for the first time, our people always find it bad. Often it is bad . . . but if the iron has been badly manufactured one should not find this surprising because it is difficult to have things done well at the first trial. If one keeps supplying the manufacturers with good samples and helps them in correcting their faults, one will eventually obtain products as good as those that are manufactured in foreign countries "[2]. This he wrote in 1670. But the following year even his faith began to be shaken and he wrote in a discouraged mood " *je ne sais plus qu'en croire* "[3]. Too many guns blew up on being tested.

The final outcome of fifteen years of efforts was a mixture of some success and much failure. The factories established in Périgord and Angoumois gave satisfactory results. By 1680 they were manufacturing iron guns that were " certainly lighter and better than those of Sweden " and could be produced in " quantity sufficient to satisfy the needs of the ports of the Western coast "[4]. But the manufactures established in Nivernais and Burgundy turned out to be a complete failure and admittedly it was there that the greatest efforts had been spent.

[1] Clément, *Lettres*, vol. 3, part 2, p. 8.
[2] Clément, *Lettres*, vol. 3, part 1, p. 76.
[3] Clément, *Lettres*, vol. 3, part 1, p. 379.
[4] Clément, *Lettres*, vol. 3, part 2, p. 379.

The reason for Colbert's very modest results lies essentially in the fact that he was too much in advance of his times. Chemistry had not yet discovered the negative role of sulphur and the positive role of phosphorus in the casting of iron. There was no way for the technicians of Colbert's time to know that the iron ore of Périgord was fitted for the contemporary methods of casting while the iron ore of Nivernais was not. The brittleness of the cannon cast in one place and the reliability of the cannon cast in another remained an unsolved mystery[1]. On the economic and social level, Colbert had intelligent, devoted and very active collaborators, but the country as a whole did not follow him. The aristocracy was lagging behind the times[2]. The "Third Estate" was moving slowly and along overgrown paths. Already before the death of the great Minister (1683), all that remained of his industrial construction showed traces of weakness and fatigue. The situation grew progressively worse until the 1730's[3] and it was not until the second half of the eighteenth century that France was able to reverse the trend and build an important armament industry[4].

11—The European situation in regard to the production of guns about the middle of the seventeenth century was vastly different from that prevailing two centuries before. The geographical distribution of the industry had radically

[1] Cf. Wertime, *Steel*, pp. 173 *ff*.

[2] As an example, one may take the attitude of the French noblesse in regard to science. Sirot, lieutenant-general of the French army wrote in 1683 that " *la noblesse regardait les sciences comme l'écueil des grandes actions et elle était persuadé qu'elles amollisaient le courage et donnaient trop de circonspection* ".

[3] Gille, *Origines*, pp. 33-4. After 1693, because of the troubled conditions in France, many iron-workers moved from Alsace, Lorraine and Franche-Comté to Germany and Switzerland. This emigration was a further blow to France's metallurgical and armament industry. Cf. Scoville, *Huguenots*, p. 171.

[4] For the developments after 1750 cf. Basset, *Historique*, and Bonaparte-Favé, *Études*.

changed. More important than that, European productive potential had increased enormously, and Europe had become much more formidable. The most relevant fact was the appearance of effective iron guns. This gave Europe the possibility of expanding her artillery park at a relatively low cost, while progress in technology and business organization allowed more efficient use of available resources.

Any effort to evaluate total European production is bound to be subject to an exceedingly large margin of error, but some estimates, no matter how approximate, may at least serve to give some idea about orders of magnitude. About 1650 Sweden was able to produce probably 1,500 to 2,000 metric tons of cast iron cannon per year[1]. England produced less

[1] Table 1 shows that just after the middle of the seventeenth century Sweden could easily export more than 1,000 tons of cast iron cannon per year.

In 1655 the Swedish Crown established a royal monopsony for all cast iron cannon produced in Sweden. The management was entrusted to B. O. Cronberg who was in charge until 1662. From his accounts (*Rechnung über Eiserne Stücken* . . . 1655-63; in Kammararkivet, Stockholm) it appears that between June 1655 and November 1662, 10,135 cannon for a total weight of 10,253 tons (=75,390 skepps) were sold to the Crown or exported under licence. This would give an average of about 1370 tons per year.

In November 1662 the administration of the Crown's monopsony was taken over by the *Generalfaktorikontoret* headed by Abraham van Eijck and Johan von Friesendorff. According to a statement by van Eijck (cf. *Svenskt Biografiskt Lexicon* ad vocem) between November 1662 and November 1666 the *Generalfaktorikontoret* sold 9,457 tons of iron cannon (=69,534 skepps) i.e. a yearly average of about 2,360 tons.

The greater part of the output came from the factories at Finspong, Nävekvarn, Åckers, Bränn-Ekeby, Fada, Huseby, Svärta, Julita, and, in the second part of the century, also from Stavsjö, Hällefors and Ehrendal. Each of these factories could normally produce about 150 tons of iron cannon per year or more. Stavsjö alone at the end of the century could produce up to 300-400 tons of cannon per year (cf. Jakobsson, *Artilleriet*, pp. 30-2nn. and here below appendix 1).

According to a report by the *Bergskollegium* of 1697 (Jakobsson, *Artilleriet*, p. 29) the Swedish cannon industry entered a period of depression after the establishment of the Crown monopoly in 1655. But the figures quoted above and the data about exports (table 1) do not seem to confirm such a view.

than 1,000 tons[1]. These were by far the most important areas of production. The other main areas were Biscay in Spain, Western Germany, the Tula region in Russia, and Périgord in France. We possess some quantitative information, only for the Tula region which was able to produce possibly 250 to 300 tons per year[2]. Anyhow it is unlikely that the total production of all these areas exceeded the total combined production of England and Sweden. If this was the case, we may calculate a total maximum productive capacity potential of about 5,000 tons per year of cast iron cannon. To this the production of bronze cannon should be added. Considering that in the biggest European navies iron guns had become predominant after 1650 and that iron guns were largely used also on land (although mostly in fortresses) one may venture to say that the total European production of bronze cannon can hardly have exceeded 5,000 tons per year. But this is pure speculation. We are on firmer grounds when we try to assess the qualitative gains made in European armament production. By the early sixteenth century naval bronze guns had " attained so high a state of perfection that they remained substantially unaltered throughout the next century and a half "[3]. By 1650 naval iron guns were not as good as bronze ordnance, but had reached a satisfactory degree of efficiency. Field artillery was the weak point of European munitions and it was in this sector that revolutionary changes occurred in the course of the seventeenth century.

At the beginning of the seventeenth century the so-called leather guns appeared. Romantic writers have created around them a glorious legend, but in reality leather guns never were a practical nor efficient weapon. In shooting power they were admittedly inferior to metal ones. Moreover they had an

[1] English output of guns *and* ammunition has been estimated all together at 800-1000 tons around 1600 (cf. above footnote[1], p. 40). After that time the charcoal crisis must have adversely affected the levels of production.

[2] Strumilin, *Istoriia*, pp. 104*ff*.

[3] Clowes, *Sailing Ships*, part I, p. 63.

exceedingly short life as individuals. Because of these rather substantial defects, they also had a very short life as a species. But times were ripe for change. In April 1629 Stockholm's royal foundry produced the first 3-pound "*regementsstycke*" (See page 72); a piece that, while weighing only 123 kg. and being therefore highly mobile, could fire three shots in the time that it took a musketeer to fire one [1]. The long quest for effective field artillery, a quest that had begun in the fifteenth century was therefore solved by European technicians in the first half of the seventeenth century. The immediate results were visible in inter-European wars. The successful campaigns of Gustavus Adolphus cannot be adequately understood if one does not take into due account the technological achievements of the Swedish foundries. But the new weapons soon opened a new chapter also in the history of European expansion. With the appearance of the "*regementsstycke*" the balance of power pointed to a further remarkable shift in favour of Europe.

In the descriptions of European expansion the references to European superiority in armament are generally given in static terms. The fact is, however, that after the first wave of expansion in the fifteenth century the European potential in armament production increased dramatically from a quantitative as well as from a qualitative point of view. This made any adjustment of the non-European peoples extremely difficult and their defence problematic, especially because the

[1] On the leather guns in general, cf. Hime, *Leather guns*; Meyersson, *Läderkanonen* and bibliographies given by them. On the leather-guns allegedly manufactured in Italy in the early 1630's cf. Montù, *Artiglieria*, vol. I, pp. 678-80. On the "regementsstycken" cf. Jakobsson, *Beväpning*. pp. 182, 214, and 223. The first 3-pounds "regementsstycken" manufactured in April 1629 had an average weight of 123 kg. In the following years other pieces were cast and their average weight was brought down to 116 kg. The average weight of a normal 3-pounder was 500 to 550 kg. if cast in iron and 400 kg. if cast in bronze. By the early eighteenth century the 3-pounds "regementsstycke" had been improved to the point that it could fire 8 to 9 shots in the time that it took a musketeer to fire one single shot (see illustration facing p. 72).

European progress in the manufacture of guns was accompanied by an equally remarkable progress in the construction of men-of-war and by the development of new techniques of naval warfare.

12—It has been indicated in the previous paragraphs that until the middle of the seventeenth century the main shortcomings of artillery for land warfare were slow rate of fire and lack of mobility. The limitations in mobility, however, were overcome in naval warfare and this accounts for the early, extensive and successful adoption of cannon on board European vessels[1]. Guns made in Tournai were aboard the ships that Louis de Male sent to attack Antwerp in 1336[2]. Genoese galleys had on board fire-arms in 1338 and Venetian boats carried bombards in 1380[3]. Guns were possibly aboard Spanish ships in

[1] Many inaccurate statements have been made about the first appearance of cannon aboard European vessels. Since the publication of Sir Nicholas Harris Nicolas's book in 1847 on the History of the Royal Navy, many historians have asserted that several of Edward III's ships were equipped with cannon as early as June 1338. The statement has been proved incorrect by Tout, *Firearms*, pp. 668-9. Guglielmotti, *Marina Pontificia*, pp. 37-8, on the basis of the Genoese chronicle by Giorgio Stella, asserted that a Genoese vessel was equipped with a bombard in 1319, but the " *artificium longum et ingens* " mentioned in the Genoese text, was certainly not a bombard. It was a device for the ejection of Greek fire (" *artificium longum et ingens ad instar tubae in quo ignis magna quantitas et frequenter accendibilis ferebatur* "). On the tubes squirting fire aboard medieval galleys cf. Oman, *Middle Ages*, vol. 2, pp. 46-7.

[2] Henrard, *Documents*, p. 240.

[3] In October 1338 a French fleet appeared in Southampton water. Some of the galleys were from Genoa, manned by Genoese in the service of the French King. They had on board *pot de fer* with gunpowder and forty-eight iron bolts presumably to be used for breaking in the gates of the town (Ruddock, *Italian merchants*, p. 32). In 1380 according to Genoese chroniclers, the Venetians used bombards on some of their vessels (Montù, *Artiglieria*, vol. 1, pp. 119-21). The Venetian " *galere da mercato* " however, had only bowmen aboard (normally 20 to 30) until the middle of the fifteenth century. In 1461 bombards having been included in the normal armament, governmental regulations provided that six gunners should be on board each galley. In 1486 the number of gunners for each " *galera da mercato* " was brought up to eight (cf. Sacerdoti, *Galere*, p. 81).

1359 and 1372 and by 1381 Catalan merchantmen carried artillery[1].

These developments came to coincide with a complex set of circumstances which I will cite here only briefly: the closer contacts between Mediterranean and Northern navigation[2]; the use of compass and the development of open sea navigation in the Atlantic area[3]; the shortage of labour due to recurrent plagues after the middle of the fourteenth century and the improvement in the standards of living of the masses[4] which made it more difficult to recruit oarsmen for the galleys; the expansion of trade in the course of the fifteenth century[5]. It is difficult—not to say impossible—to assess the relative importance of each one of these circumstances, but there is

[1] De Artiñano, *Arquitectura naval*, pp. 43-4.

[2] For examples of reciprocal influences between Northern and Mediterranean traditions in shipbuilding cf. among others Guiard, *Industria naval*, pp. 28ff.; Da Fonseca, *Galeões*, chapt. 1-5; Lane, *Venetian Ships*, p. 37.

[3] The astrolabe is described by Philopanus of Alexandria in the sixth century A.D. and an actual Persian astrolabe probably of the tenth century has been preserved. The magnetic compass was used by the Europeans for navigation after the beginning of the new millennium, and it was possibly borrowed from the Chinese via the Arabs. A.D. 1270 is the date of the first recorded use of a chart on board a ship. (Cf. Gille, *Développements*, p. 82, Derry-Williams, *Technology*, pp. 201 and 205, and Lane, *The invention of the compass*, pp. 605-17.) Although the knowledge of the compass and of nautical charts is very old, astronomic navigation developed only in the course of the fifteenth century. By the end of the same century the best Portuguese navigators could calculate fairly accurately their position at sea by a combination of observed latitude and dead reckoning. They estimated the geographical length of a degree at about $17\frac{1}{2}$ Portuguese leagues (106-560 metres) with an error of a little over 4%. (Cf. Boxer, *Portuguese Expansion*, pp. 10-11 and the bibliography quoted in it; Barbosa, *Ciencia nautica*; Rey-Pastor, *Ciencia*; Lapeyre, *Ruiz*, pp. 183-95 and Mauro, *Portugal*, pp. 53-70.) Many of the deep-sea Atlantic pilots still relied on their knowledge of nature but they were incomparably superior to Mediterranean pilots who were unable to master the new techniques of open sea navigation for quite some time (cf. Tucci, *Pratique vénitienne*, pp. 72-86 and Tenenti, *Cristoforo da Canal*, p. 42).

[4] Cf. Bridbury, *England*, pp. 103-8.

[5] The thesis of a stagnation of trade and production in the later Middle Ages is questioned among others by Bridbury, *England*, especially chapt. 2 and Cipolla, *Depression*, pp. 519-24.

no doubt that as a whole they exerted a remarkable impact on the development of shipbuilding and especially on the development of the sail boat. By the end of the fifteenth century the sailing ship had developed to such a point that, while its " rig would have appeared utterly strange to a navigator of the earlier age . . . it seems no exaggeration to say that the ship captains of the age of the great geographical discoveries, or even those of a generation before, would have had but little to learn before taking charge of a ship of Nelson's day " [1].

This progress, no matter how substantial, was of course " purely empirical and often fortuitous " [2]. It was unequal, unsystematic, full of successful experiments as well as unconsequential trials [3]. Oversimplifying the matter we may say that the main aspects of the progress were: the adoption after 1300 by Mediterranean merchantmen of the square-rig on the main mast [4] and the consequent transition from the one-masted to the three-masted ships [5]; the noticeable increase in tonnage of merchantmen during the fifteenth century [6] ; the greater reliance on artillery for attack and defence.

[1] Lane, *Venetian Ships*, p. 35.

[2] De Artiñano, *Arquitectura naval*, p. 49. Also in the relatively advanced seventeenth-century Holland, shipbuilding was " exclusively based on tradition and experiences: there was no question of scientific shipbuilding" (cf. Van Kampen, *Scheepsbouw*, p. 240).

[3] The character of the progress in shipbuilding was unsystematic. Only by doing some harm to reality, we classify systematically the various types of sailing vessels that the Europeans used at the waning of the Middle Ages (cf. De Artiñano, *Arquitectura naval*, p. 79).

[4] Lane, *Venetian Ships*, p. 37*ff.*

[5] Lane, *Venetian Ships*, p. 38*ff.*; Da Fonseca, *Caravela*, passim; Singer *Technology*, vol. 3, pp. 474-6; Derry-Williams, *Technology*, p. 203.

[6] Lane, *Venetian Ships*, p. 47 states that " about 1400 the biggest Venetian merchantmen had been but little over 400 tons, but in 1450 there were six merchantmen of 600 tons or more in the Venetian fleet and at the end of the century there was one of over 1000 tons. The size of the round ships built by the Signoria for military purposes underwent an even greater development. Such a ship of 2400 tons is reported in 1486 . . . The Venetian round ships for war at that time were officially rated at 1200 to 1500 tons. It was not found profitable to build merchantmen of such enormous tonnage but 600 tons ships became more and more common".

Such developments were the result of effective interplay between Mediterranean and Northern ideas of build and rig: the caravel as well as the carrack were neither essentially Northern nor Southern in type [1]. There is no doubt, that from 1250 to 1450, the differences between the North and the South tended to level out [2]. However, after the middle of the fifteenth century a new important difference developed between Atlantic and Mediterranean naval powers, namely a difference in attitudes toward the type of ship to use in warfare.

A long tradition going back to Roman times had established a kind of " division of labour " in Mediterranean waters between the " long ship " equipped with oars (the galley) and the " round ship " dependent on sail, the former being mainly used as warship and the latter as merchantman. This " division of labour " was shaken at the end of the thirteenth

---

Melis, *Marina Mercantile*, pp. 2-3 states that in the course of the fifteenth century merchantmen of 750 tons and more became quite common. For Spain cf. De Artiñano, *Arquitectura naval*, pp. 50-1. For Portugal, Godinho (*Découvertes*, p. 19) writes that " between 1450 and 1550 the average Portuguese tonnage has at least doubled ". For England cf. among others Carus-Wilson, *Bristol*, p. 16 who remarks that " early in the fifteenth century few ships can have carried more than 100 tuns of wine . . . But by the middle of the century ships from Bordeaux brought an average of 150 tuns " and there were ships which could carry as much as 500 tuns of wine. For the northern areas, we know that at the beginning of the fourteenth century the normal size of an Hanseatic ship was about 75 tons. Around 1400 the traditional " *Kogge* " was substituted with larger vessels of the " *Holk* " type. Around 1440 the average size of the Hanseatic vessels was about 150 tons. Thirty years later, when the caravel-type vessels were being introduced in the Hanseatic fleet, the average tonnage was around 300 tons. For all this cf. Pagel, *Hanse*, p. 256 and Olechnowitz, *Schiffbau*, pp. 7 and 8.

Clowes, *Sailing Ships*, pp. 56-9 warns about a source of confusion in all measurements prior to 1660, " that is the habit of using side by side and often without any proper distinction the two distinct measurements *tons burden* and *tuns and tonnage* ".

[1] For the caravel cf. Lane, *Venetian Ships*, pp. 52-3. For the carrack cf. Singer, *Technology*, vol. 3, p. 476.

[2] Singer, *Technology*, vol. 3, p. 474.

century by the appearance of the "great galley" which was an hybrid vessel "designed to combine not only some of the advantages of oarship and sailing vessel but also those of war-ship and merchantman"[1]. Further shaking occurred in the course of the fifteenth century when well-gunned round ships were used by Venice as auxiliaries to her armadas or to patrol the seas and hunt the ever-present pirates[2]. However, up to the end of the seventeenth century the galleys, and the galleys alone, remained the backbone of the Mediterranean war fleets. This was true for Venice as well as for Genoa, Turkey, or the Holy Order of Malta[3].

[1] Lane, *Venetian Ships*, p. 24. The first appearance of the great galley allegedly occurred around 1295 (Lane, *Venetian Ships*, p. 13).

[2] Lane, *Venetian Ships*, p. 48.

[3] Cf. Tenenti, *Cristoforo da Canal*, pp. 36-49. For Venice cf. Lane, *Venetian Ships*, p. 48. For Mediterranean powers in general cf. Moryson, *Itinerary*, p. 137: " in warr uppon that calme sea, they altogether use gallyes, whereof the greatest are called gallyons, the midle gallies and the least galliasses and frigotts. And only the king of Spaine at Naples and in the havens of that kingdome and in the port of Genoa as likewise that Citty in the same port and the Venetians in the port of Venice may be said able to arme a navye of gallyes . . . And howsoeuer the Pope hath some fewe gallyes and the Duke of Florence and the Knights of Malta have likewise some fewe gallyes, whereof they arme some part yearely to spoyle the Turkes uppon that sea, yet the number of them is so small as they deserue not to be called nauy"; p. 144: "(in Venice) they shewed me many gallyes new built, and some 100th old, but strong, lying at anchor, and together with the navye they have alwayes abroad, this state can arme 1200th other say 1300th gallies, and of late in tenn dayes they had armed 30 great gallyes ready for seafight ".

In 1618, thirty years after the defeat of the Armada, the following estimate of the Mediterranean fleets was made in Rome (*Calendar of State Papers and Manuscripts*, Venice, xv (1617-19), p. 272), " Numbers of Ships now in the Mediterranean,

At Denia in Spain, 7 galleys with Don Melchior Borgia; good new ships with 1,000 Spaniards.

At Marseilles, 20 sailing ships and 12 galleys with 1,500 French and 204 pieces of ordnance.

At Naples, 25 galleons and 24 galleys, with 15,000 troops of divers nations and 805 pieces of bronze.

In Sicily, five high decked ships, with 12 galleys carrying 3,000 men and 140 pieces of ordnance.

Serviceable enough in the Mediterranean however, the galley could not stand up to the long rollers and the fierce sou' westerlies of the Atlantic. As the potentialities of the round ship were gradually developed in the course of the fifteenth century, Atlantic naval powers turned to the sailing vessel and made of it the core of their fighting navies. It has been recently suggested that " it was the English who upset the convenient division of labour " between galley and sailing ship and made of the latter a successful naval fighter [1]. It is difficult however to say who was the first: most probably there was a series of multiple and interdependent influences among Atlantic nations. Henry VII of England (1485-1509) had especially built for his war navy in 1487 two sailing ships manned with guns, the *Regent* and the *Soveraign*, which represent a good and early example of the new developments that were taking place in the Atlantic area. Garcia de Resende (1470-1536) reports that in Portugal King John II (1481-95) " used to spend much money in building great vessels manned with guns. But, as he was ingenious in every task and knew very much in matter of artillery, in order to protect the coast with more security and less expense, after much experimentation he discovered and directed how many a great cannon might travel in small caravels and fire so low that their shot

---

At Malta, 2 galleons, with four well-armed galleys.

The Venetians, 24 ships, 6 galeasses, 60 galleys, with 9,500 foot and 550 pieces of bronze.

The Dutch come to help the Venetians, 18 sailing ships with 300 foot and 120 pieces.

Turks in the Archipelago, 15 square ships and 80 galleys with 9,000 men and 500 pieces.

Morescoes of Africa, 100 sailing ships with 6,000 Moors and 600 pieces of all kinds ".

This estimate should not be taken too literally. However, it demonstrates that as late as 1618, long after England and Holland had discarded the oar-propelled vessels, the galley was still the backbone of the Mediterranean navies. Notice that in the document the term " galleon " is used to indicate a large galley.

[1] Lewis, *Armada*, pp. 64-5.

went skimming over the water[1]. He was the first who made this invention. A few of such caravels could force many big ships to surrender because they were heavily gunned, but at the same time they were also small and highly manoeuvrable so that the big vessels could hardly hit them; and for a long time the caravels of Portugal were very much feared on the seas "[2].

Exchanging oarsmen for sails and warriors for guns meant essentially the exchange of human energy for inanimate power. By turning whole-heartedly to the gun-carrying sailing ship the Atlantic peoples broke down the bottleneck inherent in the use of human energy and harnessed, to their advantage, far larger quantities of power. It was then that European sails appeared aggressively on the most distant seas.

13—Aboard the sailing ship, guns were first placed on the decks of the castles. Later on, as the guns became heavier, the larger ones were carried on the upper deck firing over or through the bulwarks while the lighter pieces were carried inside—rather than above—the fore castle and the after castle[3]. A caravel could, under special circumstances, carry up to 30-40 pieces, but ordinarily it did not carry more than 15[4]. Bigger ships carried much more: Henry VII's *Soveraign* had 141 guns, but 110 were iron " serpentines " that is light breech-loaders mostly mounted in the castles[5].

At the beginning of the sixteenth century an important innovation was introduced: the cutting of ports in the actual hull of the ships—as distinct from the superstructures—so that cannon could be mounted not only on the upper deck or on

[1] On the meaning of the phrase cf. Da Fonseca, *Caravela*, pp. 458-9.
[2] De Resende, *Chronica*, chapt. 181.
[3] Lewis, *Armada*, p. 59.
[4] Da Fonseca, *Caravela*, p. 461. The great galley could carry up to 30-50 guns. Cf. De Artiñano, *Arquitectura naval*, p. 82; Tenenti, *Venezia*, p. 174, n.2; Moryson, *Itinerary*, pp. 142-4.
[5] Clowes, *Sailing Ship*, vol. I, p. 60.

the castles but also on the main deck. Traditionally the date of the innovation is fixed at 1501 and the innovation itself is attributed to a Frenchman. The discovery was of very great importance: it gave the bigger ships the possibility of increasing their armament vastly. Mounting the guns on the main deck not only made it possible to mount many more, but it also made possible the use of much bigger pieces without imperilling the stability of the vessel. The English warship *Harry Grace à Dieu* built in 1514 according to the new technique, carried no less than 186 guns among which there were two brass culverins of about 4,500 lbs. each and a brass curtall of about 3,000 lbs. all placed on the lower deck[1]. The *Harry* was the crack ship of her day: she was launched in the presence of the Court, the ambassadors of both the Emperor and the Pope and a distinguished assembly of bishops and nobles[2]. The " demonstration effect " set immediately to work. The *Harry Grace à Dieu* was followed in 1527 by the French *Grand François*, in 1534 by the Portuguese *Sao João* which is said to have carried no fewer than 366 guns, in 1554-9 by the Swedish *Elefanten* with 71 cannon of which 24 were of bronze[3].

What these monsters looked like, one may infer from the painting by an unknown artist, a detail from which is reproduced between pp. 72-3. With their colourful flags and

[1] Clowes, *Sailing Ship*, vol. 1, pp. 63-4.

[2] Keble Chatterton, *Ship-models*, p. 6.

[3] Anderson, *Sailing Ship*, pp. 125-7. According to Anderson (who possibly followed an indication by Börjeson) the Swedish *Elefanten* was built in 1532. The statement howeyer is not completely correct. In 1532 Gustav Vasa had built for his navy a *Stora Kravelen* (Great Caravel) of huge proportions, but there is no evidence to prove that the name of the ship was " Elefanten " nor do we possess information about the armament of the ship and its arrangement aboard.

In 1554-9 on the other hand, a huge ship—again a *Stora Kravelen*—was built in Sweden and this one was certainly named *Elefanten*. According to Ekman, *Skeppstyperna*, pp. 214 and 227 " guns must have been placed below the deck, this being probably the earliest instance in Sweden ", but this particular point still needs further clarification. The *Elefanten* sank in 1564 north of Calmar.

their fantastically ornate castles they diffused an aura of grandeur and pageantry. They were magnificent as well as formidable but they were very clumsy to manoeuvre. In order to take the greatest possible advantage of the invention of the gunports and make the maximum use of the effect of the broadside, the pendulum had swung to the opposite of the " *muito ligeiras e pequenas caravelas de Portugal*". The great ship had become a sea-fortress rather than a manoeuvrable weapon of war: " a sluggish mover, clumsy to steer, very high in freeboard and cumbered with flimsy castles in bow and stern "[1].

Inevitably the pendulum had to move back. Shipbuilders tried to improve upon the manoeuvrability of the great sailing ship without affecting fire-power and just after 1550 their efforts resulted in the legendary galleon, a boat formidable in armament and swift in manoeuvring that could serve at the same time as a deadly warship and as an efficient merchantman. In relation to the previous type of great ship, the galleon was longer for its beam and with a hull built to some extent on galley lines; it was lower in freeboard and much less " castled " especially in the bow (not to speak of improvements in the deck arrangements)[2]. Its name (which originally covered quite different types of vessels)[3] and its shape, indicate that its genesis was influenced by the design of the dexterous galleys and this fact in its turn can reasonably indicate a Spanish origin[4]. Yet, there is no doubt that those who adopted and perfected the new type of vessel most quickly

[1] Lewis, *Armada*, p. 25.

[2] As has been pointed out " it is difficult to define exactly the galleon as an unmistakably distinct type of naval construction . . . A specific galleon type never existed ". Cf. Lopes de Mendonça, *Navios*, pp. 25-31; De Artiñano, *Arquitectura naval*, pp. 98-9; Anderson, *Sailing Ship*, p. 125 and Boxer, *Fidalgos*, p. 13. It is generally admitted however that all the galleon-type vessels showed in relation to the other ships some common differentiating characteristics that I have indicated above in the text. On such characteristics cf. among others Da Fonseca, *Galeões*, pp. 151-67.

[3] Cf. De Artiñano, *Arquitectura naval*, p. 100.

[4] Anderson, *Sailing Ship*, p. 126.

[83]

and got the best out of it were eventually the English and the Dutch.

14—The Mediterranean people lagged behind[1]. If there were some who advocated the adoption of the new types of vessels, there were too many who stuck to the glorious old traditions, who emphasized the advantages of the galley without recognizing its disadvantages, who thought that the effective destruction of the enemy could only be obtained by the time-tested techniques of ramming and boarding. Also, the physical conditions of the environment were more favourable to the traditionalist's views in the Mediterranean than in the Atlantic. When the Northern galleons began to bother the Venetian navigation in the Mediterranean, lengthy discussions took place in Venice on how to cope with the molesting intruders. The traditionalists who favoured the use of the galleys as the main fighting force turned out to be the vast majority. After an early experiment with sailing warships in the first decades of the sixteenth century, this type of vessel was discarded for naval action until the beginning of the following century. A

[1] Ruddock, *Italian merchants*, pp. 223-5 shows that the development in the building and rigging of sailing ships and the increasing use of gunfire during the second half of the fifteenth century were responsible for the decadence of Venetian navigation in Atlantic waters. By the 1490's increasing numbers of Venetian agents in England shipped their exports from Southampton on English and Spanish vessels bound for Italy, being no longer willing to pay the high freight charges of the galleys.

For the sixteenth century, cf. Tenenti, *Cristoforo da Canal*, pp. 36-44 and especially p. 48: " *de toute évidence la Méditerranée ne vivait plus à l'heure de la modernité et l'Atlantique venait de prendre une avance decisive . . . De Marseille à Constantinople, d'Alger à Barcelone et de Messine à Venise, la galère, avec les navires du même type, continue à être reine . . . Tout l'univers méditerranéen vit dans le cadre technique et humaine des bateaux à rames et ne va pas au delà d'une surprise ou d'une admiration passive devant les exploits de quelque rares galions que les affrontent* ".

The Mediterranean peoples lagged behind the Atlantic nations not only in the technique of naval warfare but also in the technique of open sea navigation. On this point cf. Tucci, *Pratique vénitienne*, pp. 72-86; Tenenti, *Cristoforo da Canal*, p. 42; Teixeira da Mota, *Art de naviguer*, pp. 127-48.

" *galeone* " was eventually produced in 1608, but it turned out to be a clumsy " floating fortress ". There was no tradition of galleon building in the Venetian arsenal nor were the crews sufficiently expert in the manoeuvring of the big men-of-war. Incapable of accomplishing the transition to the new ways of naval warfare, Venice had to call on England and Holland in order to resist Spain in 1616-19 and the powerful English and Dutch galleons came to the Mediterranean to protect what in the previous centuries had been the greatest sea-power of Europe [1].

Spain herself was half Atlantic and half Mediterranean, and the Mediterranean tradition weighed heavily on her development as a sea power. It has been written that the defeat of the Armada in 1588 was due to the failure of the Spaniards to discard Mediterranean conceptions of naval warfare [2]. The thesis is too extreme, because institutional arrangements and the attitude of the crown bear their good share of responsibilities [3], but it does contain more than a grain of truth.

[1] Cf. Tenenti, *Venezia*, pp. 174-86.    [2] Lewis, *Armada*, pp. 61-80.
[3] According to Lewis, *Armada*, pp. 61-80, the design of the Spanish vessels was less fit for modern naval warfare than that of the English. He attributes this inferiority of the Spanish ships to the influence of the Mediterranean traditions of ramming and boarding. But there are more factors to take into account. Since 1512, when Henry VIII set up the Navy Office as an independent service responsible for the national defence, a permanent navy had been established in England and the Crown built a number of vessels especially designed for naval warfare. In Spain this important step was never taken. The Crown had few vessels of its own and it generally resorted to the expedient of hiring merchantmen for war purposes. In 1584 Martin de Recalde petitioned to be allowed to fly the royal standard because without it his vessels would to be taken for merchantmen. (Cf. Fernandez Duro, *Disquisiciones*, vol. 5, p. 28.) In the fleet of Don Alvaro de Bazan at Terceras in 1582-3 only three ships belonged to the Crown (*ibid.*, p. 29).

The Spanish government seized private vessels on every occasion and for every purpose, where in England royal ships would have been employed. In 1601, the Duke of Medina Sidonia wrote that " the King should build the vessels he requires and not take them from private individuals, ruining them " (cf. *ibid.*, p. 48). As a matter of fact the Spanish system had a double disadvantage. The Crown put special pressure on the merchants to

The Spaniards kept overloading their ships with soldiers for boarding tactics and proved incapable of dismissing altogether the oar-propelled galleys [1]. The Italian experts kept claiming unreasonably that " to hit the enemy at long distance with artillery cannot be the purpose of a navy, the main object being that of ramming and boarding " [2]. But the English Commission of Reform of 1618 declared: " Experience teacheth how sea-fights in these days come seldome to boarding or to great execution of bows, arrows, small shot and the swords, but are chiefly performed by the great artillery breaking down masts, yards, tearing, raking and bilging the ships, wherein the great advantage of His Majesty's navy must carefully be maintained by appointing such a proportion of ordnance to each ship as the vessel will bear " [3]. Unencumbered by the outdated traditions of the Mediterranean type, limited in the availability of manpower [4], incorrigibly addicted to privateering [5], the English came to rely exclusively on

---

build larger ships than they otherwise would have done, in order to have at its disposal large vessels to " hire " in case of war. The result was that too many Spanish vessels had drawbacks both as merchantmen and as men-of-war. Cf. Lapeyre, *Ruiz*, p. 213.

[1] When the Spaniards decided to invade England, they planned to include in the Armada 40 galleys and 6 galleasses. In 1588 the original plan was changed and the Armada sailed from Spain with 4 galleys and 4 galleasses. England at that time had only one galley " which she wisely kept out of harm's way in the Thames " (cf. Lewis, *Armada*, pp. 59 and 62).

[2] Gentilini, *Bombardiere*, pp. 26-7. According to Italian experts such a Da Canal and Busca the main purpose of naval artillery was that of hitting and disorganizing the enemy just before boarding the enemy's vessel. Guns should therefore be discharged at closed distance. Cf. Tenenti, *Cristoforo da Canal*, p. 38.

[3] Quoted by Robertson, *Naval armament*, p. 21.

[4] Toward the end of the sixteenth century, compared to the population of Italy (about 12 million people) or of Spain (about 8 million people) the population of Holland (scarcely more than one million) or of England (less than 5 million) looked very small.

[5] " The English "—said Botero—" would be a fine and praiseworthy race if they were not so given to robbing the ships of Christian merchants "

manoeuvring by the wind and the effectiveness of the broadside[1]. Few in numbers but aggressive and tenacious, scarcely imaginative but receptive and skilful[2], they produced, as Botero said, "vessels very light and very well gunned"[3]

---

(cf. Botero, *Relationi*, part 2, book 1, p. 257). Professor Davis (*Shipping Industry*, p. 45) believes that the English needed swift and well-gunned vessels in order "to stand up to the corsairs based on the Moorish ports" of the Mediterranean. It is not difficult to prove that the most redoubtable pirates in the Mediterranean waters were actually English (cf. Tenenti, *Venezia*, pp. 78-114 and pp. 174-95). Piratical and privateering operations obviously called for swift, highly manoeuvrable and well-gunned ships.

[1] In the words of King Philip II of Spain, the English liked "to fight at long distance in consequence of their advantage in artillery" (quoted by Lewis, *Armada*, p. 73).

[2] Those were the times when the English, confronted with growing foreign competition in the textile sector, were able to adopt new methods of production, shift to new types of products and outsell their foreign competitors. Those were also the times, as we have noticed in previous paragraphs, when the English, faced with dangerous shortage of copper and foreign exchange, skilfully developed new techniques for the making of ordnance. In establishing the new drapery, the English borrowed the idea from the Dutch. For casting their first iron cannon they used French gun-founders. In packing the hull of their ships with cannon, they were quick in adopting a French invention. When renewing their navy they adopted the galleon type from the Spaniards. In each case they did not show much originality but an exceptional capacity for picking up profitable ideas, perfecting others' innovations, adapting their tools and their skills to new situations. In all fields they exhibited a feeling for practicality that expressed itself in products which were handy to use and cheaper to produce. Their attitude and success remind us of the attitude and success of the Japanese in our own times. The formula of the success possibly resided in those virtues that one perceives in Elizabethan English travellers: people like Fynes Moryson or Peter Mundy never tired of travelling, observing, inquiring and learning.

[3] Botero, *Relationi*, part 2, book 1, p. 257: "*legni leggerissimi e benissimo forniti di artiglieria*". Just after the end of the sixteenth century, looking critically at the ships of the country that had been for a long time the greatest and most brilliant sea power in Europe, Fynes Moryson noticed that "Italian shipps are heavy in sayling and great of burthen . . . whereas the English shipps are swift in sayling and light of burthen" (cf. Moryson, *Itinerary*, pp. 136-7).

that " in a thousand ways bothered the huge ships of Spain " [1].
The Dutch followed the same line [2]. Within Europe herself,

[1] Botero, *Aggiunte*, p. 67: " *i legni destri e leggeri de gl'inglesi insultarono e in mille maniere travagliarono la grandezza delle navi dell'armata spagnola* ". Lewis, (*Armada*, pp. 67-8) maintains that " the Spanish ships *looked* big, the English relatively small. The Spaniards had more majesty. They stood much higher out of the water, since they retained the high forecastles now discarded by the English. But this retention was a weakness. They were the worse sailors for it, much less amenable to the helm than their English rivals ". As far as real tonnage is concerned, the Spanish vessels were certainly not bigger than the English ones. The point made by Lewis had previously been made in his own times by the Marquis de Seignelay in his Report on the English Navy (1671), when he remarked: " *En général les Anglois frégatent beaucoup davantage leurs vaisseaux qu'en Hollande ni en France; ils mesnagent jusqu'à un pouce de hauteur, et font en sort qu'un vaisseau de deux mille tonneaux ne paroist guère davantage à la mer qu'un vaisseau de France ou de Hollande de mille deux cents ... Les raisons pourquoy leurs vaisseaux paroissent beaucoup plus bas que les nostres sont:*

1—*Le mesnagement qu'ils observent dans l'élévation d'entre deux ponts, ne donnant que six pieds et six pieds et demy de hauteur dans la batterie basse à leurs vaisseaux du premier rang. . . .*

2—*La maxime qu'ils ont qu'un vaisseau basty au tiers est trop court, qui est cependant la mesure ordinaire de tous les charpentiers de Hollande et d'une grande partie de ceux de France. . . .*

3—*Le grand élancement qu'ils donnent à l'étrave. . . .*

4—*Les allonges de revers rentrent beaucoup davantage que celles de France. . . .*

*Ils prétendent que cette manière de construction est beaucoup meilleure parce qu'elle rend le vaisseau plus léger et que, outre cela, étrécissant le pont, il faut moins de monde pour faire leurs manoeuvres. . . .*" (Clément, *Lettres*, vol. 3, part 2, p. 326).

[2] The Dutch were able to put to an end the Portuguese maritime predominance in the East owing not only to a much larger navy but also to better ships. At the middle of the seventeenth-century, Father Vincenzo Maria (*India Orientale*, p. 458) noticed that " the (Portuguese) galleons are noteworthy because of their great size and their many facilities. Each one looks like a castle and is furnished with 80 or more bronze guns. The deck is so spacious, that the sailors often play ball. The rooms are numerous, spacious and with plenty of headroom so that the galleons resemble comfortable houses rather than vessels. The ropes are handled for the greatest part with the aid of capstans. The planking is thick enough to resist gunshots. In short, these vessels would be unequalled if they were not such sluggish movers and could be better manned. The Dutch vessels which are handier to manoeuvre by the wind, overcome the Portuguese galleons very easily. The Dutch can take to flight when the wind is favourable to the enemy and attack when the enemy is handicapped by low wind. To

supremacy was gained by those nations which shifted more completely to guns and sails. The era of human energy was over and the era of the machine was beginning to open up.

the Dutch any small wind is enough, while for the Portuguese vessels a half-gale is necessary for movement ". What Father Vincenzo Maria said with words, a seventeenth-century artist expressed graphically in a nice picture reproduced by De Artiñano, *Arquitectura naval*, p. 105.

Owing to the danger of their huge, unhandy ships being intercepted by the swift Dutch men-of-war, the Portuguese abandoned their use of carracks and galleons in the Macao-Japan trade after 1618 and employed instead small coasting vessels of the type known as *galiotas* leaving to the Dutch the mastery of the high seas (Boxer, *Great Ship*, p. 14*ff.*).

On the superior qualities of Dutch vessels in comparison to those of Spain cf. Usher, *Shipping*, pp. 195*ff.* On the Dutch and English Indiamen cf. also Fayle, *Voyages*, pp. xxxi*ff.* On the French Indiamen cf. Weber, *Compagnie Française*, pp. 241-63.

# CHAPTER II

# GUNS AND SAILS
# OVERSEAS

1—Thanks to their vicinity to Europe, the Moslems became acquainted with Western artillery when this was still in its infancy and they were quick to borrow it. In 1331 the Moorish King of Granada Mohammed IV attacked Orihuela and Alicante and allegedly used artillery[1]. From Spain the new technique moved to North Africa and the Middle East. Cannon was used in these areas by the Mamluks possibly in the 1350's[2], certainly by the 1360's[3]. The Ottomans manufactured cannon in Asia Minor in 1364 and used guns in 1387 against the Karamans and in 1389 in the plain of Kossovo against the coalition army of Serbia, Bosnia, Herzegovina and Albania[4].

[1] It is difficult to say when the Moslems first began to use ordnance. One finds the same difficulties that one encounters when dealing with the origins of Western artillery: obscurity of texts, misleading use of technical terms still in the process of formation, contradictory statements by different chroniclers, etc. There is no doubt that the Moslems knew " Greek fire " and used incendiary rockets before 1331. But the first use of cannon in the modern sense of the word seems to have occurred at Orihuela and Alicante. For this episode cf. Fernandez Duro, *Disquisiciones*, vol. 1, p. 18; some authors however (e.g. Sarton, *Introduction*, vol. 3, p. 725) maintain that the evidence is not conclusive.

[2] The fact is stated by later chroniclers, Ibn Buhtur and Ibn Iyas. Cf. Ayalon, *Mamluk*, p. 3.

[3] According to two reliable eye-witnesses, the encyclopedist Al-Qalqashandi (*Subh al-a' shā*, vol. 2, p. 144) and the historian Ibn Khaldun (*Kitab al-ibar*, vol. 5, p. 456) cannon were used in Alexandria and Cairo in the years 1366-8.

[4] Dr. Ayalon, (*Mamluk*, p. 7, n.22 and p. 98) on the basis of information supplied by Prof. Wittek (*ibid.*, pp. 141-4) states that " the Ottomans began to use artillery only as late as 1425 ". But it is difficult to agree with this view. Daniemend (*Osmanli Tarihi*, vol. 1, p. 73) maintains that an iron

As has been indicated in the previous chapter, fifteenth-century artillery was good only for battering walls, but it was precisely this quality that made it attractive to the Turks. Moslem armies had always enjoyed an indisputable superiority over their Western adversaries in the open field. Their advantage resided in the larger size of their forces, better discipline and superior tactics based on the high mobility of their light cavalry[1]. The only efficient obstacle that the Europeans could oppose to the Turkish forces were defensive bastions. Against the walls of fortresses and towns, the dreaded Moslem horsemen were powerless and when faced with good battlements the Turks had to resort to long sieges for which they were organizationally unprepared[2]. In artillery they found the kind of weapon they most badly needed.

---

cannon was manufactured in Bursa (Asia Minor) in 1364 and that cannon was used by the Ottomans in their second war against the Karamans. Prof. Wittek dismisses these assertions on the basis that Daniemend does not quote his sources. However, from reliable Indian sources we know that the Turks introduced cannon into India in 1368 (see below footnotes [1] and [3], p. 106). The Ottomans allegedly used cannon also at Kossovo: this is not only stated by Daniemend (*Osmanli Tarihi* vol. I, p. 73) but has been generally admitted by historians since the times of von Hammer (*Geschichte*, vol. I, p. 210).

[1] Oman, *Middle Ages*, p. 346 and Oman, *Sixteenth Century*, pp. 758-9. Cf. also the remarks by Moryson (*Itinerary*, p. 35) early in the seventeenth century: " the advantage of the Turkes horse swift to pursue or save themselves over the horse of Germany, howsoever able to endure assault, yet uppon any disaster unfitt to escape by flight and other like advantages of warr on the Turkes part many and easy to be named, have made the Germans unable to withstand the great power of the Turkes. . . ."; (p. 47): " in warr they are only fitt for light horse, neither use the Turkes any great horse armed, nor themselves (either horsemen or footmen) weare any defensive armor, but they only for offence carry lances and shields and good short swords ". Montecuccoli, *Aforismi*, p. 499 wrote: " *nelle scaramucce ha troppo vantaggio il Turco, come unico e proprio suo modo di battagliare, avendo egli cavalli piu' veloci e piu' agili dei nostri e meno aggravati dagli arnesi di briglie, selle e armature* ".

[2] The most important part of the army consisted of the cavalry who could not face a winter campaign because of inadequate supplies of fodder and because of unsuitable ground conditions. The wars waged by the Turks consisted generally of short, rapid, summer campaigns. Cf. Monte-

It is truly remarkable how quickly the Moslems learned the new technique. But no less remarkable is the fact that they never succeeded in going beyond the initial stage. They never developed artillery into a field weapon. Occasionally the Mamluks used light guns mounted on camels and the Ottomans used guns at Kossovo and at Mohacs. But one perceives a distinct reluctance on the part of the Moslems to make use of artillery in battles of movement: a reluctance that developed into sheer inability. There were various reasons for this. To begin with, the Moslems did not feel a strong need for supplementary new weapons in open fighting. They were perfectly conscious of their tactical and strategic superiority and on the other hand early artillery was conspicuous for inefficiency in the field. Furthermore, ingrained traditions and social structures stood in the way of an extensive adoption of field artillery. As Dr. Ayalon has brilliantly shown, " horsemanship and all it stood for were the pivot round which the whole way of life of the Mamluk upper class revolved and from which it derived its courtly pride and feeling of superiority ". No Mamluk knight would have ever agreed to be deprived of his horse and to be reduced to the humiliating status of a foot soldier. On the other hand, as long as the social structure of the kingdom remained essentially feudal, the backbone of the army was necessarily represented by the knights and there was no possibility of giving a major role to other corps. Artillery was left to the black slaves who were the most despised human element in the kingdom: an unfortunate lot of people whose only chance of military advancement was by being castrated and incorporated into the corps of eunuchs[1].

The Ottomans were slightly more flexible, for one of their main corps, the Janissaries, had been mainly composed of

---

cuccoli, *Aforismi*, pp. 471 and 474 and Oman, *Sixteenth Century*, pp. 758-9.
[1] For all that precedes cf. Ayalon, *Mamluk*, chapt. 3 and especially pp. 61-71.

infantry archers before the introduction of fire-arms. The Janissaries were very early equipped with hand-guns and in all likelihood this was one of the main reasons for the final victory of the Ottomans over the Mamluks in the first decades of the sixteenth century[1]. But also in the case of the Ottomans, a traditional taste for the *mêlée* and for horsemanship, and the social predominance of the mounted warrior, acted as powerful obstacles to the adoption of field artillery. Essentially the Ottomans made good use of guns only in siege operations[2].

There was something primeval and instinctive in the hatred with which these warriors whose not too distant ancestors lived as nomads in the steppes, used guns against the walls of their enemy's urban settlements. In their primitive fury they mostly strove for huge guns that hurled enormous stone balls. The story of their conquest of Constantinople is very well known but it is of such significance that it is certainly worth re-telling. The walls of Constantinople, even in their days of decay under the Paleologi, were still the most formidable system of defences in Europe. These walls gave nightmares to Mohammed when he took in hand the reduction of the fabulous town: the Turkish chroniclers tell us of the nights in his tent when the obsessed Mohammed, incapable of rest, kept drawing plans and inventing schemes to destroy the sturdy defences of the besieged town. Only artillery could help him out, and of this he was aware. It so happened that a skilled Hungarian gun-founder named Orban, who was

[1] Ayalon, *Mamluk*, pp. 86-97.
[2] Dr. Ayalon overstates the case of the use of artillery by the Ottomans. The superiority of the Ottomans over the Mamluks in the matter of fire-arms mostly consisted in their use of hand-guns. On the other hand, Dr. Ayalon (*Mamluks*, p. 112n. 3a) maintains that the Ottomans developed "no constructional difference between siege artillery and field artillery". Actually at the end of the seventeenth century the Turks had 12-pounders and 3-pounders that they used as field guns, but—as Marsigli (*Etat Militaire*, part 1, p. 23) writes—these pieces were " of the same manner " as the bigger bronze guns "and the difference consisted only in the calibre and the length of the barrel."

in the service of the Greek Emperor, was dissatisfied with the pay he got from the Byzantines, and came to the Turkish camp offering his skills for better remuneration. Mohammed welcomed the renegade most generously, and Orban produced a gun of extraordinarily great size. The piece was tested against an unlucky Venetian galley that happened to pass in the straits: one huge stone ball hurled from the gun was enough to crack the ship and sink it. Mohammed exulted and in his excitement ordered Orban to produce a second gun twice as big. So Orban produced " *Mahometta* " a huge gun of fantastic size, made of hooped iron, which could throw stone balls of about one thousand pounds weight. It took from 60 to 140 oxen to draw the gun, more than one hundred men to manoeuvre it, and two hours to reload it. The noise it made when shooting—chroniclers say—caused miscarriages among pregnant women. It was by far the greatest gun ever built. But it was a failure. It cracked on the second day of the siege and went permanently out of order on the fourth or the fifth day. The guns of lesser calibre, however, successfully carried on their task; the town was taken and days of un-restrained savagery, unimaginable cruelty, unspeakable horror followed[1].

There are two points in this story which are especially worth emphasizing. The first relates to the origin of the renegade gun-founder. According to the chroniclers, he was an Hun-garian[2], therefore a "Westerner". It is difficult to say how reliable the tradition is, but even if it were proven false, its very existence is significant. Although the Moslems had gun-founders of their own, whenever the possibility arose, they always tried to get Western technicians: " *les Turcs les retiennent quand ils les peuvent attraper* ", wrote a seventeenth-century French economist[3]. In many a case, they did not have to

[1] On the story of the great cannon of Mohammed II, cf. Hammer, *Geschichte*, vol. 1, pp. 510ff; Gibbon, *Decline and Fall*, chapt. 58; Oman, *Sixteenth Century*, p. 357.

[2] According to one source, however, Orban was a Dacian.

[3] De Montchrétien, *Traicté*, p. 51.

" capture " the needed craftsmen. Then, as always, there were many " technicians " ready to sell their skills—to the devil, if the price were high enough and Orban, if such a man ever existed, was no exception [1]. The eagerness that the Turks showed in obtaining Western gun-founders clearly indicates that although they adopted Western techniques very early, they never succeeded in going beyond the stage of " follower country ". The West kept moving ahead, and especially after the middle of the fifteenth century it moved progressively faster. This brings us to the second relevant point of the story, namely the obsession of the Turks with huge guns.

To be sure, when confronted with the descriptions that the contemporaries offer of the huge Turkish guns, it is difficult to escape those feelings of scepticism that Voltaire sharply expressed in the " *Essai sur les moeurs* " [2]. However the concrete evidence that we possess seems to support the descriptions by the old chroniclers more than the criticism by Voltaire. In 1867 the Sultan Abdul Aziz sent as a present to Queen Victoria a fifteenth-century Turkish cannon. It is not one of the biggest that the Turks ever possessed; nevertheless its calibre measures 25 inches, the barrel casing is $5\frac{1}{2}$ inches thick and the monster as a whole weighs no less than 18 tons and 7 hundredweight: to this day it can be admired (and measured) at the Tower of London (p. 33). Botero certainly indulged in exaggeration when he wrote early in the seventeenth century that " the Turks have such huge guns that they can tear down battlements only by their noise " [3], but we possess enough evidence [4] to prove that behind the hyperbole there was an undeniable reality.

---

[1] Many European renegades entered the service of the Moslems, and Western merchants went on selling " strategic materials " to the Turks despite papal excommunications and prohibitions of all kinds. " Our Christians supply the Turkes with all warlike munitions " was sadly remarked by a sixteenth-century writer.

[2] Voltaire, *Moeurs*, vol. 12, pp. 100-1.

[3] Botero, *Relationi*, part 2, book 4, p. 339.

[4] I have mentioned above in the text that at the Tower of London there

For the manufacture of the huge Turkish guns, much copper was needed, but the Ottomans possessed rich mines in Anatolia and plenty of slaves to operate them[1]. Serious difficulties hindered the transportation of the big guns, but the Sultans resorted to the drastic solution of casting the pieces on the very place of the operations[2]. In their obsession, they never admitted the shortcomings of huge cannon, nor did they realize that it was becoming obsolete. As late as the eighteenth century, Baron de Tott related this humorous episode of the Turkish-Russian war (1768-74): " On the castle which commanded the Strait, the Turks had placed an enormous piece of ordnance which would carry a marble ball of eleven hundred pounds weight. This piece, cast in brass, in the reign of Amurath, was composed of two parts, joined together by screw ...[3] I could not make use of this enormous cannon in the outworks, and the Turks murmured at my paying so little regard to a piece of artillery which, no doubt, had not its equal in the Universe. The Pacha made some remonstrances to me, on that head. He agreed with me that the difficulty of charging it would not allow, in case of an attack, firing it more

is a fifteenth-century Turkish gun that weighs more than 18 tons. In Lisbon there is a Turkish gun that weighs more than 19 tons and was supposed to throw stone shots of more than 100 pounds: it was cast in 1533 and was later captured by the Portuguese (Cordeiro, *Apontamentos*, pp. 82-3). Another Turkish gun captured by the Austrians in 1717 measured 25 feet in length (Basset, *Historique*, p. 942). Hammer, *Geschichte* vol. 1, p. 666 tells that he had himself seen a great cannon of the Dardanelles in which a tailor who had run away from his creditors concealed himself for several days. For further evidence see below footnote [1], p. 102.

[1] Anhegger, *Bergbaus*. Cf. also the reports by the Venetian Ambassadors in Alberi, *Relazioni*, series 3, vol. 1, p. 66. From Anatolia (the Turks) obtained also saltpetre for gunpowder and iron. Cf. *ibid.*, pp. 146 and 222.

[2] Moryson, *Itinerary*, p. 41: "for offensive weapons they (the Turks) carry store of artillery but for great part in rude matter to be cast in the field". Cf. also Ffoulkes, *Gun-Founders*, p. 27. At the siege of Rhodes in 1480 Mohammed II ordered 16 great guns 18 feet long and of 24 to 30 inches calibre to be cast on the spot.

[3] The gun was therefore of the same type as the Turkish piece preserved at the Tower of London.

The "gun" of the de Millimete manuscript

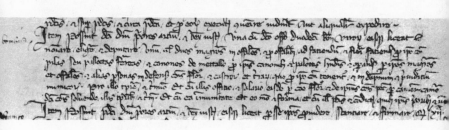

The famous Florentine document that, under the date 11th
February 1326, refers to the acquisition of *pilas seu palloctas ferreas
et canones de mettallo* for the defence of Florence

*Below*, Mons Meg at Edinburgh Castle; *right above*, the Dardanelles guns at the Tower of London. These Turkish guns date from the fifteenth century; *right below*, a Mogul gun: the Raja Gopal in Tanjore, a monster that weighs no less than 40 metric tons and shows the influence of Turkish technology

Two iron guns of the time of Henry VIII in the collection of the Royal Artillery Museum at the Woolwich Rotunda

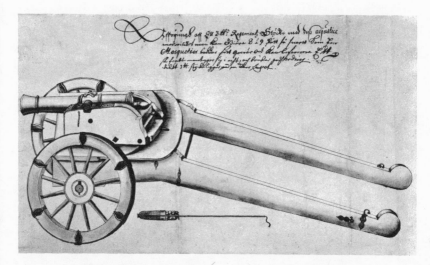

Swedish *'regementsstycke'* as represented in a MS by Möllerheim dated 1706. The caption indicates that the piece could fire 8 to 9 shots in the time it took a musketeer to fire one

'Cannon-merchants' of the eighteenth century. Drawing by C. A. Ehrensvärd (1745-1800)

The Swedish warship *Vasa*, built in 1628, in dry-dock after she had been raised from the sea-bed

he gun foundries at Julita from the painting by the Dutch artist llart van Everdingen (cf. appendix 1). The date of the painting c. 1650. Although the installations are rendered with the tmost fidelity of detail, the landscape is imaginary

The embarkation of Henry VIII for the Field of the Cloth of Gold (*detail*). Thi

icture by an unknown artist was probably painted not earlier than about 1550

The Mediterranean view of naval warfare: galleys overcome sailing ships. The picture relates to an engagement between galleys of the Holy Order of Malta and Turkish vessels that took place in 1645

The Atlantic view of naval warfare: the sailing ship overcoming galleys in a painting by the Dutch artist Hendrik Cornelisz Vrooms

The Chinese bronze gun *Fa King*, as represented in the seventeenth-century treatise *Ch'ou hai t'u pien*

Chinese light gun of the eighteenth century. (From Amiot, *Art Militaire*, p. 383)

Old Chinese guns in the provincial Museum at T'ai-yüan, capital of Shansi. The bombard in the foreground is clearly dated 1377 (cf. Goodrich, *Note*, p. 211). The guns in the background closely resemble the guns drawn and described by Father Amiot (cf. figure below)

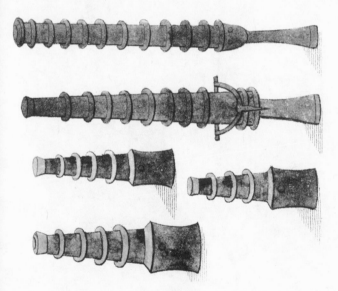

Chinese guns seen by Father Amiot in military storehouses and described by him in his *Art Militaire, planche* XXI and pp. 384-5. The two pieces above are *Pe-tse-pao*. The three pieces below are *Ma-ti-pao*. According to Father Amiot the guns looked very old when he saw them in the eighteenth century. 'The rings around the barrels are made of iron and prevent the barrel from breaking or exploding: an event that would invariably occur if it were not for such precautions'

*Left,* a Chinese war-junk, as represented in the seventeenth-century treatise *Ch'ou hai t'u pien.* It is clear that this type of vessel was still conceived for the time-honoured tactic of boarding and ramming. *Below,* an Elizabethan warship, probably the *Ark Royal,* from an engraving by C. J. Visscher

A Chinese dream. Fearing the Western vessels and their fire-power, the Chinese and Japanese rulers repeatedly issued orders that while a Western ship was in port, guns, or at least the light pieces, should be temporarily removed from the ship. In this eighteenth-century painting, the artist represents a Western ship at anchor on the Chinese coast. Guns have been removed and are visible ashore in a shed. In another shed one notices the porcelain that will be exported by the Westerners

than once, but he urged, this single discharge would be so destructive and reach so far, that it would be, alone, sufficient to destroy the whole fleet of the enemy. It was easier for me to give way to this prejudice than overthrow it, and, without changing my plan of defence, I could, by cutting through the epaulement in the direction of this piece, allow it room to be fired, but I was willing first to judge of its effect.

" The crowd about me trembled at this proposal, and the oldest among them asserted, there was a tradition that this piece, which had never yet been discharged, would occasion such a shock as must overturn the castle and the city. It was indeed possible it might shake some stones out of the wall, but I assured them they would not be regretted by the Gran Seigneur . . . Never certainly, had any cannon so formidable a reputation. Friends and enemies were alike to suffer from its fury. To load this piece of artillery it required no less than three hundred and thirty pounds weight of powder, and I sent to the Head Engineer to prepare a priming. All who heard me give this order immediately disappeared, to avoid the predicted danger. The Pacha himself was about to retreat, and it was with the utmost difficulty I persuaded him that he ran no risk, in a small kiosk, near the corner of the castle, from whence he might observe the effects of the ball.

" Having succeeded in this, nothing remained but to inspire the engineer with courage, who, though he was the only one who had not fled, shewed no great resolution in the remonstrances he made to excite my pity. I, at last, rather silenced than animated him, by promising to expose myself to the same danger. I took my station on the stone-work, behind the cannon, and felt a shock like that of earthquake. At the distance of three hundred fathoms I saw the ball divide into three pieces, and these fragments of a rock crossed the straits, and rebounded from the water to the opposite mountain . . ." [1].

The episode related by Baron De Tott was certainly not the last of its type in the fantastic story of the Turkish artillery.

[1] De Tott, *Memoirs*, vol. 2, part 3, pp. 66–9.

As late as 1807, when Sir John Duckworth's squadron forced the Dardanelles, the English sailors, to their incredulous astonishment, saw many a stone ball of enormous size being noisily hurled against their vessels[1].

Until the middle of the fifteenth century also Western gunfounders, striving for super-weapons, had dreamed of monstrous guns, but at the very moment when Mohammed II was firing " *Mahometta* " the technicians in the West reversed the prevailing trend and devoted great efforts to the production of light field artillery. The Turks altogether failed to recognize the importance of the innovation and did not keep up with the new developments. Their undisputed superiority in battles of movement and the feudal structure of their army contributed to this failure. Also, with the sixteenth century, the Ottomans entered a period of social unrest and economic difficulties that hampered change and adaptation. Whatever the cause, it is certain that they continued to devote their main efforts to the production of siege ordnance[2] and lagged behind the West both in the production and the use of field artillery. As long as this type of cannon was in its infancy in Western Europe, the lag did not noticeably affect the balance of power. But in the course of the seventeenth century and especially after the appearance of the Swedish " *regementsstycke* " European progress in the manufacture of highly mobile field-guns with a good rate of fire became rapid and substantial. In the second half of the century, Raimondo Montecuccoli, the general who routed the Turkish army at the battle of St. Gothard (August 1664) wrote on the basis of his own experiences: " This enormous artillery (of the Turks) produces great damage when it hits, but it is awkward to move and it requires too much time to reload and sight. Furthermore it consumes a great amount of powder

[1] Robertson, *Naval armament*, p. 67.

[2] The Turks acquired special expertise in using siege artillery. They developed the technique of using composite batteries in which huge guns operated together with medium calibre pieces in demolishing walls. This technique is described by Colliado, *Platica*, p. 13.

besides cracking and breaking the wheels and the carriages and even the ramparts on which it is placed ... Our artillery is more handy to move and more efficient and here resides our advantage over the cannon of the Turks "[1]. With an artillery that was, as Baron de Tott saw it, " formidable in appearance from the width of its bore, but little to be dreaded after the first discharge from the slowness with which these enormous pieces must be served "[2], the Turks were hopelessly doomed[3].

[1] Montecuccoli, *Aforismi*, p. 457. The views expressed by Montecuccoli are supported by numerous other sources. Father Vincenzo Maria (see appendix II) noted at the middle of the seventeenth century that " the Turks make little use of artillery and indeed seem not to care for it except for siege operations ". Earlier in the century, Fynes Moryson (*Itinerary*, p. 41) wrote that " the great armyes of the Turks may be attributed to their small skill and rare use of fighting with guns, which only some part of the Janizaries useth, though they have great store of artillery, which in like sort they cannot generally so well manage as the Christians ". The Turks failed to develop field artillery and when attacked by the Russians in 1768 they did not have many a field-gun although they had plenty of huge and clumsy siege ordnance, cf. the remarks by Baron de Tott, *Memoirs*, vol. 2, part 3, p. 114: " such was the ignorance of the Turks that their army wanted a field artillery without which the greatest abilities could effect but little "; p. 155: " the first work of the new foundry (that De Tott organized) was to be a train of field artillery with which the Turks were entirely un-provided ". Also Monsieur de Peyssonnel who was rather critical of some of the remarks by De Tott, admitted that the Turks had no " furnace proper for casting the small field-pieces of which they are in want and which Baron De Tott undertook to fabricate " (De Tott, *Memoirs*, vol. 2, part 4, p. 257).

[2] De Tott, *Memoirs*, vol. 2, part 3, p. 38. The relative abundance of copper supplies and the primitive passion for huge siege-guns were certainly among the main causes of another Turkish failure. They did not develop the art of casting iron guns. As late as the second half of the eighteenth century, Monsieur de Peyssonnel remarked that " the Turks have no iron cannon and either know not how or disdain to make it. All their artillery is of brass nor have they any other on board their ships; for though we find pieces of iron ordnance in some of their fortified places or on board their merchant ships, these have all been taken in war or purchased from Swedes, Danes, or the Europeans " (cf. De Tott, *Memoirs*, vol. 2, part 4, p. 256).

[3] See below Epilogue.

2—On land the balance of power between the Turks and the Europeans turned definitely against the Turks in the course of the seventeenth century. On the seas, it had turned against them more than a century earlier.

On the 7th of October 1571 at Lepanto a Christian fleet of 208 galleys, including 6 immense galleasses engaged a Turkish fleet of 230 galleys. After a ferocious fight that lasted three hours, 80 Turkish galleys were sunk, 130 were captured and only 40 escaped from the wing. The West rejoiced and the whole Christian world joined in boasting of the importance of the great victory. The Pope exulted more than anybody else and in his excitement declared that by divine grace he had " seen " the whole course of the battle while sitting in his chair in St. Peter's at Rome.

The Turks did not appear very shocked. " The infidels only singed my beard; it will grow again " said the Sultan reportedly and it does not seem that such a complacent reaction was a mere piece of propaganda. His main strength was on land and not on the sea[1]. The Turks also knew that they had enough resources to rebuild their navy in a matter of months, as in fact they did.

Assessing the historical importance of the battle, Western historians (except when writing text books) generally tend to lean more toward the interpretation of the Sultan than toward that of the Pope. " A great victory without consequences ", they say and blame the lack of unity in the Christian field, the rivalries between Venice and Spain and the involvement of Spain with England and Holland. However, Lepanto did not have " great consequences " essentially because it was not a " great victory ". Lepanto was an anachronistic battle, fought with galleys and a lot of boarding and ramming, at a time when novel types of vessels and weapons were opening

[1] Moryson (*Itinerary*, p. 58) noticed that " no doubt the gallies of the Turks are neither so well built nor so swift in saile, nor so fitte to fight, nor so strong, nor built of so durable timber as those of the Spaniards, Venetians and other Christians their enemyes ". Cf. also appendix II.

a new era in naval warfare and showing the way to a new naval strategy. At Lepanto the victors were no less anachronistic than the vanquished: both parties were prisoners of outdated traditions and techniques. In the light of history, at Lepanto everybody lost.

Less glamorous and less publicized, the victories of the Portuguese against the Moslems in the Indian Ocean during the first half of the sixteenth century were historically of a much greater significance[1]. Immediately after the arrival of Vasco da Gama at Calicut, the Moslems realized that the presence of Christian vessels in the Indian Ocean opened a new front, threatened their position and upset the traditional balance of power. In 1507 a fleet with no less than 15,000 men left Egypt under Admiral Mir Hussain aiming at the destruction of the Portuguese. But the Portuguese defeated it off Diu in 1509[2]. The attack was renewed and new expeditions were launched, but despite isolated success, the Moslems failed in their efforts and the Christians established their sovereignty over the Ocean.

It has been suggested that the failure of the Moslems was mainly due to the lack of timber supplies. According to this view, " the total absence of timber on the Red Sea and the Persian Gulf" greatly hampered the rulers of Egypt (before 1517) and of Turkey (after 1517) in their efforts to build a fleet for use in the Indian Ocean[3]. It cannot be denied that the lack of timber created problems for the Moslems, but this kind of difficulty they most certainly managed to overcome. In fact they armed one fleet after another in the Red Sea in the course of the sixteenth century[4]. The main reason for their failure lay rather in their outmoded techniques of naval warfare.

[1] It is significant that, as Moryson (*Itinerary*, p. 34) wrote, " the Turks more feare the Spaniards at sea because they have been heretofore fouly defeated by the Portugalls having forts in the Red Sea ". Between 1580 and 1640 Portugal belonged to the Spanish monarchy.

[2] Serjeant, *The Portuguese*, p. 41, *n.*4.

[3] Boxer, *Portuguese in the East*, p. 197 and Boxer, *Four Centuries*, p. 15.

[4] Serjeant, *The Portuguese*, pp. 15, 19*ff.* and passim.

The Turks as well as their traditional foes, the Venetians and the Holy Order of Malta, did not realize the importance and the implication of the naval revolution that the Atlantic powers had accomplished. They remained " medieval " when the modern age had already begun. They used guns on their ships (although in their own primitive way) [1] and they made use of sailing vessels. But essentially they remained heavily dependent on human energy: they stuck to the old tactic of ramming and boarding and the galleys were always the backbone of their fighting force [2]. Against the Portuguese on the Ocean they fought as they did at Lepanto. In 1551-2 when Piri's fleet moved to the Persian Gulf, in 1576-7 when a naval expedition was led by 'Aly Bey against Muscat, in the defence of Aden with Admiral Khidr Beg, it was always the large galleys, the *qādyrgas*, that carried the weight of the battle [3]. The Portuguese used galleys also but the backbone of their fleet was the large ocean-going gun-manned sailing vessel [4]. In a small closed sea the big galleys still had a few chances. It is not fortuitous that neither the Portuguese nor the Dutch ever succeeded in establishing themselves on the

[1] The passion for huge cannon never deserted the Turks. In 1516 a Turkish galley came out of Aden and attacked Portuguese vessels. The Turks had placed aboard the galley a huge gun (a *basilisk*), that was said to throw a shot of three-quarters of a hundredweight. When the gun was fired, the recoil was so great that the galley turned over till the Portuguese could see her keel (cf. Whiteway, *The Portuguese*, pp. 39-40 and Serjeant, *The Portuguese*, p. 170, *n*. H). In the eighteenth century Monsieur de Peyssonnel noted that " the Turkish ships of the line have all in their upper tire four or five guns of an enormous calibre which carry stone balls of several hundred weight " (cf. De Tott, *Memoirs*, vol. 2, part 4, p. 240).

[2] Cf. the description of the Turkish warships given by Hāǧi Halifa and reproduced by Kahle (ed.) in Piri Re'is, *Bahrije*, pp. xxxiv-xxxviii.

[3] Serjeant, *The Portuguese*, p. 179n. DD and p. 180n. EE. Cf. also the Ramūzī illustration reproduced in Kahle, *Piri*, p. xxxvii.

[4] In his expedition to Aden (A.D. 1517) Lopo Soares de Albergaria had 15 *naos* (large sailing vessels), 10 *navios* and *caravelas* (sailing ships smaller than the *naos*), 8 galleys, 1 *caravelao*, 1 *bargantin* and 1 Indian junk. In his expedition to Hermuz (A.D. 1520) Diego Lopes de Sequeira had 11 *naos*, 2 galleons, 5 galleys, 4 square rigged ships, 2 brigantines and 2 caravels (cf. Serjeant, *The Portuguese*, pp. 170-1, notes H and I).

shores of the Red Sea. But on the ocean the galleys had no chances whatsoever. When they were not sunk by the guns of the great sailing ships they were easy prey to the fury of the elements[1].

Late in the sixteenth century the Turks learned how to man ocean-going vessels. In the early decades of the seventeenth century the " Moors " of the North African coast put together a considerable fleet of sailing vessels for privateering activities[2], but the Empire as a whole never made up for the late start. Western naval technology kept moving ahead faster and the Turks lagged hopelessly behind—more and more so in the course of the centuries[3].

3—Having outflanked the Turks—Ottomans as well as Mamluks—the Europeans were confronted with peoples of vastly different technologies and civilizations: on the one hand the very primitive peoples of the Americas and Africa and on the other hand the highly developed and sophisticated peoples

[1] As in 1554 when the fleet of Sīdī ' Alī Ra'īs was destroyed by a storm.

[2] " Within some sixteene yeares last past the generall peace of Christendome made our soldiers for want of meanes to live turne pyratts who having no safety in the ports of Christian Princes retyred themselves to Algier in Barbary, the people whereof and of the parts adioyning are most daring of all the Turkes. They gladly intertayned these pyratts and were content at first to have share of the spoyles and to goe with them to sea, but of late they have gotten some 60 or 80 good shipps of warr from the Christians by their meanes and from them have learned such skill to saile by the compasse as they have been able to man these shipps with Turkes and have had the dareing to rob uppon the Ocean which they never knew nor durst behold in any former age " (Moryson, *Itinerary*, p. 60). By 1618 an unofficial estimate of the " numbers of ships in the Mediterranean " (see above chapt. 1, footnote [3] p. 79) confirms the recital by Moryson and indicates that while the " Turks in the Archipelago " remained faithful to the galley, the " Morescoes of Africa " had assembled a fleet of sailing ships. Cf. also marsigli, *État Militaire*, part 1, pp. 144-5.

[3] In the eighteenth century Monsieur de Peyssonnel, who was sympathetic to the Turks, admitted that the Turkish vessels were rather cumbersome. Hassan Pacha brought improvements " into the building and rigging of ships, lowered their decks, rendered their sterns less lofty, raised their masts and provided them with better tackling and a more regular artillery ". (De Tott, *Memoirs*, vol. 2, part 4, p. 250).

of Asia. The first, of course, had never dreamed of fire-arms, and we can paraphrase Paolo Giovio by saying that the noise of European artillery was enough to induce them " into the worship of Jesus Christ ". As to the second, the picture is noticeably less simple.

Says an ancient Chinese text: " Among the hills in the Western parts (of China) there exist beings in human shape, a foot or more in height, who are by nature very fearless. If offended they cause men to sicken with (alternate) heat and cold. They are called *Shan-sao*. By thrusting bamboos into fire, and producing a crackling sound the *Shan-sao* are frightened away "[1]. According to a tradition widely accepted among Chinese antiquarians, gunpowder and fire-works were developed in order to scare away the little demons with a noise that magnified the crepitating sound of the burning bamboos[2]. Precisely when this began, we do not know. There is no doubt, however, that as early as the tenth century A.D. the Chinese were using gunpowder and, by that time, not only to drive away the malignant *Shan-sao* but also in actions of war[3]. Whether the Chinese had invented the noisy compound or had borrowed it from Brahmin chemists is a question that does not need to detain us here[4].

Both in India and China metallic guns, in the modern sense of the word, appeared long after gunpowder had began to be used and after a long series of experiments with all kinds of rockets, missiles, incendiary projectiles, etc. etc.[5] Chinese bombards dated 1356 and 1357 have been preserved in Chinese Museums and there is no doubt that weapons of this kind were

[1] Mayers, *Gunpowder*, p. 77.

[2] Fire-crackers are known in China by the name of *p'ao-chu* which literally means " crackling bamboo ".

[3] Mayers, *Gunpowder*, pp. 85*ff.*; Wang-Ling, *Gunpowder*, pp. 160-2; Needham, *Science*, vol. 1, pp. 131 and 134.

[4] The thesis of the Chinese origin is more generally accepted. For the thesis of the Indian origin cf. Mayers, *Gunpowder*, pp. 81*ff.*

[5] Mayers, *Gunpowder*, pp. 83-93; Wang-Ling, *Gunpowder*, pp. 160-78; White, *Medieval Technology*, pp. 96-9.

used by the Chinese before the middle of the fourteenth century[1]. From China the knowledge of gunpowder and firearms spread to Korea, Japan, Java and other parts of Asia[2]. For India, Ferishta relates that in the 1360's guns were largely used in the Deccan both by the Raja of Vijayanagar and by Muhammad Shah Bahmani. Actually Muhammad Shah gave special attention to artillery, added to his army a special branch for it, and employed " Rumis " (Turks) and " Farangi " (Europeans) well acquainted with the art of gunnery "[1].

[1] Goodrich, Note, p. 211 has pictures of Chinese bombards dated 1356 and 1357. These bombards have trunnions on their barrels which may indicate an already advanced stage of cannon manufacture. According to Wang Ling, Gunpowder, pp. 172-3 guns made of metallic barrel were first used in China around 1275. White, Medieval Technology, p. 99, challenges this view and favours the hypothesis of the European origin of modern artillery, but his criticism is not entirely convincing. On this question cf. also Chow Wie, Chung Kuk Ping Ji, pp. 234-8.

[2] According to tradition the Koreans were introduced to the use of cannon by the Chinese at the end of the fourteenth century. Yu Sungyong, a prime minister of the Yi dynasty during the Japanese invasion of 1592-9, wrote that " in our chosen Korea from the first there was no powder. At the end of Koryn (A.D. 1372) a Chinese merchant named Lee Hang stayed at the home of a general in charge of weapons ... This was the first time our chosen Korea had gunpowder and fire-arms. It was started by Choi Mushen " (Yu, Su-A-Mun Jip, pp. 283-5). Boots, Korean Weapons, pp. 20-1 adheres to the view that fire-arms were first used in Korea at the end of the fourteenth century, but the analysis of some texts brought to my attention by Mr. S. Y. Kwack leads me to believe that this event could have occurred some time earlier. As regards Japan, there are numerous references to the existence of guns prior to the arrival of the Portuguese, although it is generally agreed that guns were not used extensively for military purposes until the end of the Tembun era (1532-54) (cf. the Japanese bibliography quoted and summarized by Brown, The Impact of Firearms, pp. 236-7 and, in addition, Arisaka, Heikkiko, pp. 35ff.). In Java the knowledge of fire-arms was probably introduced by the Mongols (cf. Schlegel, Invention of Fire-arms, p. 6). As to Malacca, when the Portuguese set foot in the country in 1511, according to their chroniclers they captured 3,000 pieces of artillery. We are not told what kind of guns these were, but a modern author believes that it was a question of " small arms which came from foundries in Pegu and Siam, iron casting having been introduced into these countries from China " (cf. Meilink-Rollosz, Asian Trade, p. 123). Also the people of the Philippines allegedly had some knowledge of fire-arms before the arrival of the Europeans.

Ferishta wrote these lines more than two hundred years after the event [2], but he is generally a very careful and reliable historian and we have no reason to doubt his recital. We have previously noticed that by 1368 both Europeans and Turks were acquainted with artillery, and on the other hand the reference to Turkish gunners is not at all surprising because it is well known that Turkish influences were very strong in those parts of India in the fourteenth century [3]. In Gujarat, guns were used in the battle of Malwa in A.D. 1421 and in A.D. 1457 in the bombardment of Mandalgash. In the second half of the century, Sultan Mahmud Beghra had, beside field and siege guns artillery which was used in naval battles [4].

Further research will undoubtedly add much needed detail to this fragmentary and incomplete recital. Much information is still badly needed on the problem of the direction in which the new technology travelled, its velocity and the agents of its propagation. But a few points seem reasonably clear. It is certain that artillery was known in Asia, long before the arrival of the Portuguese. It is likely that Chinese guns were at least as good as Western guns, if not better, up to the beginning of the fifteenth century [5]. However, in the course of the fifteenth

[1] Nadvi, Use of cannon, pp. 406-7.

[2] Ferishta was born in A.D. 1550 or 1570 and died either in 1612 or in 1623. The first draft of his history was presented to his patron-king in 1606 but was subsequently revised.

[3] The impact of Turkish technology on Indian cannon manufacture remained strong throughout the sixteenth and seventeenth centuries.

[4] Nadvi, Use of cannon, p. 407. Cf. also Crawfurd, Dictionary, p. 22.

[5] The Museum für Völkerkunde in Berlin acquired a small bronze gun (35 centimetres in length) that came originally from the Great Wall in China and that was manufactured in 1421 at the time of Emperor Yung-loh (Gohlke, Gewehr, pp. 205-6; for the use of guns in China under Emperor Yung-loh cf. Mayers, Gunpowder, p. 94). Such a piece is not very dissimilar from the small hand-guns that were made in Nuremberg about the same date (cf. Rathgen, Pulverwaffe, pp. 28-9). As to heavy guns, one notices that extant Chinese bombards dated 1356, 1357 and 1377 have trunnions on their barrels (cf. pictures published by Goodrich, Note). Trunnions came into general use in the West more than a century later.

century, European technology made noticeable progress and by 1498 " the armament of the Portuguese ships was something totally unexpected and new in the Indian (and China) seas and gave an immediate advantage to the Portuguese " [1]. European artillery was incomparably more powerful than any kind of cannon ever made in Asia, and it is not difficult to find in contemporary texts echoes of the mixture of terror and surprise that arose at the appearance of European ordnance. The following passage from the *Rajavali* relates the first arrival of the Portuguese at Ceylon: " and now it came to pass that a ship from Portugal arrived at Colombo, and information was brought to the King that there were in the harbour a race of very white and beautiful people who wear boots and hats of iron and never stop in any place. They eat a sort of white stone and drink blood. And if they get a fish they give two or three *ridé* in gold for it, and besides, they have guns with a noise like thunder and a ball from one of them, after traversing a league, will break a castle of marble "[2].

The Portuguese arrived in China in 1517, but the fame of their guns had preceded them since 1511 when they took over Malacca, or even before[3]. *Fo-lang-ki* was the name given to the frightening contrivances by those who reported about them: the name possibly meant " Franks "[4] and the scholar Kou Ying-Siang had to warn his people that " *Fo-lang-ki* is the name of a country and not of a gun "[5].

When the Portuguese fleet under Fernao Peres cast anchor off a quay of the port of Canton in 1517, the first thing they did was to fire a salute with cannon. In the words of Professor

---

[1] Panikkar, *Asia*, p. 29. For a detailed and technical analysis of the overwhelming superiority of Western armament at the very beginning of the sixteenth century cf. Rathgen, *Pulverwaffe*, pp. 11-30.

[2] Tennent, *Ceylon*, vol. 1, p. 418.     [3] Pelliot, *Le Hōja*, pp. 204-7.

[4] Pelliot, *Le Hōja*, p. 204, *n.*244. On the term " Franks " as applied indiscriminately by the Easterners to all Europeans cf. among others the Florentine " merchant " Francesco Balducci Pegolotti (*Pratica*, p. 22) who wrote in the fourteenth century that in China " *franchi appelan'eglino tutti i Cristiani delle parti di Romania innanzi verso Ponente* ".

[5] Mayers, *Gunpowder*, p. 96 and Pelliot, *Le Hōja*, p. 204, *n.*244.

T. T. Chang " it had never before occurred to the Chinese that in some part of the earth a demonstration of war implements could be also an expression of respect or courteous recognition " [1]. The populace was scared and the scholar-officials protested. The dreadful tales that they had heard about the " barbarians with the big nose " and their formidable weapons were abundantly confirmed. Wrote censor Ho Ao a few years after the event: " the *Fo-lang-ki* are most cruel and crafty. Their arms are superior to those of other foreigners. Some years ago they came suddenly to the city of Canton and the noise of their cannon shook the earth " [2]. And the scholar-official Wang-Hong reiterated: " The *Fo-lang-ki* are extremely dangerous because of their artillery and their ships . . . No weapon ever made since memorable antiquity is superior to their cannon " [3].

The roar of European ordnance awoke Chinese, Indians and Japanese to the frightening reality of a strange, alien people that unexpectedly had appeared along their coasts under the protection and with the menace of superior, formidable weapons and ruthlessly [4] interfered with the natives' life. For many a responsible Asian, merchants apart, it was a nightmare. How to deal with the " foreign devils " ? To fight them or to ignore them? To copy and adopt their techniques and give up local habits and traditions or to sever

---

[1] Chang, *Trade*, p. 64. Cf. also Pelliot, *Le Hōja*, p. 123, *n.*77.

[2] Quoted by Chang, *Trade*, p. 51.    [3] Pelliot, *Le Hōja*, p. 107, *n.*42.

[4] In the Europe of the fifteenth, sixteenth and seventeenth centuries, despite some noticeable progress brought about by Renaissance and Reformation, " turbulent noblemen, ignorant clergymen, and filthy and ferocious day-labourers " were not a minority group. Moreover, the sample of European population with which the non-Europeans unexpectedly and unwillingly came in contact was, in general, unfortunate. Cultivated, understanding and generous individuals were not totally absent, as the cases of Bartolomeo de Las Casas in the West and Matteo Ricci in the East may easily prove, but they were conspicuous for their rarity. The great majority of the Europeans who went overseas—sailors, soldiers, merchants and missionaries—were people who, no matter how admirable for bravery, endurance, ingenuity or fervour, did not distinguish themselves for good manners or education and had little talent for public relations.

all contacts with them and seek refuge in a dream of isolation? To be or not to be? The fog of Hamletic doubt began to pervade the soul of Asia—a doubt that was to plague Asia for centuries[1], a dilemma that was tragically unanswerable because both alternative solutions implied surrender and the only alternative to surrender was death.

4—Inevitably, an armament race developed. Cannon became a highly coveted commodity: a much sought after and well rewarded object of trade, the perfect gift for obtaining favours from a local ruler[2], the precious jewel of a princely

[1] This conflict is best represented by the famous theory of the bifurcation between "foundation" (*t'i*, literally 'corpus') and "function" (*yung*). Developed by the influential scholar Feng Kuei-fen (1809-74) after the shock of the Opium War, the theory essentially stated: "If we keep Chinese ethics and famous (read: Confucian) teachings as an original foundation and let them be supplemented by the methods used by the various nations for the attainement, would it not be the best of all procedures?". In other words, this suggested using Western means for Chinese ends, retaining Confucian values while utilizing Western tools, supporting China's traditional civilization while importing Western technology (cf. Fairbanks, *China's response*, p. 387). The idea was further emphasized by Chang Chih-tung whose formula was "Chinese learning as the structure and western knowledge for practical use". But history proved the inapplicability of such wishful thinking. As Yen Fu pointed out, criticizing Chang Chih-tung, "Chinese knowledge has its foundation (*t'i*) and function; western knowledge has also its foundation and function". Technology has its roots in science and science in philosophy. The Chinese could never learn western science without modifying their philosophy (Mu, *Hundred Flowers*, p. 94).

[2] The instances of guns presented by Europeans to local rulers in order to obtain special permissions or privileges are so numerous that one can hardly cite even a small proportion of all the known cases. For artillery presented by the Dutch and the English to Japanese rulers cf. Boxer, *Jan Compagnie*, pp. 25*ff*. and Hyma, *The Dutch*, pp. 145 and 157. For the delivery of Portuguese artillery to the Japanese cf. the letter that Otomo Yoshishige, Daimyō of Bungo, wrote to the Bishop of Nicea in 1568 (Brown, *The Impact of Firearms*, p. 242, *n*. 31). Instances of cannon and ammunition presented by the English to the Chinese in the course of the seventeenth century are quoted by Morse, *Chronicles*, vol. 1 pp. 37 and 56.

dowry[1]. There was nothing that cannon could not buy—in fact as well as in fancy. In an old Javanese poem the beautiful princess Tarurôgô is sold to a Dutchman for three pieces of artillery.

Of course, the Europeans were not always willing to give away the weapons on which their supremacy rested. Often guns were turned over to the natives. In some cases the Europeans wanted to obtain from the local authority special privileges for their trade[2]. In other cases it was a question of helping one potentate against the other according to the policy of " divide and rule "[3]. Money minded and motivated

---

For cannon offered by the English to the ruler of Ikkeri in India, in 1637, cf. Mundy, *Travels*, vol. 3, p. 88.

Particularly significant is the letter written by Minamoto Iyeyosu to the King of Siam on ceremonial gifts. The Japanese lord bluntly stated that " guns and gunpowder are what I desire more than gold brocade " (Satow, *Notes*, p. 145).

In connection with this tradition of providing guns by way of gift, one may mention a curious episode that occurred in 1684 on the coast of China. An English vessel had brought to Foochow " things serving for warr, videlizet brass guns, musquetts, gunpowder and lead " hoping to sell them " to his Imperiall Majesty in his warrs against the rebells of Tywan ". The Chinese officials claimed the material as a gift to the Emperor. The English answered that the Company was a body of traders and could not afford to give such expensive presents, but sent out these for sale. Thereupon the Chinese officials assumed an appearance of great wrath maintaining that good subjects needed no arms for their protection while evil rebels must not be supplied with them. The English made such defence as they could and obtained exemption for the lead, as it " mought be applyed to other uses besides warrfare ", but in order not to " hazarde the whole shipp " and the rest of the cargo, they left most of the cannon and ammunition in the hands of the Chinese officials as a present for the Emperor (Morse, *Chronicles*, vol. 1, p. 54).

[1] " The Kinge of Acheijn sent a peece of ordinance, such as for greatnes length [and workmanship], the like is hardly to bee found in all Christendome, which hee gave in marriage with his daughter to the King of Ior, a town lying by Malacca, upon the coast of Sian " (Linschoten, *Voyage*, vol. 1, pp. 109-10).

[2] See above footnote [2], p. 109.

[3] Around 1514-15 the Portuguese supplied the Persians with fire-arms and taught them the art of casting ordnance in order to increase the

by profit, many a European was ready to sell anything to anybody[1]: for pepper, good brass ordnance was sold to " Babarautt, the arche pyratt "[2]. But it has to be admitted that the export of Western cannon to Asia never amounted to more than an insignificant portion of European cannon production.

On the other hand, the Asian potentates did not like to remain dependent on the Europeans for their armament. Whenever they could, they tried to set up gun foundries of their own and gun-founders were as eagerly sought after as cannon[3]. In principle the Europeans were opposed to the idea of giving away their techniques. The Portuguese severely punished those who taught the natives the art of gunnery[4]. To the Japanese officials who asked him to teach them gunnery, Pieter Nuyts, Dutch governor of Taiwan, replied: "Japan rules the land with bow, arrow and sword, my country only with fire-arms, wherefore I cannot teach you this art "[5]. At Batavia, considering that the gun foundry was " too close to the natives and Javanese, from whom this art should certainly be kept secret ", the Dutch

---

difficulties of the Turks against whom the Persians were chronically at war (Godinho, *Repli vénitien*, p. 299). In 1541-2 the Portuguese gave cannon to the Abyssinians to help them against Ahmad Grāñ (Serjeant, *Portuguese*, p. 102).

[1] The selling of cannon brought high profits. Cf. Raychauduri, *Coromandel*, p. 195 with special reference to guns sold by the Dutch to Indian rulers.

[2] Mundy (*Travels*, vol. 2, p. 316) states that while in Bhatkal in 1637 " we mett with Babarautt's frigatts, from whome wee receaved some pepper in exchange of a brass gun ".

[3] In 1643 two Dutch vessels were seized by the Japanese near the city of Nambre or Nambu. One Japanese authority accounts for the sparing of the lives of the Hollanders by the fact that three of them were made gunnery instructors (Hyma, *The Dutch*, p. 288 n.6). In 1675 the captain of the *Flying Eagle* was asked, and in some measure forced, to leave two gunners in Formosa to instruct the artillerymen against the Manchus (Morse, *Chronicles*, vol. 1, p. 44).

[4] Cf. the story told by Varthema and reproduced below at pp. 112-13.

[5] Boxer, *Jan Compagnie*, p. 28.

shifted the foundry to a less conspicuous place within the Castle walls [1]. In 1645, Pieter Antoniszoon Overtwater, chief of the Dutch factory in Nagasaki, wrote that " these mortars are great jewels and one may well ask whether it had not been wiser never to have taught this proud and haughty nation about them . . . (as to the request by the Japanese authorities for the loan of a gun-founder) we ought to be rather evasive and fob them off with polite nothings " [2]. But in the course of time the Asian potentates always found some Europeans ready to teach them the art of making cannon. Ludovico Varthema reports that: " Being then arrived in Calicut (A.D. 1506) I found two Christians who were Milanese. One was called Ioan-Maria and the other Piero-Antonio, who had arrived from Portugal with the ships of the Portuguese and had come to purchase jewels on the part of the King. And when they had arrived in Cochin, they fled to Calicut. Truly I never had greater pleasure than in seeing these two Christians. They and I went naked after the custom of the country. I asked them if they were Christians. Ioan-Maria answered: ' Yes, truly we are '. And then Piero-Antonio asked me if I was a Christian. I answered: ' Yes, God be praised '. Then he took me by hand, and led me into his house. And when we had arrived at the house, we began to embrace and kiss each other, and to weep. Truly, I could not speak like a Christian: it appeared as though my tongue were large and hampered, for I had been four years without speaking with Christians. The night following I remained with them, and neither of them nor could I eat or sleep for the great joy we had. You may imagine that we could have wished that that night might have lasted for a year, that we might talk together of various things, amongst which I asked them if they were friends of the King of Calicut. They replied that they were his chief men, and that they spoke with him every day. I asked them also what was their intention. They told me that they would willingly have returned to their country, but that

[1] Boxer, *Jan Compagnie*, p. 27.    [2] Boxer, *Jan Compagnie*, p. 38.

they did not know by what way. I answered them: ' Return by the way you came '. They said that was not possible, because they had escaped from the Portuguese and that the King of Calicut had obliged them to make a great quantity of artillery against their will, and on this account they did not wish to return by that route. And they said that they expected the fleet of the King of Portugal very soon. I answered them, that if God granted me so much grace that I might be able to escape to Cananor when the fleet had arrived, I would so act that the captain of the Christians should pardon them, and I told them that it was not possible for them to escape by any other way, because it was known through many nations that they made artillery and many kings had wished to have them in their hands on account of their skill, and there-fore it was not possible to escape in any other manner. And you must know that they had made between four and five hundred pieces of ordnance large and small, so that in short they had great fear of the Portuguese. And in truth there were reasons to be afraid, for not only did they make the artil-lery themselves, but they had also taught the Pagans to make it, and they told me, moreover, that they had taught fifteen servants of the King to fire *spingarde*. And during the time I was here, they gave to a Pagan the design and form of a mortar, which weighed one hundred and five *cantara* and was made of metal. There was also a Jew here who had built a very beautiful galley, and had made four mortars of iron. The said Jew, going to wash himself in a pond of water, was drowned. Let us return to the said Christians. God knows what I said to them, exhorting them not to commit such an act against Christians. Piero-Antonio wept incessantly, and Ioan-Maria said it was the same to him whether he die in Calicut or in Rome, and that God had ordained what was to be " [1].

Eventually, nostalgia and remorse won the case and the two gun-founders planned to escape, but they were discovered and

[1] Varthema, *Travels*, pp. 260-2.

lynched. This was the end of the story of Ioan-Maria and Piero-Antonio but other European gun-founders were to come to Asia, as renegades or otherwise. In 1505 four Venetians arrived in Malabar to cast cannon[1]. In 1649 after years of "polite nothings" the Dutch had to comply with the requests of the Japanese and the gunner Schaedel along with three other Dutchmen was sent to Yedo where they instructed the natives about guns and gunnery[2]. In China the Jesuits generously offered their services in exchange for the authorization to open Jesuit missions. Actually, the Chinese had cast *fo-lang-ki* at least since 1522: in that year they had got the help of two countrymen of theirs who were serving aboard Portuguese ships and were induced to desert by the clever and scheming Ho Jou[3]. The event was gloried over in the official imperial histories and the Imperial Ministry of the Interior "recapitulating the previous merits of Ho Jou" eventually appointed him to the post of assistant-under-prefect in the under-prefecture of some under-division of the territory of Peking[4]. However, it does not seem that left to themselves the Chinese could go very far in the production of cannon. The Jesuits made themselves very useful as inter-mediaries between the Imperial officials and the Portuguese authorities whenever the former wanted to buy Western guns in Macao. Most willing to oblige, they offered further services as instructors in the art of gunnery and gun-casting. To this job they were certainly well fitted. In the defence of Macao against the Dutch in 1622 it was the Italian Jesuit and mathematician Padre Giacomo da Rho who with a lucky cannon-ball struck the enemy's barrel of gunpowder

[1] Whiteway, *Portuguese*, p. 37; Pieris, *Ceylon*, vol. 1, p. 445, *n*.18.

[2] The Japanese repeatedly asked the Dutch for an expert gunner as instructor. Cf. Boxer, *Jan Compagnie*, pp. 26-7 and 39.

[3] Pelliot, *Le Hôja*, pp. 199-207. Pelliot quotes another text according to which experiments in casting "*fo-lang-ki*" were possibly made before 1522.

[4] Pelliot. *ibid.*

and caused it to explode in the midst of the attacking party with devastating effects. Also in Macao, it was the Jesuits who showed great dexterity in gunnery when, angry at the Dominicans over a hot dispute, they took up their guns and blew up the monastery of St. Dominic [1]. The Chinese could hardly have got better teachers. In the last days of the eighteenth century, an English diplomat travelling through China still heard about " the two Jesuits Schaal and Verbiest (who) took great pains to instruct them (the Chinese) in the method of casting cannon " [2]. As Dr. Chiang puts it, " while Buddha

[1] Boxer, *Fidalgos*, pp. 81 and 97. On Father Giacomo da Rho (1593–1638) and his action in the defence of Macao cf. also Pfister, *Notices*, pp. 188–91.

[2] Barrow, *Travels*, p. 302. Father Johann Adam Schall von Bell (1591–1666) was of German origin. At the request of the Chinese Court he built and operated a cannon foundry in the vicinity of the Imperial Palace, early in the 1640's. He allegedly erected an altar at his furnace and performed Christian rites before the casting of guns. The Chinese Emperor gave orders to let him perform his rites undisturbed (Väth, *Schall*, pp. 111-14. Cf. also Pfister, *Notices*, p. 165 and Hummel, *Eminent Chinese*, vol. 2, p. 622). Scholars debate if he was the author of a Chinese book on gunnery or if he just provided technological information (Väth, *Schall*, p. 370).

Father Ferdinand Verbiest (1623-88) was born in the Southern Low Countries. At the instance of the Chinese Court he took over the manufacture of cannon in the 1670's. After having restored about 300 old clumsy bombards, he produced 132 small and highly manoeuvrable pieces (Bosmans, *Verbiest*, pp. 392-400. Cf. also the *Huang Ch'ao Wen Hsien T'ung K'ao*, chüan 194, p. 14). Before consigning the weapons to the Imperial Army, Father Verbiest made arrangements for a solemn and public benediction of the guns. He had also inscribed on each piece the name of a Saint and the symbol of Jesus (Pfister, *Notices*, p. 348). Father Verbiest wrote a book in Chinese on the casting of guns and their use (Bosmans, *Verbiest*, p. 398 and Pfister, *Notices*, p. 359). On all that precedes cf. also Duhalde, *History*, vol. 2, pp. 79ff.

Beside Schall and Verbiest, other Jesuits contributed to the diffusion of Western military techniques among the Chinese. Han Lin, who wrote two treatises dealing with the use of fire-arms, had received instruction in such matters from the Italian Jesuit Father Alfonso Vagnoni (1566-1640) (Hummel, *Eminent Chinese*, vol. 1, p. 274). Fathers J. de Rocha, N. Longobardi, E. Diaz and F. Sambiaso are also to be mentioned among those who instructed the Chinese on the use of artillery (cf. Lin, *Essai sur Duhalde*, p. 15).

came to China on white elephants, Christ was borne on cannon balls ".

5—If some progress was achieved by the Chinese in the making and use of ordnance after their first contact with the Portuguese, it was remarkably slow. More than half a century after that first contact, Father Martin de Rada could still write that " Chinese artillery (at least that which we saw and although we entered an armoury in Hocchin) is most inferior, for it consists only of small iron guns "[1]. Father Matteo Ricci held no different opinion: " the arms supplied to the army are practically worthless for an offensive against an enemy or even for self-defence "[2]. Also a Chinese text candidly admitted: " the Fo-lang-ki use fire-arms with great skill. The Chinese on the contrary blow off their fingers or their hands or even their arms . . ."[3].

By 1624 a Chinese military treatise boasted of some substantial progress maintaining that the Chinese " using their ingenuity improved upon the cannon of the Western bar-barians and produced a gun larger in size and more flexible in use than the fo-lang-ki. The name of the gun is fa-k'uang ". According to the same text, the power of the fa-k'uang was such that a stone ball shot from it " could pierce a wall, penetrate into a house, break a tree, turn human beings and animals into a mess of blood and also penetrate into a mountain for several feet "[4]. This huge gun was admittedly " useful only in storming a fort or in trying to capture a strategic place ". Another military treatise indicates that guns of different calibres and dimension were being envisaged if not constructed, beside numerous other more or less fantastic contrivances for vomiting fire[5], but to the eyes of a well-informed European writer at the middle of the seventeenth century the guns of

[1] De Rada, *Relation*, p. 273.   [2] Trigault, *China*, p. 90.
[3] Pelliot, *Le Hōja*, p. 93, n.14.   [4] Hu, *Ch'ou hai t'u pien*.
[5] Mao, *Wu-pei-chih*, especially vol. 50 but also vols. 51 to 56.

China still looked " few and poor ". The efforts by Father Verbiest in the 1670's did not substantially change the picture and China lagged hopelessly behind the West[1].

The reasons for the Chinese failure to produce satisfactory artillery despite the technical assistance of the Jesuits, a good supply of raw materials, native wit and ingenuity, are not easily analyzed. To ask why the Chinese did not produce good artillery is equivalent to asking why they did not industrialize, and to this kind of question there can hardly be an answer—or, rather, there are answers which are as vague and indeterminate as the question itself. But I would be inclined to remark that what was at issue was not only technical skill, but also taste, cultural pride and institutions. Ming Ch'ing China was " a Confucian and phisiocratic State " where skilled artisans were not very numerous and did not have much status[2]. On the other hand, the demand was not such as to induce them to apply themselves to the adoption and development of Western technologies. The Imperial Court never developed that kind of enthusiasm for cannon that inspired the more technically-minded and more warlike monarchs of the West. Fearing internal bandits no less than foreign enemies and internal uprisings no less than foreign invasion, the Imperial Court did its best to limit both the spread of the knowledge of gunnery and the proliferation of artisans versed in the art. " In the reign of Yung Loh fire-arms had already been obtained, but they

[1] For the middle of the seventeenth century cf. Brusoni, *Osservazioni*, pp. 97-8 and Semedo, *Histoire*, p. 145. In the second half of the following century, Father Amiot gave a precise and detailed description (with measures and weights) of some of the cannon used by the Chinese troops: it appears that the few guns used were generally old and outdated, some dating back to 1636 (Amiot, *Art militaire*, pp. 375-84). At the end of the eighteenth century, according to De Guignes (*Voyages*, vol. 3, pp. 35-6) " the greatest part of the guns that exist in China " were old pieces manufactured by Fathers Schall and Verbiest. De Guignes also noticed that the Chinese often used cannon balls made of dried mud. Cf. also Barrow, *Travels* p. 302 and Keberg, *Ostindische Reise*, p. 101.

A gun made of bamboo (described by Father Amiot in his *Supplement*, p. 360) was the Chinese equivalent of the Western leather-cannon.

[2] Ho, *Ladder of success* pp. 41ff. and 56ff.

were not permitted to be known publicly. Although in 1422 the proposition of Chang Fu for the placing of guns at the Ta T'ung and other frontier passes for defence against the enemy was acceded to, yet these formidable weapons were not allowed to be seen and the Emperor set great store by them "[1]. By 1570 cannon had become well known to the populace and guns were placed at the gates of practically all walled towns[2]. Still, the Imperial Court was very suspicious and did not like the idea that its subjects could play around with the art of gunnery[3]. The attitude of the Imperial Court was also heavily influenced by the fact that Chinese rulers had always been apprehensive of foreign influence, for they realized that the idea of the " barbarians " being superior to Peking would be political dynamite[4].

On the other hand, when an Emperor adopted a more sympathetic attitude toward the Western " barbarians " and their technology, conservative circles and officials busily manoeuvred to hinder the change. Sometimes it was just a question of feelings of envy and suspiciousness because of

[1] Reproduced by Mayers, *Gunpowder*, p. 94. A Chinese hand-gun manufactured at the time of Emperor Yung Loh is described by Gohlke, *Gewehr*, pp. 205-6.

[2] De Mendoza, *History*, p. 130: "in everie citie they have certaine houses where they make their ordinance and artilerie continuallie: they doo not plant them on castles (for that they have not the use of them in all the kingdome), but uppon the gates of their cities, which hath mightie great and thicke walles and deepe ditches".

[3] On a few occasions the Imperial Government hired Portuguese guns as well as Portuguese gunners, but then it sent them home as quickly as possible. The history of these episodes is told in details by Boxer, *Expedições militares*. One may also consult Pfister, *Notices*, p. 214 and Boxer, *Fidalgos*, p. 75.

The idea of the Celestial Court was that the loyal subjects should not play around with any kind of arms. As Nieuhoff noticed in the seventeenth century (*Embassy to China*, p. 156) "nobody (in China) is suffered to wear arms within a city, nor the souldiers nor commanders nor the learned philosophers, unless they are upon the march and going to the wars. Neither are suffered to have arms in their houses or to ride armed otherwise than with a dagger to defend themselves against highwaymen".

[4] Mu, *Hundred Flowers*, p. 76.

the repute acquired by some foreign "barbarian" at the Imperial Court [1]. But there was more than that. Among the gentry and the scholar-officials the prevailing cultural traits were not favourable to innovation. Of course it is not difficult to find examples of scholar-officials who recommended the adoption of the new weapons and the development of their manufacture. Wang Hong sent Portuguese guns to the Imperial Court in 1522 urging that they be used against the Mongols [2]; Hsü Kuang-chi strongly recommended the acquisition of guns in Macao in 1619 and again in 1630; Sun Yüan-hua wrote a report in 1621 recommending the adoption of Western cannon; Chü Shih-ssü managed to obtain Western guns through the intercession of missionaries and allegedly used them in the defence of Kuei-lin in 1648 [3]. But the efforts of a few were not enough to compensate for the immobile conservatism of the many. The superior performance of Western science in matters of astronomy with all the implication that this had for the Chinese calendar and the Imperial administration, was too much of a shock to the scholar-officials to be accepted as a matter of course. The idea that the stylish poems and formal essays they learned were useless

[1] As an example one may quote the persecution of Father Schall at the instigation of Imperial astronomers. Opposition to Western influences often originated also from the squabbles between eunuchs and scholar-officials. If one group showed some interest in Western contrivances, the rival group would immediately take the opposite attitude.

[2] Pelliot, Le Hōja, pp. 199-201.

[3] Hummel, Eminent Chinese, vol. 1, pp. 200, 317, 318 and vol. 2, pp. 686 and 912. It is interesting to note that among the scholar-officials who favoured the adoption of Western technology there were many who had adopted the Christian faith and were in close contact with the Jesuits. Once the mental block that stood in the way of the adoption of " things barbarian " was removed, there was no limit to what could be absorbed. But the majority of the scholar-officials could not break through that mental block. As Mei Weng Tin (1632-1721) wrote in one of his poems: " How can I detach my life from the Confucian wisdom/ and devote my life to the Western theories?/ If I were to study astronomy without becoming Catholic/ our friendship would be insincere/ how in this world can one go back on one's origins? ".

in the light of the engineering knowledge of the West, was more than they could bear. As the Chinese writer who conceales himself under the pseudonym of Mu Fu-Sheng cogently puts it " military defeat was the technical reason why Western knowledge should be acquired, but it was also the psychological reason why it should not be. Instinctively the Chinese preferred admitting military defeat, which could be reversed, to entering a psychological crisis: people could stand humiliation but not self-debasement ... The mandarins sensed the threat to Chinese civilization irrespective of the economic and political issues and they tried to resist this threat without regard to the economic and political dangers. In the past the Chinese had never had to give up their cultural pride: the foreign rulers always adopted the Chinese civilization. Hence there was nothing in their history to guide them through their modern crisis "[1]. Cultural pride stood tenaciously in the way of change. Traditional tastes and ingrained sets of value also opposed it. To the majority of the scholar-officials of Ming and early Ch'ing China nothing could be less attractive than noisy weapons and military innovations. Genteel initiates in an essentially humanistic culture, the officials of the Celestial Empire " were amateurs in the fullest sense of the word, without interest in progress, leanings to science, sympathy for commerce or prejudice in favour of utility. Amateurs in government because their training was in art, they had an amateur bias in art itself for their profession was in government "[2]. Their culture being firmly established on tradition, they could not be persuaded—as Father Le Comte (1655-1728) noted—" to make use of new instruments and leave their old ones without an especial order from the Emperor to that effect. They are more fond of the most defective piece of antiquity than of the most perfect of the modern, differing

[1] Mu, *Hundred Flowers*, pp. 76-7. A corroboration by contrast of the thesis of Mu is to be found in the fact quoted in the preceding footnote.

[2] Levenson, *Confucian China*, pp. 16-19.

much in that from us (Europeans) who are in love with nothing but what is new "[1].

Below the Imperial Court and the scholar-officials, cultural traits were not more favourable to change. The whole of Chinese society was imbued with a taste for tradition, individual virtuosity and colourful performance. Last but not least, both upper and lower classes shared an intense contempt for soldiers and military matters. " The military is one of the four conditions which are considered mean among them " wrote Father Ricci [2]. And Semedo added: the weakness of their army is due: 1, to the long periods of peace they enjoyed; 2, to their high esteem for letters and their contempt for military matters; 3, to their way of appointing the army-captains, namely on the basis of (literary) examinations and not on the basis of military expertise [3].

Nothing, I think, can better serve than the following delightful episode to illustrate the prevailing Chinese aura of patrician detachment and amateurish style. When in 1626 Yüan Ch'ung-huan had to defend Ning-yüan against the attacking Manchus and eventually decided to resort to " foreign guns ", the general direction of artillery operations was put in the hands of his Fukienese cook who, incidentally, put up a very good show [4].

If a Fukienese cook was good enough as captain-major of artillery against the " barbarians " who were pressing against

[1] Le Comte, *Empire of China*, p. 68. As indicated by Professor Chen, *Lin Tse-hsü*, pp. 58-60, conservatism was particularly strong in the provinces where still at the middle of the nineteenth century most of the governors resisted any innovation and especially the adoption of Western techniques.

[2] Passages from Ricci's letter are reproduced by Staunton (ed.) in De Mendoza, *History*, p. lxxviii. Commenting upon Ricci's remarks, Geronimo Roman, factor of the Philippines at Macao, added (*ibid.* p. lxxx): " the soldiers of this country are a disgraceful set ... What can the soldiers be in a country where their position is looked upon as dishonourable and occupied by slaves? ". On the social position of military personnel in Ming-Ch'ing China cf. Ho, *Ladder of Success*, pp. 59ff.

[3] Semedo, *Histoire*, pp. 145-6. The remarks by Brusoni, *Osservationi*, p. 98 are taken literally from Semedo's work.

[4] Hummel, *Eminent Chinese*, vol. 2, p. 954.

China from the steppes, much more was needed to fight against the "barbarians" who were coming from the sea. But the scholar-officials of the Celestial Empire did not have much more at their disposal.

6—The disadvantage of the Chinese in matters of artillery in relation to the European powers was felt not so much on land as on the seas. As has been repeatedly said in the first chapter and will be emphasized again in the epilogue, until the middle of the seventeenth century the Europeans were unable to produce effective light field artillery. Their guns lacked mobility and in the open field their fire could be overwhelmed either by a massive assault or by manoeuvre. On the sea things looked quite different, and it was impossible for the Chinese or any other people to cope with the formidable European vessels[1].

It has been highly fashionable in the last few decades to sing the virtues of the Chinese junk, and there is no doubt that, as far as seaworthiness and navigational qualities in general go, these laudatory songs are deserved. The Chinese

[1] When a large number of junks could be assembled around an isolated Western vessel, there were hopes of success for the Orientals, but even in such cases chances were limited. In 1565, 8 to 10 Japanese junks and no less than 50 *fumé* attacked a Portuguese carrack. The carrack had only eighty Portuguese sailors on board and many of those on shore could not get back to the ship in time, but thanks to their cannon the few Portuguese were able to repel the Japanese boarders. The Hirado flotilla withdrew with a loss of over two hundred casualties and returned crestfallen to base (cf. Boxer, *The Great Ship*, p. 31).

More than once European vessels were taken or destroyed when the local authorities succeeded in sending aboard trouble-makers disguised as merchants or envoys, but this of course does not affect the argument developed in the text. The main weakness of the Europeans lay in the incongruousness of their position: much stronger from a military point of view because of their formidable weapons, they were not in China or Japan for conquest but for trade, not for glory but for money. If on the one hand they were often ready to use force, on the other hand they needed peaceful contacts for carrying on business.

junk could compare honourably with Western sailing vessels for mercantile endeavours or voyages of discovery ,[1] and the successful explorations of admiral Cheng Ho in the early fifteenth century are an excellent proof of this, if any proof is needed. The problem, however, was that the junk never developed into a man-of-war [2]. Like the Mediterranean galley,

[1] While many a Western traveller in the Far East during the thirteenth and fourteenth centuries spoke with enthusiasm of the huge ocean-going junks (cf. Hudson, *Europe*, p. 164), after the end of the fifteenth century it was the Western sailing ship that captured the imagination of the Orientals. In the *T'ai-wan Fu-chih*, an eighteenth-century text mostly based on earlier sources, one reads: " the people which we call red-haired barbarians are the Dutchmen. They are also called *Po-ssu-hu* . . . The sails of their boats are like spider's webs so that they can be turned in all directions for wind and go anywhere they want " (cf. Chang, *Trade*, p. 117).

In 1581 one of the most powerful feudal lords in Japan, the Daimyō of Kitanoshō, Shibata Katsuie, told visiting missionaries that " he would be delighted if the Great Ship would come to this Kingdom of Canga, and if it were necessary he would lend ten, fifteen or twenty thousand *taels* to the Portuguese which he would do solely to gratify his desire to see so new a thing as the Great Ship " (cf. Boxer, *The Great Ship*, p. 41).

The Japanese called the Western carracks and galleons " *kurofune* " or " black ships ". The great impression that these vessels made on the Japanese is reflected in the fact that they became the favourite theme of one of the most characteristic forms of art of old Japan, the so-called " *Namban-byoby* " or " Southern Barbarian screen ". For a brief account of the development of this type of artistic production and the influence on it of the changing patterns of European-Japanese relations, cf. Boxer, *Fidalgos*, pp. 20-6.

[2] An expert such as Capt. Audemard ( *Jonques*, p. 31) wrote on this point: " *les constructeurs (chinois) de cette époque* (sixteenth-eighteenth centuries) *ne se sont pas preoccupés de realiser le bâtiment de guerre aux sens exact du mot. Le bâtiment employé à cet effet n'est, à des rares exceptions près, qu'une jonque ordinaire de commerce montée par des soldats armés de quelque instruments de combat* ". Cf. also Worcester, *Junks*, vol. 2, p. 348ff. In regard to the Korean and Japanese navies, Admiral Ballard ( *Japan*, p. 51) wrote that " their fighting ships only differed from their traders—when they differed at all—in having more oars and a better design for speed and handiness in manoeuvring. The principal method of attack was by boarding ". This statement needs however some qualifications. Under the leadership of their great admiral Lee Sün-sin the Koreans equipped their men-of-war with long-range artillery and adopted those " methods of naval warfare toward which Drake and Howard were moving at almost the same time " (Under-

the Chinese war-junk remained essentially a vessel suited for ramming and boarding. With very high castles and no portholes for guns in the hull, the war-junk was fit only for the traditional way of fighting and such it remained.

Geronimo Roman, factor of the Philippines at Macao wrote about 1584: " The King of China maintains a numerous fleet on this coast, although he is not at war with any one. In an island called Lintao, which is situated near this town (Macao), there is an arsenal, the director or *haytao* of which is continually occupied in superintending the building and equipment of vessels . . . The admiral has the title of *Chunpin*. It is a very high rank, although inferior to the *Tutan*. He has a numerous guard and many drums and trumpets, which make a most agreeable music to the ears of the Chinese, but an insufferable din to ours.

" (The Junks) have some small iron guns, but none of bronze; their powder is bad . . . Their arquebuses are so badly made that the ball would not pierce an ordinary cuirass, especially as they do not know how to aim. Their arms are bamboo pikes, some pointed with iron, others hardened by fire, short and heavy scimitars, and cuirasses of iron and tin. Sometimes a hundred vessels are seen to surround a single corsair, those which are to windward throw out powdered lime to blind

---

wood, *Korean Boats*, pp. 79-81, Marder, *From Jimmu Tennō to Perry*, pp. 24-5 and *Hankuk Haeyang Sa*, pp. 220-5. On Admiral Lee, cf. also Lee, *Lee Chungmu Kong*). Hideyoshi's naval force was defeated by the Koreans (A.D. 1592) because it was " merely an instrument for carrying soldiers ". While the Koreans " had no muskets but plenty of cannon ", aboard their ships, " the Japanese had plenty of muskets but few cannon". After the defeat, the Japanese realized that their inferiority in naval warfare lay in the lack of artillery and they took steps to equip their ships with cannon (Brown, *The Impact of Firearms*, p. 252). This new trend was however interrupted in the 1630's when the Shogun Tokugawa Iyemitsu, with the aim of stamping out Christianity in Japan and insulating the country from disrupting foreign influences, forbade the sailing of Japanese ships to foreign countries and the construction of all vessels of ocean-going capacity. These decrees ushered in a period of Japanese impotence. (Cf. Marder, *From Jimmu Tennō to Perry*, p. 31.)

the enemy, and, as they are very numerous, it produces some effect. This is one of their principal warlike stratagems " [1].

The tone of the letter is definitely that of scorn but the matter of the substance is perfectly confirmed from other sources [2]. The Chinese threw arrows and fire-rockets other than lime powder [3], but it remains true that their naval tactics were and continued to be based exclusively on ramming and boarding: " All their use," wrote Father Gaspar de Cruz, " is to come many together, to compass the adversary ship and to board it " [4]. As late as 1624 the military treatise *Ch'ou hai t'u pien* maintained that " fire arms can be used on large boats but the waves make aiming very hard. Chances of hitting the enemy are very slender. Even if one enemy boat should be hit, the

[1] Reproduced by Staunton (ed.) in the introduction to De Mendoza, *History*, pp. lxxix-lxxx. The " stratagem . . . of the powdered lime " was also used by the Indian pirates: cf. Vincenzo Maria, *Viaggio*, p. 245.

[2] Cf. the report by Gaspar de Cruz reproduced in Boxer (ed.), *South China*, pp. 112-13: " The Chinas have a common saying for to show the nobleness of their kingdom, that the King of China can make a bridge of ships from China unto Malacca. . . . The greatest ships they call junks, which are ships fit for war, made like great carracks, in the which they make great forecastles and high, and likewise abaft, to fight from them in such manner that they over-master their adversaries. And because they use no ordnance, all their use is to come many together, and compassing the adversary ship, they board it; and at the first onset they cast a great deal of lime to blind the adversaries, and as well from the castles as from the tops they cast many sharp pikes burned at the end, which serve for top-darts, of a very stiff wood. They use also great store of stone, and the chiefest they labour for, is to break with their ships the dead-works of their adversaries, that they may be masters over them, having them under them, and being destitute of anything to shelter them; and as soon as they can enter they come to the pike or handy blows, for the which they have long lances and broad-swords hanging at their sides ". Cf. also Father Semedo (*Histoire*, p. 145): " aboard the (Chinese) warships there are few and small guns, but the Chinese do not know how to aim them well ". An important study of Chinese war-vessels and Chinese techniques of naval warfare is that by Capt. Audemard, *Jonques*.

[3] Cf. above footnote [2]. Cf. also the passage by Mundy, *Travels*, vol. 3, part 1, pp. 228-9 who refers to the attack of Chinese junks to an English vessel in 1637 and reports that " balles of wylde fire, rocketts and fire-arrows flew thicke as they passed by us ".

[4] Cf. above footnote [2].

enemy would not thus incur severe losses. The purpose of having fire arms aboard is purely psychological, namely that of disheartening the enemy "[1].

The Chinese, like the Turks and the Indians, lagged hopelessly behind the times in understanding the true potentialities of naval artillery and in learning the new naval tactics that artillery was mercilessly imposing. When they eventually realized that times had changed, it was too late. In the nineteenth century Feng Kuei-fen wrote: "The most unparalleled anger which has ever existed since the creation of heaven and earth is exciting all who are conscious in their minds and have spirit in their blood: their hats are raised by their hair standing on end. This is because the largest country on the globe today, with a vast area of ten thousand *li*, is yet controlled by small barbarians . . . Why are they small and yet strong? Why are we large and yet weak? . . . What we have to learn from the barbarians is only one thing, solid ships and effective guns "[2].

7—In other parts of Asia, the diffusion of European technology encountered a less tenacious resistance. Unlike the Chinese, the Japanese never took their country as the centre of the world. Traditionally they looked beyond their border for foreign customs and techniques to copy and assimilate. For centuries their model had been China. When the Europeans arrived in Asia, the Japanese were not as hampered as the Chinese by

[1] Hu, *Ch'ou Lai Tu pien*. The passage was faithfully reproduced by Tchen Meng-Lei in his eighteenth-century encyclopedia with reference to the *Ta Fou Tch'ouan* (great Foukienese boat): cf. Audemard, *Jonques*, p. 53.

[2] Teng-Fairbank, *Response*, pp. 52-3. The beginning of industrialization in China was strictly connected with the need to provide the country with modern and effective weapons for military defence. In the private and public writing of the pioneers of Chinese industrialization such as Lin tse-hsü and Tseng kuo-fan, "ships and guns" were the main, almost obsessive argument for industrialization. Cf. Chen, *Tseng kuo-fan*, chapts. 1-3 and Chen, *Lin tse-hsü*, pp. 2-4 and 11-21.

self-centred cultural pride[1]. " The Japanese "—wrote Linschoten at the end of the sixteenth century—" are sharpe witted and quickly learne anything they see "[2], and Mendes Pinto observed: " They are naturally addicted to war and in war they take more delight than any nation that we know "[3]. Under the leadership of their warlike barons, the Japanese set about copying Western fire-arms and succeeded in producing some cannon and great quantities of arquebuses[4]. In order to resist the Japanese invasion of the 1590's the Koreans too turned eagerly to the new weapons. They actually did better than the Japanese in the production of artillery although it seems that they lagged behind the Japanese in the production of hand-guns[5]. In India, Ceylon became a well-known centre

[1] Cf. the remarks by Mu, *Hundred Flowers*, p. 17.

[2] Linschoten, *Voyage*, vol. 1, p. 153. Other contemporary statements on the extraordinary receptivity of the Japanese were made by Mendes Pinto, Jorge Alvares and Father Frois and are quoted by Le Gentil, *Fernão Mendes Pinto*, p. 155.

[3] Le Gentil, *Fernão Mendes Pinto*, pp. 151-8 and M. Collis, *The Grand Peregrination*, p. 148.

[4] Cf. Mayers, *Gunpowder*, pp. 97-8, Le Gentil, *Fernão Mendes Pinto*, pp. 151-8, and especially Brown, *Impact of Firearms* where the recent Japanese bibliography is quoted. According to Prof. Brown (*op. cit.*, p. 238) just after the middle of the sixteenth century " the manufacture of fire-arms was confined to the island of Kyushu, where the Portuguese vessels called, but within a few years blacksmiths from the main island were journeying to Kyushu to study methods of making this new type of weapon. The more famous gunsmiths founded schools . . . Sakai in the province of Izumi and Yokkaichi and Kunitomo in the province of Kai became particularly famous as centres for the production of fire-arms ". In general it was a question of matchlocks; cannon was produced only in very limited quantities (Brown, *op. cit.*, p. 244).

In the early seventeenth century, Cocks (*Diary*, vol. 1, p. 34) wrote that the Dutch employed Japanese workers at their factory in Hirado and were able to produce " as formall ordnance as we doe in Christendom " that neither for " workmanship nor stuffe did not stand in halfe the price it cost them in Christendom ".

For pictures of Japanese guns of the seventeenth century cf. Arisaka, *Heikkiko*, pp. 198 ff.

[5] *Hankuk Haeyang Sa*, pp. 219-25 and Boots, *Korean Weapons*, pp. 22-3. Cf. also Underwood, *Korean Boats*, pp. 59, 79-81 and Brown, *The Impact of Firearms*, p. 243. Among contemporary sources cf. Yu, *Su-A-Mum Jip*

for the production of fire-arms[1] and great quantities of ordnance, often of the Turkish monstrous type, were currently manufactured in the Moghul Empire[2].

Despite some local successful achievement, however, no place ever developed manufactures that would even faintly compare with European products. Western guns were always much superior to any non-European product and their superiority was universally recognized[3]. Europe never lost

---

pp. 128, 597-603, 708-22. Korean fire-arms produced at the end of the sixteenth century ranged from the light *Sung-ja* muskets (the smallest had calibre of 19 mm. and a length of 560 mm.) to the heavy *Pao-Kus* (whose largest types had a calibre of 3.5 inches and a weight of about one thousand pounds). For pictures of Korean guns of the late sixteenth and early seventeenth centuries cf. Arisaka, *Heikkiko*, pp. 193ff.

[1] Linschoten, *Voyage*, vol. I, p. 81, wrote that " the natural born (people of Ceylon) or Chingalas make the fairest barrels for peeces that may be found in any place ". Cf. also Maffei, *Historie*, p. 39. Other travellers noticed that excellent gunpowder was also manufactured in India: cf. Tavernier, *Travels*, vol. 2, pp. 268-9 and De Laet, *Description*, p. 115.

[2] On the artillery of Indian Moghuls cf. Irvine, *Army*, pp. 113-51 and Rathgen, *Pulverwaffe*, pp. 196-217. Among the guns manufactured in India during the sixteenth and seventeenth centuries, there were pieces with monstrous proportions, weighing as much as 35, 40 or even 50 metric tons (Rathgen, *Pulverwaffe*, p. 208 and Irvine, *Army*, p. 118ff.; for contemporary narratives cf. De Laet, *Description*, p. 115). More than to the " orientalische Pracht-und Prahlsucht der Grossen " (Rathgen, *Pulverwaffe*, p. 217), the fact should be related to the impact of Ottoman technology. Throughout the sixteenth and seventeenth centuries, Turkish influences were strongly felt in India in the manufacture of ordnance (Goetz, *Aufkommen*, pp. 226-9) and many Turks served the Moghuls as gun-founders as well as gunners (Irvine, *Army*, pp. 152ff).

[3] The Europeans made cannon overseas. One of their main centres of production in Asia was Macao where, in the first half of the seventeenth century, a Manuel Tavares Bocarro operated a renowned gun-foundry (cf. appendix I). The foundry provided with guns all the Portuguese colonies in Asia and on occasion also native rulers. Another Portuguese centre of cannon production was Goa. The Dutch set on foot cannon production at their factory in Hirado (Japan) but in the course of time their main centre of cannon production was Batavia. Guns were also cast by the Spaniards in Gavite (Philippines) but few in number and poor in quality.

The products of all these foundries could hardly compete with the products of European manufactures, the main reason being that European

her formidable advantage in armament production—neither quantitatively nor qualitatively. Despite the fact that the "know-how" was broadcast by renegades, Jesuits, and official missions of "technical assistance", non-European countries never succeeded in filling the vast technological gap that separated them from Europe. On the contrary, in the course of time the gap grew conspicuously larger [1].

"It might be supposed"—wrote an eminent scholar— "that an ignorant man, some edible materials and a cookery book compose together the necessities of a self-moved activity called cooking. But nothing is further from the truth. The cookery book is not an independently generated beginning from which cooking can spring; it is nothing more than an abstract of somebody's knowledge of how to cook: it is the stepchild, not the parent of the activity. The book, in its turn, may help to set a man on to dressing a dinner, but if it were his sole guide he could never, in fact, begin: the book speaks only to those who know already the kind of thing to expect from it and consequently how to interpret it" [2]. Commenting upon this tasty piece of wisdom, another scholar remarked

---

foundries in Asia were generally operated with relatively unskilled native labour. The Japanese maintained that they "would rather have one of those (guns) cast in Europe than ten of such as were ever cast (by Europeans) in Japan" (Boxer, *Jan Compagnie*, p. 25).

[1] When Sir John Duckworth's squadron forced the Dardanelles in 1807, the Turks were still employing for the defence of the Straits old guns that hurled huge stone balls (see above footnote [1], p. 98). In 1841 during the Opium War, when, as P'an Shih-ch'eng put it, "the English barbarians were discourteous", the Chinese still employed Portuguese guns cast in 1627 (Chen, *Lin tse-hsü*, p. 14). As to the artillery of the Indian Moghuls, a British observer noticed in 1746 that "having never experienced the effect of field pieces, they (the Indians) have no conception that it is possible to fire with execution the same piece of cannon five or six times in a minute; for in the awkward management of their own clumsy artillery, they think they do well if they fire once in a quarter of an hour" (Irvine, *Army*, p. 116. Compare this statement with that by Baron De Tott about the Turkish artillery, quoted above at p. 99).

[2] Oakeshott, *Education*, p. 15.

that " at first sight the problem might appear to be merely one of introducing new methods of production and the instruments, tools or machines appropriate thereto. But what is really involved is a vast change in social beliefs and practices. . . ." Technical knowledge is " the expression of man's response to the changing problems set by the environment and by his fellow men . . . For meeting any new situation, new thoughts, new aptitudes, new action will be required. But knowledge has to grow: capital has to be created afresh on the basis of continuous experiment, and new hopes and beliefs have to evolve. It is because all these new activities are not independent of the existing institutions into which they have to be fitted, and which have in turn to be adjusted to them, that the process of change is so complex and, if it is to proceed harmoniously, necessarily so slow "[1].

To admit the new role of field artillery in battles of movement and to adopt new strategies accordingly, the Mamluks had to sacrifice the role and prestige of their feudal cavalry, namely the social position and prestige of the dominating class. This in its turn presupposed the disruption of feudal structures and a profound social revolution for which the kingdom was totally unprepared[2]. Before accepting Western techniques, the Chinese had to undergo " a wholesale change of the world-view, a Copernican revolution of a minor order "[3]. Powerful socio-cultural factors were opposing the assimilation and diffusion of Western technology. In Europe the situation was vastly different. The European knights of the early Renaissance nourished ideas in regard to fire-arms which were not different from those of the Mamluk horsemen, but by 1500 European affairs were coming more and more under the control of new social groups that had a taste for organization rather than splendour, for efficiency rather than gallantry. And such groups could count on an increasingly numerous class of craftsmen with a taste for mechanics

[1] Frankel, *Economic Impact*, pp. 22-4.
[2] Ayalon, *Mamluk*, p. 61.          [3] Mu, *Hundred Flowers*, p. 17.

[130]

and metallurgy. The very factors that had originally favoured the development of the new technology continued to operate and fostered its further progress powerfully: as has been indicated in the previous chapter, European shipbuilding and manufacture of ordnance moved rapidly ahead during the centuries that followed the first direct contact of the Portuguese with the peoples of Asia.

It has also to be said that with few exceptions, when an innovation is first introduced, its advantages over established traditions are not always very obvious. The first European field guns were certainly not conspicuous for their efficiency. The attitude of the Turks toward early field artillery, as the attitude of the Venetians toward the early galleons, cannot be simply discarded as a piece of human stupidity. At their first appearance, innovations are less valuable for their actual advantages than for their potential of future developments and this second quality is always very difficult to assess.

The result of the interplay of all these and other factors and circumstances, whatever their respective weight, was one and unequivocal. After the end of the fifteenth century the original " disequilibrium " between Europe and the rest of the world grew larger instead of levelling out. And for the less " developed " countries things turned progressively for the worse.

# EPILOGUE

1—When Vasco da Gama dropped anchor in the harbour of Calicut, a native asked what the Portuguese were looking for in Asia. The answer of da Gama allegedly was " Christians and spices ". When Albuquerque attacked Malacca in 1511 he told his officers that they had to exert themselves to the utmost in the coming battle because of two reasons: " the great service we shall perform to our Lord in casting the Moors out of the country and quenching the fire of the sect of Mahomet . . . and the service we shall render to the King Don Manoel in taking this city because it is the source of all the spiceries and drugs ". Bernal Diaz speculating about the motives that had driven him and his like to the Indies, wrote that they had left Europe " to serve God and his Majesty, to give light to those who were in the darkness and to grow rich as all men desire to do ".

Through the idea of mission and crusade the conquistadores succeeded where the medieval merchants failed and were able to reconcile the antithesis between business and religion that had plagued the conscience of medieval Europe. One has no reason to doubt the sincerity of their statements, but one may wonder about their realism and the validity of their rationalizations. That the Europeans were more often than not imbued with religious zeal and intolerance is a fact that does not need to be proven. But it is doubtful whether the religious element was as relevant among the motives that drove people overseas as it was among the forces that helped them once they were there. Religious convictions nourished boldness in battle, endurance through ordeals, truculence after victory.

But, missionaries apart, when the Europeans undertook the perilous journey, they were dreaming more about Mammon than about lost souls to enlighten. Ogier Ghiselin de Busbecq, the sixteenth-century diplomat was an inveterate pessimist, but he cannot have been far from the truth when he wrote that for the " expeditions (to the Indies and the Antipodes) religion supplies the pretext and gold the motive "[1].

European expansion after 1400 can hardly be depicted as an extension of the Crusades[2]. It cannot be described as the result of Malthusian pressures either. Recurrent epidemics were constantly checking population growth and no population pressure of any relevance was felt in Europe till the second half of the eighteenth century[3]. On the other hand the number of Europeans overseas remained very exiguous until the

[1] Some governments gave a prominent position to the religious element in their plans. When Legaspi sailed from Mexico to the Luzon Islands, political annexation and religious conversion were both included in his commission. Both Spain and Portugal gave large administrative powers to the clergy in overseas territories. This was not just propaganda. But we may repeat what Prof. Cortesao (*Nautical Science*, p. 1079) wrote of Prince Henry: if he were moved considerably by religious zeal when he began the direction of explorations, " after the early years of his career he was above all the administrator of an economic enterprise of national magnitude and international consequence ".

[2] See below footnote [3], p. 134.

[3] In Portugal people knew that " *as nossas conquistas defraudavan muito este reino de gente* " (Cordeiro, *Apontamentos*, p. 66) and overseas expansion was regarded as the cause of underpopulation at home rather than the effect of overpopulation. The same can be said about Spain (Bourne, *Spain*, p. 251). As for England, from about 1550 to the Restoration in 1660 there were people who believed that the country was overpopulated. It is also true that real wages fell after 1510 and reached their lowest point around 1597 (Phelps Brown & Hopkins, *Prices*, p. 189). But to talk of a " Malthusian crisis " as Phelps Brown and Hopkins do, seems to me a gross exaggeration, although I admit that the widespread idea of overpopulation induced many to support the colonial movement and was an influential factor in gaining the government's support for the work of expansion. From 1660 to the middle of the eighteenth century the general attitude was completely different and although emigration was always of small volume it was viewed with great alarm. Cf. Beer, *Colonial system*, pp. 32-52.

nineteenth century [1]. Those who left Europe were few. Those who arrived at their destination were half as many [2]. And a large proportion of those who survived the ordeals of the journey and the dangers of life overseas returned to Europe as soon as they could.

European expansion was essentially a commercial venture [3],

[1] According to Boxer (*Four Centuries*, p. 20) "it is unlikely that there were more than 10,000 able bodied Portuguese men overseas in an empire which extended from South America to the Spice Islands in the sixteenth century" but this estimate may turn out to be too low. As Boxer himself points out (see below footnote [2],) the fleet of 1571 alone brought to Goa at least 2,000 people. According to Rosenblat, *Población*, p. 57 the white population of Brazil in 1650 amounted to about 70,000 people but this in its turn may be too large a figure. For the American territories of the Spanish Empire, a generous estimate by Rosenblat (*Población*, p. 57) puts the total white population at about 650,000 souls for 1650. The white population of the Dutch and English possessions was very small. In conclusion, it is probably safe to say that around 1650 there were less than one million whites overseas including those born abroad.

[2] It is difficult to overestimate the hardships of travel to the Indies in those days. Slow passages, bad and often insufficient food, overcrowding and lack of sanitation were the causes of exceedingly high mortality on board the Indiamen. The Portuguese fleet of 1571 reached Goa with only about half of the 4000 men who had embarked at Lisbon (Boxer, *Four Centuries*, p. 20). On a vessel that left Lisbon in 1656, seventy passengers died before reaching Goa. In the following year, out of seventeen missionaries who left Lisbon, two died and one lost his mind during the journey, and another died just after reaching Goa (Bosmans, *Verbiest*, pp. 209-10). In 1676 the Dutch ship *Asia* was held for nine days " under the equinoctial line " by lack of wind : because of " the extreme unhealthy wheather " sixty-two persons died in that short period of time " so that we expected every soul should die out of the ship " (cf. Schweitzer's account in Fayle, *Voyages*, p. 178).

These were actually the fortunate cases when the ships were able to reach their destination. But it was " almost impossible for two or three ships to make so considerable a voyage, without some lett or misfortune " and often ships were lost with all or part of their crew because of fires, explosions, storms, pirates, enemies, etc. For some information on the length and the perils of the passages and life on board Indiamen cf. Fayle, *Voyages*, pp. xxxiii-xliii. For the eighteenth century cf. Nixon, *Health*, pp. 121-38 whose conclusions are valid also for previous centuries.

[3] Cf. Boxer, *Portuguese in the East*, pp. 192 and 214: " a cynic might observe that if it was Christians and spices which had brought the Portuguese to the Orient, it was the spices which were mainly instrumental

and the fact that the colonial policies of the European powers had a very pronounced mercantile tone was the natural consequence of the basic motives behind that expansion. King François I of France was flippantly rude when he styled King Manoel of Portugal " *le roi épicier* " but he was historically correct. One may only add that the States General of Holland and the rulers of England and Spain were no less favourably inclined to " grocery " than Dom Manoel.

A wide range of economic opportunities magnetized the Europeans overseas. The spice trade, of course, always gave promise of lucrative results. But there was more than that. The Portuguese became increasingly interested in the spice trade toward the end of the fifteenth century. Earlier in the century they crept along the African coast looking for ivory, ebony, slaves, gold, grain and fish[1]. In the sixteenth and seventeenth centuries, when the Europeans had established themselves in the Indian Ocean and the China seas, they did not limit themselves to the spice trade. They were at that time interested in a wide range of commodities from saltpetre to copper, silk and porcelain. The current textbooks of

---

in keeping them there ... The old idea of ' the Conquest, Commerce and Navigation ' of the Eastern Seas as an extension of the Crusade against the Muhammadans had been greatly watered down if it had not totally disappeared ". Cf. also Cortesao, *Nautical Science*, p. 1079*ff*. For the early English settlements in America cf. Beer, *Colonial System*, p. 29: " though the religious motive figured very prominently in the writing of the day— the spread of Christianity is specifically mentioned as one of the objects in view in nearly all the Colonial charters from that of Gilbert on—yet it cannot be considered as one of the determining causes of the movement. While superficially prominent, the idea was fundamentally subordinate. The individual who settled in America was primarily interested in gaining what was at best a precarious livelihood; the colonizing companies were mainly intent upon earning some return on their capital; and the government was not, except to a very minor degree, influenced by the prospective of conversion of the aborigines ". For the Dutch cf. Hyma, *The Dutch*, p. 159, who remarks that the Dutch never complained about certain inconveniences caused by Japanese officials " who searched their vessels for crucifixes or bibles. The Dutch were there to make money not Christians ".

[1] Godinho, *Découvertes*, pp. 42-6.

economic history are wrong when they give the impression that the only activity of the European adventurers in Asia was that of supplying the West with Eastern products. The Portuguese, the Dutch and the English were the middlemen in a vast network of commercial activity among Asian nations and a good deal of European imports were actually paid for with the income derived from invisible exports of shipping and commercial services[1]. Opportunities were many, risks high but profits higher[2].

Religion supplied the pretext and gold the motive. The technological progress accomplished by Atlantic Europe during the fourteenth and fifteenth centuries provided the means. As has been indicated in the Prologue, the "motives" were already active in the Mediterranean Europe as early as the thirteenth century. The Italians and the Catalans were economically very advanced but they did not succeed in out-flanking the Moslem blockade because they were not supported by adequate technology. They made some use of the energy of the wind and later that of gunpowder, but only in a sub-sidiary way. Essentially they relied on human muscular energy for movement and fighting. But a crew could hardly master the ocean by the use of muscular energy, and when confronted with an enemy it had to yield to superior numbers if the fight were decided by a final mêlée. The link between the Mediter-ranean and Atlantic developments was Columbus. He had to

[1] The Europeans were very actively engaged in bringing Japanese silver to China (Boxer, *The Great Ship*, passim), Japanese copper to China and India (Glamann, *Trade*, pp. 175-6 and passim and Glamann, *Japanese copper*, passim), cloves to India, Indian cotton textiles to South East Asia (Ray-chaudhuri, *Coromandel*, especially chapt. 8), Persian silk and carpets to India and Japan (Vincenzo Maria, *Viaggio*, pp. 111-12). "Invisible" exports were vitally important for Europe because of the "one-way" nature of the trade between Europe and Asia: on this point cf. my next book *The Chinese and the Clock*.

[2] According to Raychaudhuri, *Coromandel*, p. 211, Western activity in Asia was characterized by the prevalence of a "policy of trading for a high rate of gross profit per unit, the illogical conclusion of the universal mercan-tile effort to buy cheap and sell dear".

borrow "Atlantic vessels, Biscayan sailors and Portuguese nautical techniques"[1]. His role and relevance through the genesis of the project was that of agent of Genoese capital[2]. The contribution of the Mediterranean world to European expansion at the end of the fifteenth century was financial and commercial rather than technological.

The gunned ship developed by Atlantic Europe in the course of the fourteenth and fifteenth centuries was the contrivance that made possible the European saga. It was essentially a compact device that allowed a relatively small crew to master unparalleled masses of inanimate energy for movement and destruction. The secret of the sudden and rapid European ascendancy was all there: in the skill acquired by Atlantic nations in the use of the sailing ships and in their having understood that " sea fight in these days come seldome to boarding or to great execution of bows, arrows, small shot and the sword but are chiefly performed by the great artillery "[3].

When the sailing vessels of Atlantic Europe arrived, hardly anything could resist them. As Albuquerque proudly wrote to his King in 1513, " at the rumour of our coming the (native) ships all vanished and even the birds ceased to skim over the water ". This was not rhetorical prose. Within fifteen years after their first arrival in Indian waters the Portuguese had completely destroyed the naval power of the Arabs and their King could justifiably style himself " Lord of the Conquest, Navigation and Commerce of Ethiopia, Arabia, Persia and India ". Meanwhile business and technology were rapidly

[1] Godinho, *Découvertes*, pp. 50-1.

[2] Cf. Caddeo, *Historie*, vol. 2, appendix F, pp. 346-65. The position of Columbus as the *longa manus* of Genoese capitalism explains the question formulated by Hudson, *Europe*, p. 216: " what was it that induced Ferdinand and Isabella to make such a contract with an indigent Genoese adventurer? . . . . It is clear that for some reason Columbus was regarded as indispensable for the success of the scheme. But he could only have been regarded as indispensable if he were believed to have a secret, to know something which no one else knew. This secret could not have been any general cosmographical theory based on well-known literary sources ".

[3] See above, chapt. 1, footnote [3], p. 85.

advancing in Europe and before the non-Europeans had absorbed the shock of the first contact with the Atlantic vessels, more efficient and more numerous vessels arrived. The caravels and the carracks were followed by the galleons. The Portuguese fleets were followed by the vastly more formidable fleets of the Dutch and the English. The arrival of the new invaders coincided with the outbreak of bloody struggles among the whites. But if the Europeans were tragically divided, their opponents were often no more united and they proved unable to take full advantage of the fratricidal quarrels of the Europeans.

2—The relative advantage of the Europeans was on the seas. On land they remained for a long time highly vulnerable. As has been repeatedly pointed out in the previous chapters, the Europeans were unable to produce an effective, mobile field artillery until the fourth decade of the seventeenth century. Before that date, their land artillery could be moved only with great difficulty. Moreover, its rate of fire could be easily overcome by masses of people. This was a serious drawback, especially overseas where the Europeans were few, and their opponents were many.

Francisco de Almeida pointed out in the sixteenth century that sea power was the key to the situation. "Let it be known" —he wrote to his King—"that if you are strong in ships the commerce of the Indies is yours, and if you are not strong in ships little will avail you any fortress on land". This was also the advice of Albuquerque who wrote to the King that "if once Portugal should suffer a reverse at sea, your Indian possessions have not power to hold out a day longer than the Kings of the land choose to suffer it"[1]. Cornelis Nieuwenroode,

[1] For Almeida cf. Boxer, *Portuguese in the East*, p. 209 and Ballard, *Rulers*, pp. 68*ff*. For Albuquerque cf. his *Commentaries*, vol. 3, pp. 259-60. *Ibid.* pp. 115-16 see another statement attributed to Albuquerque: "my will and determination is, as long as I am governor of India, neither to fight nor to hazard men on land, except in those parts wherein I must build a fortress".

chief of the Dutch factory of Hirado, expressed similar feelings when he wrote in 1623 that the Dutch had " barely sufficient force to set ashore, unless under the protection of the ship's cannon " [1]. On the other hand, the Europeans were not the only ones to realize how precarious was their position ashore. The Asians knew it too. In 1614 viceroy Chang Ming-kang presented a memorial to the throne in which one reads the following passage: " Some people are of the opinion that the Portuguese should be removed to Lang-pai or should be permitted to trade with us only aboard their ships which should remain in the open sea. In my opinion we should not resort to the force of arms without duly weighing the consequences. As Macao is within the boundary of our land and forms a part of the district of Hsiang-shan our military forces can watch over the foreigners by just guarding the surrounding sea. We shall know how to put them at death's door as soon as they cherish any disloyal design. Now if we move them to the open sea, by what means could we punish the foreign evil-doers and how could we keep them in submission and defend ourselves against them? " [2].

Actual instances of the vulnerability of the European on land are easy to assemble. In the 1620's Abraham van Uffelen the governor of the Dutch factories in Coromandel acted very arrogantly toward the local ruler. When the King decided to strike, van Uffelen could not offer an effective

[1] Boxer, *Fidalgos*, p. 90.

[2] Quoted by Chang, *Trade*, p. 120. Centuries later, in 1841, Commissioner Lin reported that " if the barbarian vessels escape outside the Bocca Tigris, it is impossible for our light ships to chase and crush them ". In an edict dated 1842, the Chinese Emperor made the following statement: in " the invasion by the rebellious barbarians, they depended upon their strong ships and effective guns to commit outrageous acts on the seas and harm our people, largely because the native war junks are too small to match them. For this reason I, the Emperor, repeatedly ordered our generals to resist on land and not to fight on seas . . . When the enemy ships come, no resistance can be offered; when they go away no means of pursuit are available . . . In my opinion what the rebellious barbarians rely upon is the fact that Chinese war junks are incapable of going out to sea to fight them " (Chen, *Lin tse-hsü*, pp. 20 and 52).

resistance and met with a miserable fate in the prisons of Golconda[1]. In 1638 Goa would certainly have been lost to the Marathas had not the Great Moghul come to the rescue of the Portuguese[2]. When the Tokugawa Shoguns decided to close Japan to Western influence and decreed the expulsion of the Europeans from the country, the Europeans had no other choice than to comply with the order and leave the country as quickly as possible.

The particular situation by which the Europeans were vulnerable on land while they looked formidable and impregnable on their vessels, explains both the characteristics of European expansion and a curious paradox. The paradox is this: while Europe was boldly expanding overseas and was aggressively imposing her predominance over the coasts of Asia, Africa and the Americas, on her eastern border she was spiritlessly retreating under the pressure of the Turkish forces. Northern Serbia was invaded by the Turks in 1459. Bosnia-Herzegovina in 1463-6. In 1470 the Venetians lost Negroponte. After 1468 it was the turn of Albania. In 1526 the army of King Louis of Hungary was massacred at Mohacs. In 1529 Vienna was besieged. In 1531 Hungary was ravaged and Suleiman retreated only because of the threat from Persia. In 1566 European forces were again retreating in Hungary. In 1596 they were badly beaten at Keresztes. As late as 1606 Western diplomats in Constantinople were fearing further attacks from the Turks and were worrying about the fate of Vienna. In 1683 the Turks were again menacing Vienna.

3—Thanks to the revolutionary characteristics of their man-of-war, it took only a few decades for the Europeans to establish their absolute predominance over the Oceans. Because their advantage resided in their men-of-war, for almost three centuries their predominance was confined to the seas.

[1] Raychaudhuri, *Coromandel*, p. 30.
[2] Boxer, *Four Centuries*, p. 39.

No serious attempt was ever made to make an inroad into Asia and extend territorial conquest. The strategy conceived by the great Albuquerque[1] was strictly followed for more than two centuries after him and apart from a small group of vociferous hot-heads[2], Europeans generally felt that any attempt to extend their control over Asian hinterlands had no chance of success. In Africa (I mean " Africa Nigra ", south of the Sahara desert) the native populations were by far less numerous and technologically more primitive than in Asia, yet the position of the Europeans ashore was no less precarious[3]. Furthermore, geophysical conditions created

[1] Albuquerque understood from the beginning the impossibility of large territorial acquisitions. He also saw that he could gain control over the Indian Ocean by occupying a number of strategic points which should serve as bases for the navy and in their turn could be defended from the sea by the gunned vessels. During his governorship (1509-15), Goa, Malacca and Ormuz were occupied respectively in 1510, 1511 and 1515 and became the strongholds of the Portuguese predominance in Asia.

[2] Don Francesco Sande, Governor of the Philippines, offered to undertake the conquest of China with an army of about 5,000 men. The Chinese, he wrote to his King, " are so cowardly that no one rides on horseback " and on the other hand he thought he could obtain assistance from the Japanese and Filipinos " who are much braver than the Chinese are ". This foolish project received support from clerical and military groups in Manila but the Crown councillors in Madrid proved to be more sensible. In 1586 King Philip II wrote to his bellicose governor that " as regards the conquest of China which you think should be undertaken forthwith, it has seemed to us here that this matter should be dropped and that on the contrary good friendship should be sought with the Chinese " (cf. Boxer, *South China*, p. L and Schurz, *Manila Galleon*, p. 68). Among the Dutch, a remarkable hot-head was Coen who in 1618 wrote to the Directors of the Dutch company: " According to the Portuguese and the Spaniards a few Christians can do a great deal against hundreds of thousands of natives. Are we weaker than they? " (Hyma, *The Dutch*, p. 116). On the failure of Coen's " big-stick " policy cf. Boxer, *Fidalgos*, pp. 90-1.

[3] To hold their own against the local inhabitants the Portuguese courted the favour of rulers with customary presents, exploited inter-tribal jealousies, used other methods such as conversion to Christianity, inter-marriage, and treaties of friendship. Only in extreme cases did they resort to armed intervention. Cf. Dike, *Niger Delta*, pp. 6-7. Toward the end of the sixteenth century, when hordes of savages pressed from the interior of the continent and pushed on to the Indian Ocean, the Portuguese suffered severe losses

an insurmountable barrier to white penetration. The Europeans of the Renaissance had learned to master the energy of the wind and of gunpowder but they were still rather crude in the more general mastery of the adverse forces of nature. " It seems "—wrote a Portuguese chronicler in the sixteenth century—" that for our sins or for some inscrutable judgement of God, in all the entrances of this great Ethiopia that we navigate along, He has placed a striking angel with a flaming sword of deadly fevers who prevents us from penetrating into the interior to the springs of this garden, whence proceed these rivers of gold that flow to the sea in so many parts of our conquest "[1]. The few Europeans who ventured into the hinterland were rapidly killed or incapacitated by malaria, tropical fevers, disease and lethal climate. As late as 1876 only ten per cent of the African continent was under white occupation[2]. In the Americas things turned out to be exceptionally more favourable to European invasion. The geophysical conditions of most parts of the continent were not forbidding. The country was not very densely populated and the natives were technologically very primitive. Moreover they turned out to be highly susceptible to European infectious diseases and the spread of deadly epidemics further weakened their already meagre possibilities of resistance[3]. Last but not least, ruthless minorities such as the Aztecs in Mexico were cruelly

---

and could save a precarious toe-hold on the coast only because of the help they received from the Mohammedans of Malindi. Cf. Penrose, *Travel*, p. 172.

[1] Quoted by Boxer, *Four Centuries*, p. 27. In 1486 King John II of Portugal claimed to have created and maintained by force a West African empire and styled himself " Lord of Ethiopia ". But as has been noted (Dike, *Niger Delta*, p. 5) these claims " were largely pretensions designed to keep out interlopers and rivals. Portuguese rule, or whatever there was of it, was strictly limited to their fortified trading posts on the coast or on adjacent islands ". About Madagascar, Father Carré wrote to Colbert in 1674 that " the island was the ruin of men and ships that had been sent there from Europe " (Kaeppelin, *Compagnie*, p. 51).

[2] Townsend, *Colonial Expansion*, p. 54.

[3] Borah, *America*, pp. 184-5.

exploiting large masses of people who were bound to welcome and help any stranger as a liberator[1]. This exceptional combination of favourable circumstances made possible the conquest of vast American territories. The European success and performance however should not be exaggerated. Claims to territorial sovereignty should not be taken as equivalent to actual conquest and until the eighteenth century the areas that came under permanent and effective European control with few exceptions were close to the sea.

Maps show better than any verbal description that until the eighteenth century European possessions the world over consisted mostly of naval bases and coastal strongholds. It is not customary when drawing maps to paint the sea-areas with the colour of the predominant nations. Yet only such a practice would give a correct idea of the nature and extent of European dominance and the role of the Atlantic European nations as world powers during the first centuries of the modern age. Within a few years after the arrival of the first European vessels in the Indian Ocean it became mandatory for non-European vessels to secure sailing permits if they did not want to be blown up by European guns[2]. The oceans belonged to Europe.


4—The eighteenth century marked the beginning of a new phase. As indicated in chapter I, European gun-founders succeeded in producing effective field artillery just before the

[1] Simpson, *Encomienda*, pp. vii-viii; and Simpson, *Many Mexicos*, pp. 22-3; Penrose, *Travel*, p. 126.

[2] The custom was first introduced by the Portuguese who were determined to break the Moslem monopoly over the spice trade in the Indian Ocean. In the course of time sea-passes were sold and were a source of income for Western companies or governments. The custom had been accepted by Indian merchants and potentates with little protest not because they liked it but because verbal protests were futile. The wars among European nations rendered the system particularly irksome for the Indians because passes had to be secured from each of the belligerent nations. Cf. Raychaudhuri, *Coromandel*, p. 126. Cf. also Tosi, *India*, vol. I, p. 93.

middle of the seventeenth century. At the beginning the "innovation" was largely applied at home where the Europeans enthusiastically used it to butcher each other on their numerous battle-fields. Even so, it further enlarged the military technological gap between Europe and the rest of the world and the balance of world power became more unbalanced than ever. As with naval artillery and sailing ships, the Europeans rapidly improved upon their new discovery before the non-Europeans were able to absorb it. The disequilibrium grew, therefore, progressively larger and it was no longer limited to sea power.

Atlantic Europe had initiated maritime expansion. Oriental Europe opened the phase of territorial expansion. First the Turkish menace was brought under control in the course of the eighteenth century. Then Russia took the initiative of the counter-attack which she successfully launched in two directions: to the East against the Hordes of the Kazaks and to the South against the Turks. The iron foundries established by the Dutch in the seventeenth century and developed by Peter the Great in the first half of the eighteenth century went some way to break the blockade of Europe on her Eastern border [1]. As G. F. Hudson puts it " the collapse of the power of the nomads with so slight a resistance, after they had again and again turned the course of history with their military powers, is to be attributed not to any degeneracy of the nomads themselves but to the evolution of the art of war

[1] At Tula on the nucleus that had been established by the Dutch in the seventeenth century (see above chapt. 1), Peter the Great built in 1712 large ironworks which in the course of time were to form the main supply of weapons for the Russian army (Amburger, *Marselis*, p. 174). In 1816, 3,562 males were ascribed to these factories (Mavor, *Russia*, vol. 1, pp. 434-5). At the middle of the nineteenth century, Scrivenor (*Iron Trade*, p. 168) wrote that " in the empire (of Russia) are four (manufacturers of fire-arms), all belonging to the Crown. The oldest and the greatest is at Tula and employs upward of 4,000 workmen ". The Russian manufacturers were not able, however, to satisfy fully the demand for cannon and Russia had to import large number of guns from Western Europe throughout the seventeenth and eighteenth centuries.

beyond their capacity of adaptation. The Tartars in the seventeenth and eighteenth centuries had lost none of the qualities which had made so terrible the armies of Attila and Baian, of Jenghiz Khan and Tamerlane. But the increasing use in war of artillery and musketry was fatal to a power which depended on cavalry and had not the economic resources for the new equipment "[1]. As to the Turks, this is the testimonial by Baron de Tott who witnessed the events as a military expert: " The Turks were slaughtered in every action by the cannon of the Russians and could only avenge themselves for their disasters by accusing the Russians of cowardly artifice. They overpower us, said they, by the superiority of their fire which, in fact, it is impossible to approach; but let them leave their abominable batteries and encounter us like brave men, hand to hand, and we shall soon see whether these infidels can resist the slaughtering sabre of the True-Believers . . . The Grand Seigneur having been informed that the howitzers had very much annoyed his cavalry, enquired of me what kind of artillery they were, for they were unknown at Constantinople . . . The destruction or at least the entire dispersion of the Turkish army by the action at Craool, had already induced His Highness to imagine that the quick fire of the Russian artillery was the principal cause of the discouragement of his troops "[2].

Overseas the impact of the new European technological developments was not felt until the end of the eighteenth century because of the difficulty of supplying a large army over long distances from the home base. As late as 1689 the forces of the East India Company were completely routed on land in India. In 1700 the Directors of the Company regarded the idea of conquering territories or planting colonies in the country as " altogether impracticable in respect of a long voyage, the diseases to which our people are liable in those hot regions and the power, force, and policy of most Indian

[1] Hudson, *Europe*, p. 268.
[2] De Tott, *Memoirs*, vol. 2, part 3, pp. 10 and 79.

nations " [1]. The conquest of the country in the second half of the eighteenth century was possible only because of the state of anarchy into which India was plunged after the death of Aurangzeb in 1707 and the defeat of the Marathas at the hands of the Afghans [2].

The Europeans' effective conquest or control of vast hinterlands came later as one of the by-products of the Industrial Revolution.

European maritime expansion was one of the circumstances that paved the way for the Industrial Revolution. To deny it on the basis that there were no West Indies merchants or East-India adventurers among the " entrepreneurs " who built factories in Europe is as sensible as to deny any relation between the Scientific Revolution and the Industrial Revolution on the basis that neither Galileo nor Newton set up a textile mill in Manchester. Inter-relationships in human history do not always work so openly and crudely.

On the other hand, there is no doubt that the Industrial Revolution in its turn added great impetus to European expansion. It multiplied the number of the Europeans both in absolute terms as well as in relation to the size of non-European population. It provided the Europeans with more powerful weapons and with efficient techniques to master the adverse forces of nature. And it gave Industrial Europe the opportunity to subjugate non-industrial economies through the policy of " free trade " and the subtle mechanism of " dual economies ". As Adam Smith saw it " in ancient times the opulent and civilized found it difficult to defend themselves against the poor and barbarous nations; in modern times the poor and barbarous find it difficult to defend themselves against the opulent and civilized ".

[1] Quoted by Thomas, *Mercantilism*, p. 10. On the campaigns of 1685 and 1689 cf. Wilson, *Early Annals*, vol. 1, pp. 102 *ff.*

[2] Gupta, *Sirajudaullah*, p. 20.

5—In the passage by Adam Smith just quoted, readers may perceive traces of a disturbing confusion between " civilized " and " technologically advanced ", a confusion that, at least in the form in which we are familiar with it, is one of the by-products of the Industrial Revolution. Queen Victoria's gunboats defeated Lin's noble efforts to put to an end the opium trade but this does not imply that the admirals of Queen Victoria were more " civilized " than Commissioner Lin. If the historical analysis of this book is correct, the technologically more advanced people are bound to prevail regardless of their degree of " civilization " which is something more difficult to define and assess.

The " Vasco da Gama's era " has now come to an abrupt end. In its uprising against Western predominance, the " underdeveloped " world seems to emphasize exclusively the importance of the acquisition of Western technology. Since Western predominance has rested on superior technology, the attitude is understandable, but it has tragic implications.

In order to acquire Western techniques, the non-European people had or have to undergo a more profound and general process of " westernization ". Paradoxically enough, in order to fight against the West they have to absorb Western ways of thinking and doing. As M. Chiang wrote, " since we were knocked out by cannon balls, naturally we became interested in them, thinking that by learning to make them we could strike back. We could forget for the time being in whose name they had come, since for us common mortals to save our lives was more important than to save our souls. But history seems to move through very curious ways. From studying cannon balls we came to mechanical inventions, which in turn led us to political reforms; from political reforms we began to see political theories, which led us again to the philosophies of the West. On the other hand, through mechanical invention we saw science, from which we came to understand scientific method and the scientific mind. Step by step we were led farther and farther away from the cannon ball—yet we came nearer and nearer to it "[1]. In this process, the goal is the technique while philosophy and social and human relations are degraded to the role of means. The machine which should serve man, becomes his master. The " Vasco da Gama's era " ends in a nightmare in which men—Westerners and non-Westerners alike—are bewildered by this confusion and the old fancy of the *apprenti sorcier* becomes tragically actual.

[1] Chiang, *Tides*, p. 4.

APPENDICES

ACKNOWLEDGEMENTS

BIBLIOGRAPHY

INDEX

# APPENDIX I

The first eleven paragraphs of chapter 1 are intended to offer a very cursory view of European armament production from the four-teenth century to the end of the seventeenth. Much detail has been sacrificed for the sake of compactness and clarity. Other material has been sacrificed because not directly pertinent to the main theses of the book. Many problems have not been fully clarified because of lack of information. I indicate here briefly some of the points that could have received better illustration or that are still in need of further research.

The story of the system used for boring cannon has been told so many times (and has been illustrated by so many plates) in the current histories of Western technology that I did not think it advisable to retell it once more. The same may be said about the history of gun carriages and the systems for sighting guns.

Strictly connected with the production of ordnance was the production of cannon balls. Innumerable types of gun shot had been devised in the course of time, offering a tragic example of the possible aberrations of human ingenuity: there were stone balls, cast-iron balls, case shots, grape shots, bar shots, double-headed bar shots, link shots, chain shots, hot shots, iron shells " filled with fireworks or wild fire ", etc. etc. The technological history of these deadly objects has been extensively told, but we know very little about the economic aspects of their production.

Similarly we know the history of gunpowder production mainly from a technological point of view. Much has been written in regard to the great change that occurred in the sixteenth century when " corned powder " took the place of the unreliable " ser-pentine powder ", but much less has been written on the economic aspects of the subject. Prof. Nef (*Industry*, pp. 59-68 and 88-98) has explored the field for sixteenth- and seventeenth-centuries England and France, but his pioneering effort has not been properly followed. We know nothing about the manufactures in Holland and the Southern Low Countries which were among the main European centres of production. And in general we know nothing about the prices of gunpowder, costs of production, size and structure of the firms, marketing of the product, etc. The same can be said for portable fire-arms. I have not devoted special attention to this type of weapon although I am perfectly aware that they played an important role in more than one episode of European expansion. They were very important in the conquest of the Philippines. They were more important than ordnance in the Spanish conquest of America. They were largely used also in naval battles well into the nineteenth century. Much too much has been written on portable fire-arms from the point of view of military, technological and art history, but very little has been written on their economic history.

Thanks to a recent work by Prof. A. R. Hall we have some information about the relations between the science of ballistics and the so-called Scientific Revolution in the seventeenth century. But we are in complete darkness about the " human aspects " of the new developments. The " art of gunnery " produced a new type of warrior, the cold-blooded, technically inclined man who in the middle of the fight had to carry out a series of measurements and calculations, no matter how rough and imprecise. This new type of fighter vividly contrasted with the hot-blooded warrior of the old days who daringly threw himself into the *mêlée* with feathers, flags and sword, screaming and shouting and perspiring as much as humanly possible.

The use of guns appealed to the appetite for the practical and the technical that characterized Renaissance Europe. As has been written " By the beginning of the sixteenth century the gun had acquired a rich store of symbolic and associative overtones and was already rivalling the sword as the embracing symbol of war " (Hale, *War*, p. 21). There were however many conservative souls who considered fire-arms a most despicable innovation. Gian Paolo Vitelli was in the habit of blinding and cutting the hands of arquebusiers, whilst Bayard shot them when captured. Cervantes wrote that " the devilish invention of artillery " enabled " a base cowardly hand to take the life of the bravest ". The history of the debate about the rights and wrongs of the use of fire-arms throws interesting light on many aspects of the history of ideas. Some work has been done on the subject and one can consult the bibliography quoted by Fuller, *Armament*, pp. 77, 86 and by Hale, *War*, pp. 23*ff*.

Many of the problems that I touched on in chapter I need further research, especially on a local basis. Much can be learned by a detailed study of the individual factories. For Sweden we possess excellent plans of the gun factories at Finspong and Julita for the seventeenth century. The plan of Julita is reproduced here facing p. 49. The plan of Finspong can be found in Bergsten, *Bergslag*, p. 170. One should add to them the description of the gun foundry at Tula in Russia around the middle of the seventeenth century (Amburger, *Marselis*, p. 119).

When estimating employment at the gun factories, one has to distinguish between skilled workers, directly employed in the production of guns and the supplementary unskilled labour employed for the production and transportation of charcoal. The first group was always very limited in size while the second group was incomparably larger. At Åkerstyckebruk in 1629 there were 15 " Walloons " (skilled labour) in addition probably to some other skilled workmen (Hahr, *Åkers*, p. 8). In 1676 the working force, excluding charcoal burners and peasants hired for transportation, seems to have amounted to 28 men (Jansson, *Bergsbruken*, p. 71). In 1695 there were at Finspong 6 hammersmiths, 14 blast-furnace workers, and 17 other workers in addition to 21 miners and an unspecified number of charcoal burners and labour employed in transportation. In 1751 at Finspong there were 16 people for administration, 10 smiths, 22 casters, 35 helpers and 12 undefined. In addition there were 474 charcoal burners, 92 men employed in transportation and 26 maids (Bergsten, *Bergslag*, pp. 210 and 212). In the light of this evidence one is inclined to believe that the figure of 200 men allegedly employed at the factory of Mr. Browne at Brenchley (Kent) early in the seventeenth century (*Calendar State Papers*, Domestic, 1619-23, vol. 105, *n*.92, Feb. 11, 1619) must have included charcoal burners.

As to the volume of production of the single foundries, we know that when Levett began the production of cast-iron cannon in England, he could produce at his foundry in Ashdown Forest about 120 iron guns in nearly two years (see above chapter I). This was in 1545. From 1604 to 1609 Thomas Browne " made and sold " at his Brenchley furnace an average of about 175 tons per year

(Schubert, *Extension*, p. 246). In 1621 his son John Browne claimed that at the same foundry he could cast 200 iron guns in 200 days (*Calendar State Papers*, Domestic, Addenda, 1580-1625, vol. 42, no. 66). In all likelihood 200 was the number of days of effective work of a furnace in a year. At Julita over the period 1632-35 the production of iron guns was as follows (Lund Univ. Library, *De la Gardieska Samlingen, Topográphica, Julita* "Rachnung oppa dhe Järnstijcken . . ."):

|      | No. of guns | overall weight in metric tons |
|------|-------------|-------------------------------|
| 1632 | 64          | 45                            |
| 1633 | 140         | 105                           |
| 1634 | 143         | 112                           |
| 1635 | 219         | 162                           |

In Nävekvarn, Bränn-Ekeby and Fada over the period 1637-46 the production of iron guns amounted to 5,893 pieces for a grand total of about 4,700 metric tons. This would give a yearly average for each factory of 196 guns or about 155 tons. (*Svenskt Biografiskt Lexicon, ad vocem* H. De Besche). At Stavsjö the production of iron guns toward the end of the seventeenth century was as follows (Jakobsson, *Artilleriet*, p. 31n.):

|      |                  |
|------|------------------|
| 1671 | 160 metric tons  |
| 1693 | 119              |
| 1694 | 288              |
| 1695 | 424              |
| 1696 | 352              |

At Finspong, according to fiscal evaluation, 1,020 metric tons of bar iron and 3,264 tons of iron cannon were produced over the period 1642 to 1648 (Dahlgren, *De Geer*, vol. 2, p. 366). Also at Finspong, 223 guns were produced in 1689 and 261 in 1690 (Bergsten, *Bergslag*, p. 176). These figures seem to indicate that the productive capacity of single plants underwent a remarkable growth in the course of the sixteenth and seventeenth century.

In regard to the production of bronze ordnance, the following figures relate to the output of the Stockholm royal foundry (Jakobsson, *Beväpning*, pp. 213-14):

| | | | | |
|---|---|---|---|---|
| 1617 | 15 metric tons | 1625 | 79 metric tons |
| 1618 | 1 | 1626 | 6 |
| 1620 | 7 | 1627 | ? |
| 1621 | 15 | 1628 | 71 |
| 1622 | 24 | 1629 | ? |
| 1623 | 26 | 1630 | 22 |
| 1624 | 78 | 1631 | 23 |

In France, one of the main foundries for the production of bronze cannon was at Douai. Around 1670 the output of the foundry averaged 144 guns of small calibre or 96 " *canons de batterie* " per year (Basset, *Historique*, p. 1038). In seventeenth-century Spain, the most important centre for the production of bronze ordnance was Seville. According to an official report dated 1679 Seville's foundry could hardly produce more than 36 guns of medium calibre per year (Carrasco, *Artilleria de bronce*, pp. 53-4).

Detailed research is needed on the relative prices of copper, iron, tin and charcoal in the various parts of Europe. When dealing with such data, researchers ought to be very careful in specifying the quality of the raw materials involved, because there were noticeable price differentials. When Professor Mankov (*Prix*, p. 97) tells us that in Russia the ratio of copper to iron was 1 to 11 around 1600, one would like to know what kind of copper and what kind of iron he is considering. In Cremona (Northern Italy) in 1580 iron was sold at the following prices:

| | | | | | |
|---|---|---|---|---|---|
| *ferro rotto* | lire | 1. | 4. | 5 | the *peso* |
| *ferro ladino* | | 3. | 13. | 0 | |
| *ferro lavorato* | | 4. | 16. | 4 | |
| *filo di ferro* | | 8. | 14. | 2 | |

Still in Northern Italy (Como) at the same date, copper was sold at the following prices:

| | | | | |
|---|---|---|---|---|
| *rame di Rosetta* | 12. | 0. | 0 | the *rubbo* |
| *rame cavato* | 13. | 11. | 8 | |
| *rame lavorato* | 15. | 19. | 4 | |
| *filo di rame* | 19. | 17. | 6 | |
| *rame filato* | 25. | 0. | 0 | |

In Sweden the ratio between " raw copper " and " osmund iron " was 1:9 around 1580 and 1:10 around 1600. The ratio between " raw copper " and " bar iron " was instead 1:5 both around 1580 and around 1600 (Heckscher, *Historia*, diagram 6). An excellent series of prices of Swedish raw copper and bar iron in Amsterdam has been published by Professor Posthumus (*Prijsgeschiedenis*, vol. 1, tables 168 and 173) for the period 1624-94. On the basis of Posthumus' data I have calculated the ratio between the prices of raw copper and bar iron in Amsterdam (cf. the following table). As one can easily notice the ratio shows remarkable fluctuations. From other data that I have collected it would seem that the ratio of copper to iron was noticeably lower in Italy and Southern Germany than in Sweden, Holland or England and this could explain why the Italians were so slow and reluctant to shift from bronze to iron ordnance.

Prices of guns are easy to collect, but no systematic research has ever been done in this regard. It seems that they grew rapidly in the course of the so-called " price revolution ". In 1546-8 ordnance from Sussex was sold at £10 per ton (Schubert, *Iron Industry* p. 253). At the end of the century the custom officials still evaluated guns on the base of £10 the ton for the assessment of the " customs and subsidies " (*Calendar of State Papers*, vol. 26, no. 52) but the market price was much higher. In the 1630's cast-iron guns were valued at about £35 or £40 per ton (*Calendar of State Papers*, vol. 230, no. 36 and vol. 340, no. 48). Prices of guns varied of course according to weight and calibre, as well as the place of origin and the name of their manufacturers. In 1671 the son of Colbert reported to his father that the prices of cast iron guns on the Dutch market " *sont différens suivant la bonté des canons et les marques de fonderies. Le meilleur vaut presentement g livres le cent . . . Les canons de 48 livres de balle et ceux de 12, 18, etc. valent 8 livres le cent* " (Clément, *Lettres, vol.* 3, part 2, p. 311). In his *Addition au memoire concernant la fonderie de canons* (Bibl. Nat. Paris, Dept, mscr. Colbert 4219, *ff.* 11-12) he added more specifically that " *le canon de Suède est marqué a plusieurs marques dont il y en a de bons et de mauvaises, les meilleurs marques sont* F, G, *et* H. *Ceux qui sont marquez de cette manière coustent beaucoup plus que les autres* ". Little or nothing is presently known about the cost of transportation of ordnance, the marketing of it, etc.

## UNITS OF BAR IRON NEEDED TO BUY ONE
## UNIT OF SWEDISH RAW COPPER IN AMSTERDAM

| | | | |
|---|---|---|---|
| 1624 | 10·41 | 1655 | 8·21 |
| 1625 | 11·22 | 1656 | 8·10 |
| 1626 | 8·74 | 1657 | 8·86 |
| 1628 | 7·75 | 1658 | 9·50 |
| 1630 | 7·09 | 1660 | 10·36 |
| 1631 | 6·15 | 1663 | 8·67 |
| 1632 | 8·69 | 1664 | 9·03 |
| 1633 | 9·12 | 1665 | 9·42 |
| 1634 | 9·28 | 1666 | 9·38 |
| 1635 | 6·62 | 1667 | 8·78 |
| 1638 | 6·36 | 1668 | 9·08 |
| 1639 | 6·53 | 1669 | 10·23 |
| 1640 | 5·87 | 1671 | 10.53 |
| 1641 | 6·40 | 1672 | 9·80 |
| 1642 | 6·80 | 1673 | 8·42 |
| 1643 | 7·49 | 1674 | 9·05 |
| 1645 | 8·33 | 1677 | 9·08 |
| 1646 | 9·27 | 1679 | 9·72 |
| 1648 | 8·17 | 1682 | 9·45 |
| 1649 | 8·22 | 1683 | 11·46 |
| 1650 | 7·61 | 1686 | 9·17 |
| 1651 | 6·33 | 1688 | 8·70 |
| 1652 | 5·92 | 1691 | 9·58 |
| 1653 | 5·36 | 1692 | 9·83 |
| 1654 | 7·12 | 1694 | 9·83 |

Another study that promises interesting results is that of the role of state intervention in the production of ordnance and ammunition (cf. Nef, *Industry*, p. 135*ff*.).

In regard to entrepreneurial history, the seventeenth century offers abundant and interesting material for research. The life and activities of the fabulous Louis de Geer (1587-1652) have been satisfactorily illustrated in the works by Dahlgren and Breedvelt (see bibliography. The short article by Carr, *Swedish Financiers* is based on Dahlgren's volumes and deals almost exclusively with the financial aspects of de Geer's activity). Another interesting " entrepreneur ", although more of a technician than businessman was W. G. de Beche (1573-1629) also from Liége. De Beche, having emigrated to Sweden in 1595 and having become the supervisor of the royal foundries, gave the first great impulse to the Swedish cannon industry, induced de Geer to extend his operations to Sweden (1615) and became his faithful partner (from 1619). Some information on the life and the activities of this enterprising " Walloon " can be found in the works by Dahlgren and Breedvelt on de Geer. They should be integrated with the *Svenskt Biografiskt Lexicon* (v. de Beche) and Hahr, *Åkers*, pp. 6-7. Yernaux, *Métallurgie* is good for the " liègeois " background of both de Geer and de Beche but it is often imprecise about their activities in Sweden.

The financial, commercial and industrial activities of the Marselis family especially in regard to the establishment of the Russian iron foundries has been amply studied by Amburger (see bibliography). Not enough is known on the activities of the members of the Trip family, especially of the two brothers Elias (1570-1636) and Jacob (1575-1663). They were prominent merchants in Amsterdam and Dordrecht and dealt largely in cannon, copper and iron. Elias imported cast-iron cannon from England (see above, footnote [1]., p. 49) and from Russia where he was for a while partner in a Dutch company for the production of ordnance (see above, footnote [4]., p. 59). In the three years period 1656-8 he imported from Sweden into Holland no less than 2,031 iron guns for a total of approximately 2,350 metric tons (Heijkenskjöld, *Styckegjutning*, pp. 75-6). In the 1640's Peter Trip in association with Gabriel Marselis, Lawrence de Geer and others sold guns and ammunition to Portuguese envoys (see above, footnote [3]., p. 32). Later in the same decade, Hendrick Trip, son of Jacob, and his brother rented the cannon factory at Julita in Sweden. Some information on the history of the Trip family can be gathered from the works by Dahlgren (*de Geer*), Barbour (*Amsterdam*, pp. 37n. and 39) and Trip.

It may be worth mentioning that as an essential part of their *technique des affaires* these cannon merchants practised a *politique des marriages*. De Beche's son Charles married Ida de Geer, daughter of Louis. Elias Trip married Maria de Geer. Jacob Trip married Margareta de Geer. A son of Elias, Adrian, married Adriana de Geer and a son of Jacob, Hendrick, married Jean de Geer. But business being business, family ties did not, on occasion, prevent one group from fighting ruthlessly against the other.

The Brownes of England, Thomas and his son John, the Mariottes and the von Triers of western Germany were also great cannon merchants but their activities have not been satisfactorily studied. On the Brownes one may consult the short note by Schubert, *Extension*. As to the Mariottes one may consult Yernaux, *Métallurgie*.

Special mention in the list of the cannon merchants of the seventeenth century is deserved by Manuel Tavares Bocarro, the man who set on foot the renowned gun foundry at Macao and whose guns sold largely all over Asia. (Cf. the bibliography quoted in Boxer, *Macau*, pp. 212-13; in addition see Viterbo, *Fundidores de artilharia*, p. 28; Amaro, *Fundições e Fundidores Artilheiros;* Teixeira, *Os Bocarros*. See also the important document in Arquivo Historico Ultramarino, Lisbon, Livro 79, pp. 1-5).

# APPENDIX II

Father Vincenzo Maria di Santa Caterina da Siena was an Italian missionary of the order of the Carmelitani Scalzi who went to India in 1655. The report of his voyage contains many an interesting observation on Eastern countries, customs and peoples. In Chapter eleven Father Vincenzo Maria gives accurate information on the Turkish navy and emphasizes two of the points I discussed above in this book, (a) that the Turks made good use of artillery only in siege operations, and (b) that in naval warfare they essentially relied on the tactic of ramming and boarding [1]. This is the translation of Chapter eleven: *On The Naval Forces and Artillery of the Turk*, " The naval forces of this Empire are in my belief greatly unequal to the land forces, not for any want of manpower, lumber, or any other thing needful for the formation of such powerful fleets as it may desire, but rather for the lack of talent, ability and inclination for such pursuits among the natives. The abundance of lumber, which they possess on the shores of the Black Sea, in Greece, and in Asia, makes it possible to assemble galliots, men-of-war and every other sort of sea-going vessel with such ease that one surely could not wish it greater. The forests are exceedingly vast, and close to the water, being thus more convenient. Adjacent to these are certain large villages exempt from the usual obligations and bound instead to prepare the material or to transport the same to the place where need requires it; so that one need but command, and in a few days as much wood as is wanted will be found in the appointed places, arranged and prepared for any undertaking, however grand. There are many places on the Black Sea where they build galleys and men-of-war continually. In addition, the Empire possesses three great shipyards, the first in Constantinople, another in

[1] Vincenzo Maria di Santa Caterina. *Il Viaggio all' India Orientale* pp. 41-3. For Turkish sources of information on the Ottoman naval forces and shipbuilding cf. Piri Re'is, *Bahrije*, pp. xxxiv-xlii.

Gallipoli, a third in Suez, the first having 144 covered vaults and the others fewer, in each of which, excepting the last, the Sultan maintains more than a thousand salaried carpenters, augmenting their number according to the occasion; and these men apply themselves to nothing else but the construction of ships of every kind for his service.

The iron which they require comes from Samacho, a place in Greece not far from Salonica, where it is extracted from the mines. The ropes are made in Constantinople. The cost of labour is minimal (I heard of this from very well-informed persons): for the outfitting of a galley a chief craftsman will get no more than 14 to 15 *sequins* it being within the power of the officers to demand that the work be done at whatever price they wish to pay. From all the preceding one can understand why it is that whenever the Turk's armada has gone down in ruins, it very soon appears restored, for neither expense nor inaccessibility of materials, nor lack of workmen hinders him. A fact of great importance, however, is this: all the ships are badly made, and last but a very short while; in three of four years they are old and no longer seaworthy because the wood is always cut in the wrong season, i.e. in the early summer, when the moisture is diffused throughout the trunk, so that it tends to decay and be eaten by worms. Moreover, they put the wood to use straightaway after cutting it, while it is still drying, and thus the hulls of the ships expand so much that sometimes before ever being launched they lie on the shore full of gaps and cracks and totally useless. And it must be added that the workmen, being paid so poorly by the Sultan, spare on the iron, whence the ships turn out so badly made, and so unseaworthy, that they are often lost before ever reaching Constantinople.

The Sultan mans his galleys with four men to the oar; first with his own slaves, who in winter are kept in custody in camps constructed for this purpose; secondarily with convicts; and lastly, with men brought from Asia, which region provides him with as great a quantity of them as he wants for this purpose, for he has imposed this duty on a great many villages, and indeed might appoint many more yet; and for every ten persons in these villages, one is chosen, who must report for service without question, or else redeem himself by sending another at his own expense. The Sultan pays to each slave, and to each of these men from Asia, 25 *sultanins*, with which they must make do until such time as they return to port, nothing further being given them save only victuals; this payment is called the *Avarische* and is raised through a tax on those lands from which children are not taken as a tribute. For the outfitting of 200 galleys, three *sultanins* are collected from each hearth, the hearth being composed of four houses. However, these Asiatics are so ill suited to the sea, that many succumb to nausea, and others perish from hardship, so that very often the armada is afflicted with sickness; and were it not for the aid of the slaves who are accustomed to the sea, it would surely be very weak and almost useless. In order to provide the fleet with sailors and soldiers, the Sultan keeps in his pay many thousands of men, whose job it is to perform whatever service is imposed on them by the Captain of the Navy; and though these people are no less spirited than bold, they are nonetheless wanting in experience, and not well suited to action on the water; whence it is, that if the Captain happens upon some vexing storm, it becomes difficult to control them, and make them do what is necessary; indeed, they are in dire peril of their lives.

Each galley carries 70 soldiers or more, up to 100, provisions being furnished by the Islands of Lesbos (*Meteline*), Euboea (*Negroponte*), and others nearby; 3,000 feud-holders (*Timari*) are bound to this service, in addition to the great number of Janissaries who volunteer to the service . . . .

. . . The Turks make little use of artillery, and indeed seem not to care for it, nor value its use except for siege operations. In naval battles they rely heavily on the sail and on boarding, so that in an encounter they seek to ram the enemy as quickly as possible, hoping to exploit their advantage in numbers; the very few guns which they do use on their ships are loaded with stone shot more often than with iron, for they believe that stone, in splintering, hits more surely and does more harm. They store the naval artillery in the *Pera*, where it is also manufactured, and the land artillery in Constantinople; both are under the command of the Captain General. The copper for its manufacture is taken from the mines which they possess in Alexandria, from whence comes also such a quantity of powder as is sufficient to their need. But a great advantage on the side of the Christians, it seems to me, is in having more guns, and greater skill in handling them . . . ."

# ACKNOWLEDGEMENTS

The author wishes to acknowledge his debt to the following for the use of illustrations:

Gun of the de Millimete manuscript: The Governing Body of Christ Church, Oxford.

Florentine manuscript: Archivio di Stato di Firenze.

Mons Meg: The Ministry of Public Building and Works (Crown Copyright).

Dardanelles guns: The Master of the Armouries (British Crown Copyright).

Mogul gun (taf. 9 from Pulverwaffe in Indien by B. Rathgen, from *Ostasiatische Zeitschrift* 12, 1925): Deutschen Morgenländischen Gesellshaft.

Tudor guns: The Royal Artillery Museum at the Woolwich Rotunda.

Foundries at Julita: Rijksmuseum, Amsterdam.

Vasa: The Maritime Museum, the Wasa Dockyard, Stockholm.

Cannon-merchants: AB Svenska Metallverken.

Swedish field-piece: Armémuseum, Stockholm.

Atlantic view of naval warfare: *Svenska Flottans Historia*.

Chinese bronze gun and war-junk: East Asian Library, University of California, Berkeley.

Elizabethan warship: The Trustees of the National Maritime Museum, Greenwich.

A Chinese Dream: Dr. F. Dahl, who kindly brought to my attention this painting at the University Library of Lund, Sweden.

The Chinese guns at T'ai-yüan (plate 10 from The Beginning of Civilization in Eastern Asia by C. W. Bishop in the 1940 Smithsonian *Annual Report*) is reproduced by courtesy of The Smithsonian Institution, and the detail from The Embarkation of Henry VIII for the Field of the Cloth of Gold by gracious permission of Her Majesty the Queen.

# BIBLIOGRAPHY

This is not intended to be a complete bibliography. Only the publications quoted in this work have been listed here. The name of Chinese, Korean, and Japanese authors have been transliterated.

ALBERI, E., (ed), *Relazioni degli Ambasciatori Veneti al Senato.* Firenze, 1840.

ALBION, R. G., *Forests and Sea Power.* Cambridge (Mass.), 1926.

AL-QALQASHANDI AHMED IBN ALI, *Subh al-a'shā.* Cairo, 1913-19.

ALBUQUERQUE, A., *The Commentaries* (ed. by W. de Gray Birch). London, 1875-85.

AMARO, F. DA SILVA, Fundições e Fundidores Artilheiros Portugueses na Asia e na Africa, in *Boletim Eclesiástico de Diocese de Macau,* pp. 680-3 (1960-1).

AMBURGER, E., *Die Familie Marselis. Studien zur russischen Wirtschaftsgeschichte* (Giessener Abhandlungen zur Agrar—und Wirtschaftsforschung des Europäischen Ostens, vol. 4). Giessen, 1957.

AMIOT, J. M., *Art militaire des Chinois* (ed. by J. De Guignes), Paris 1772 (republished in vol. 7 of the *Mémoires concernant l'histoire, les sciences, les arts, les moeurs, les usages, etc. des Chinois.* Paris, 1776-91).

AMIOT, J. M., Supplement à l'Art militaire des Chinois, in *Mémoires concernant l'histoire, les sciences, les arts, les moeurs, les usages, etc. des Chinois.* Paris, 1776-91, vol. 8.

ANDERSON R. & R. C., *The Sailing Ship.* New York, 1947.

ANGELUCCI, A., *Documenti inediti per la storia delle armi da fuoco italiane.* Torino, 1869.

ANHEGGER, R., *Beiträge zur Geschichte des Bergbaus im Osmanischen Reich.* Istanbul, 1943-5.

ARISAKA, SHO ZU, *Heikkiko,* Tokyo, Showa 21 (A.D. 1936)

ATKINSON, G., *Les nouveaux horizons de la Renaissance Française.* Paris, 1935.

AUDEMARD, L., *Les jonques chinoises*, ed. by C. Nooteboom. Rotterdam, 1957.

AYALON, D., *Gunpowder and Firearms in the Mamluk Kingdom*. London, 1956.

BAASCH, E., *Holländische Wirtschaftsgeschichte*. Jena, 1927.

BAASCH, E., Der Verkehr mit Kriegsmaterialen aus und nach den Hansestädten, in *Jahrbücher für Nationalökonomie und Statistik* 137 (1932), pp. 538-43.

BAKLANOV, N. B., MAVRODINI, V. V. and SMIRNOV, I. I., *Tul'skie i Kashirskie zavody v XVII v.*, Moscow-Leningrad, 1934.

BALLARD, G. A., *The Influence of the Sea on the Political History of Japan*. London, 1921.

BALLARD, G. A., *Rulers of the Indian Ocean*. London, 1927.

BANG, N. (ed.) *Tabeller over Skibsfart og Varetransport gennem Øresund*. Copenhagen-Leipzig, 1906-53.

BARBOSA, A., *Novos subsidios para a história da ciencia nautica portuguesa da epoca dos descubrimientos*. Oporto, 1948.

BARBOUR, V., *Capitalism in Amsterdam in the Seventeenth Century*. Baltimore, 1950.

BARROW, J., *Travels in China*. London, 1804.

BASSET, M. A., Essais sur l'historique des fabrications d'armement en France jusq'au milieu du XVIII siècle, *Mémorial de l'artillerie française*, 14 (1935), pp. 881-1280.

BEER, G. L., *The Origins of the British Colonial System 1578-1660*. Gloucester (Mass.), 1959.

BECK, L., *Die Geschichte des Eisens*. Braunschweig, 1891-5.

BERGSTEN, K. E., *Östergötlands Bergslag*. Lund, 1946.

BERGSTEN, K. E., *A Methodical Study of an Ancient Hinterland: The Iron Factory of Finspong, Sweden*. (Lund Studies in Geography, ser. B. Hunnan Geography monogr., no. 1) Lund, 1949.

BEVERIDGE, W., *Prices and Wages in England from the Twelfth to the Nineteenth Century*. London-New York-Toronto, 1939.

BISHOP, C. W., The Beginnings of Civilization in Eastern Asia, in *Annual Report of the Board of Regents of the Smithsonian Institution*, 1940, pp. 431-46.

BLAIR, F. H. & J. A. ROBERSTON (ed.), *Philippine Islands*. Cleveland (Ohio), 1963.

BLOK, P. J., *Geschiedenis van het Nederlandsche volk*. Leiden, 1913.

[165]

BOËTHIUS, B. & E. F. HECKSCHER, *Svensk Handelsstatistik 1637 1737*. Stockholm, 1938.

BOËTHIUS, B., Swedish Iron and Steel, in *The Scandinavian Economic History Review*, 6 (1958), pp. 144-75.

BOGOIAVLENSKII, M. M., *Vooruzhenie russkikh voisk v XVI-XVII*, Moscow, 1938.

BOISSONADE, P. & P. CHARLIAT, *Colbert et la Compagnie de Commerce du Nord*. Paris, 1930.

BONAPARTE, N. L. & I. FAVÉ, *Études sur le passé et l'avenir de l'artillerie*. Paris, 1846-71.

BOOTS, J. L., Korean weapons and armour, in *Transaction of the Korea Branch of the Royal Asiatic Society*, vol. 23, part 2 (1934), pp. 1-37.

BORAH, W., America como modelo? El impacto demografico de la expansión Europea sobre el mundo no Europeo, in *Cuadernos Americanos*, 6 (1962), pp. 176-85.

BORGNET, J., Analyse des chartes namuroises qui se trouvent aux archives departementales du Nord à Lille, in *Bulletin de la Commission Royale d'Histoire*, Bruxelles, 1863, series 3, vol 5, pp. 39-222.

BOSMANS, H., Ferdinand Verbiest, Directeur de l'Observatoire de Peking, in *Revue des Questions Scientifiques*, series 3, vol. 21 (1912) pp. 195-271 and pp. 375-464.

BOTERO, G., *Aggiunte fatte alla Ragion di Stato*. Venice, 1659.

BOTERO, G., *Relationi Universali*. Venice, 1659.

BOURNE, E. G., *Spain in America*. New York, 1962.

BOXER, C. R., *Jan Compagnie in Japan*. The Hague, 1936.

BOXER, C. R., *Expediçoēs militares portuguêsas em auxilio dos Mings Contra os Manchus 1621-1647*, Macau, 1940.

BOXER, C. R., *Macau na Epoca da Restauraçao*, Macau, 1942.

BOXER, C. R., *Fidalgos in the Far East 1550-1770. Fact and Fancy in the History of Macao*. The Hague, 1948.

BOXER, C. R. (ed.), *South China in the Sixteenth Century*. London, 1953.

BOXER, C. R., The Portuguese in the East, in *Portugal and Brazil*, ed. by H. V. Livermore. Oxford, 1953.

BOXER, C. R., *The Dutch in Brazil*. Oxford, 1957.

BOXER, C. R., *The Great Ship from Amaçon*. Lisbon, 1959.

BOXER, C. R., *Four Centuries of Portuguese Expansion, 1415-1825: a succinct survey*. Johannesburg, 1961.

BRAUDEL, F., *La Méditerranée et le Monde Méditerranéen à l'époque de Philippe II*. Paris, 1949.

BREEDVELT VAN VEEN F., *Louis de Geer, 1587-1652*. Amsterdam, 1935.

BRIDBURY, A. R., *Economic Growth: England in the Later Middle Ages*. London, 1962.

BRIGGS, J. (ed. & transl.), *History of the rise of the Mahomedan Power in India ... translated from the original Persian of Mahomed Kasim Ferishta*. Calcutta, 1909.

BROWN, D. M., The impact of fire-arms on Japanese warfare 1543-98, *The Far Eastern Quarterly*, 7 (1948), pp. 236-53.

BRUNET, J. B., *Histoire générale de l'artillerie*. Paris, 1842.

BRUSONI, G., *Varie osservazioni sopra le Relazioni Universali di G. Botero*. Venice, 1659.

CABARGA, S. J., *Santander*. Santander, 1956.

CADDEO, R. (ed.), *Le Historie della vita e dei fatti di Cristoforo Colombo per D. Fernando Colombo*. Milan, 1930

CARMAN, W. Y., *A History of Firearms*. New York, 1955.

CARR, R., Two Swedish Financiers: Louis de Geer and Joel Griepenstierna, in *Historical Essays presented to David Ogg* (ed. by H. E. Bell and R. L. Ollard), London, 1963, pp. 18-34.

CARRASCO, A., Apuntes para la historia de la fundicion de la artilleria de bronce, in *Memorial de Artilleria*, series 3, vols. XV & XVI, Madrid, 1887.

CARRASCO, A., Apuntes para la historia de la fabricacion de artilleria y proyectiles de hierro, in *Memorial de Artilleria*, series 3, vol. XIX, Madrid, 1889.

CARUS-WILSON, E., *The Merchant Adventurers of Bristol in the Fifteenth Century*. Bristol, 1962.

CEDERLÖF, O., *Vapenhistorisk Handbok*. Malmö, 1951.

CHANG, T. T., *Sino Portuguese Trade from 1514 to 1644*. Leyden, 1934.

CHEN, G., *Lin Tse-Hsü*. Peiping, 1934.

CHEN, G., *Tseng Kuo-Fan, pioneer promoter of the Steamship in China*. Peiping, 1935.

CHERNOV, A. V., *Vooruzhennye sily Russkogo gosudarstva v XV-XVII vv.*, Moscow, 1954.

CHESNAY, F. R., *Observations on the past and present state of firearms*. London, 1852.

CHIANG, M., *Tides from the West*. New Haven, 1947.

CHINCHERINI, A., *Lo scolare bombardiere ammaestrato*. Venice, 1641.

CHOW WIE, *Chung Kuk Ping Ji Shü Kö*, Peking, 1957.

CHRISTENSEN, A. E., *Dutch Trade to the Baltic about 1600*. Copenhagen-The Hague, 1941.

CHRISTENSEN, A. E., *Industriens historie i Danmark*. Copenhagen, 1943.

CIPOLLA, C. M., The Decline of Italy, in *The Economic History Review*, 5 (1952), pp. 178-87.

CIPOLLA, C. M., Economic Depression of the Renaissance? in *The Economic History Review*, 16 (1964), pp. 519-24.

CLÉMENT, P., (ed.), *Lettres, instructions et mémoires de Colbert*. Paris, 1859-82.

CLOWES, G. S. L., *Sailing Ships, their History and Development*. London, 1932.

COCKS, R., *Diary*, ed. by E. M. Thompson. London, 1883.

COCLE, M. J. D., *A Bibliography of Military Books up to 1642*. London, 1957.

COLENBRANDER, H. T., *Jan Pieterszoon Coen*. The Hague, 1934.

COLLIADO, L., *Platica manual de artilleria*. Milan, 1592.

COLLIS, M., *The Grand Peregrination, being the life and adventures of Fernão Mendes Pinto*, London, 1949.

CONTURIE, P. M. J., *Histoire de la Fonderie Nationale de Ruelle (1750-1940)*. Paris, 1951.

COORNAERT, E., *Les Français et le commerce internationale à Anvers*. Paris, 1961.

CORDEIRO, J. M., *Apontamentos para a Historia da Artilheria Portuguesa*. Lisbon, 1895.

CORTESAO, A., Nautical Science and the Renaissance, in *Archives Internationales d'histoire des Sciences*, 9, (1949), pp. 1075-1092.

COUTINHO, C. V. G., *A nautica dos descobrimentos*. Lisbon, 1951-2.

CRAWFURD, J., *History of the Indian Archipelago*. Edinburgh, 1820.

CRAWFURD, J., *A Descriptive Dictionary of the Indian Islands and Adjacent Countries*. London, 1856.

CUNNINGHAM, W., *The Growth of English Industry and Commerce*. Cambridge, 1919.

DA FONSECA, Q., *A Caravela Portuguesa*. Coimbra, 1934.

DA FONSECA, Q., O problema das caracteristicas dos galeões Portugueses, in *Memorias da Academia das Sciencias de Lisboa,* I, pp. 151-67.

DAHLGREN, E. W., *Louis de Geer*. Uppsala, 1923.

DANIEMEND, I. H., *Izahli Osmanli Tarihi Kronolojisi*, Istanbul, 1947.

DAVIS, R., *The Rise of the English Shipping Industry in the Seventeenth and Eighteenth Centuries*. London, 1962.

DE ARTIÑANO Y DE GALDÁCANO, G., *La arquitectura naval española*. Madrid, 1920.

DE GUIGNES, C. L. J., *Voyages à Peking, Manille et l'Ile de France, faits dans l'intervalle des années 1784 à 1801*. Paris, 1808.

DE JONGE, J. K. J., *De opkomst van het Nederlandsch gezag in Oost-Indië*. The Hague, 1862-95.

DE LAET, J., *Description of India* (edited by J. S. Hoyland and S. N. Banerjee under the title of *The Empire of the Great Mogol*). Bombay, 1928.

DEL MARMOL, E., Notes sur quelques industries namuroises aux XVIIe et XVIIIe siècles d'ápres les registres de la Chambre des Comptes, in *Annales de la Societé Archéologique de Namur* 12 (1872-1873), pp. 33-54 and 245-59.

DE MENDOZA, J. G., *The History of the Great and Mighty Kingdom of China*, ed. by G. T. Staunton. London, 1853.

DE MONTCHRÉTIEN, A., *Traicté de l'oeconomie politique*, ed. by Th. Funck-Brentano, Paris, 1889.

DE RADA, M., Relation of the Things of China, in *South China in the Sixteenth Century*, ed. by C. R. Boxer, London, 1953.

DE RESENDE, G., *Chronica de El-Rei d. João II*. Bibliotheca de Classicos Portuguezes, vol. 32-4. Lisbon, 1902.

DERRY, T. K., WILLIAMS T. I. and ass., *A Short History of Technology*. Oxford, 1960.

DE SAINT-RÉMY, P. S., *Mémoires d'Artillerie*. Paris, 1745.

DE TOTT, F., *Mémoires* (II edition with the strictures of M. De Peyssonnel). London, 1786.

DIKE, K. O., *Trade and Politics in the Niger Delta, 1830-1885*. Oxford, 1956.

DION, R., *Histoire de la vigne et du vin en France des origines au XIXe siècle*. Paris, 1959.

DI VARTHEMA, Ł., *The Travels*, ed. by J. W. Jones and G. P. Badger. London, 1863.

DOORMAN, G. (ed.), *Patents for inventions in the Netherlands*. The Hague, 1942.

DU HALDE, J. B., *The General History of China*. London, 1741.

EGERTON OF TATTON, W., *A description of Indian and Oriental Armour*, London, 1896.

EHRENBERG, R., *Hamburg und England im zeitalter der Königin Elisabeth*. Jena, 1896.

EKEBERG, C. G., *Ostindische Reise in den Jahren 1770 und 1771*, Dresden-Leipzig, 1785.

EKMAN, C., Skeppstyperna under Gustav Vasa och Erik XIV: s tid, in *Sjöhistorisk Årsbok*, 1945-6, pp. 207-28.

ELDRIDGE, F. B., *The Background of Eastern Sea Power*. Melbourne, 1945.

ELIAS, J., *Schetsen uit de Geschiedenis van ons Zeewezen*. The Hague, 1916.

ELSAS, M. J., *Umriss einer Geschichte der Preise und Löhne in Deutschland*. Leiden, 1936-40.

EVRARD, R. & A. DESCY, *Histoire de l'usine des Vennes*. Liège, 1948.

FAIRBANK, J. K., China's response to the West: problems and suggestions, in *Cahiers d'histoire mondiale*, 3 (1956), pp. 381-406.

FAYLE, C. E. (ed.), *Voyages to the Indies of Christopher Fryke and Christopher Schweitzer*. London-Toronto-Melbourne, 1929.

FEI HSIAO-TUNG, *China's Gentry*. Chicago, 1953.

FERNANDEZ DURO, C., *Disquisiciones nauticas*. Madrid, 1876-80.

FFOULKES, CH., *The Gun-Founders of England*. Cambridge, 1937.

FISHER, F. J., Commercial Trends and Policy in Sixteenth-Century England, in *The Economic History Review*, 10 (1940), pp. 95-117.

FOSTER, W., (ed.), *Early Travels in India*. Oxford, 1921.

FRANKEL, S. H., *The Economic Impact on under-developed societies*. Oxford, 1953.

FRIIS, A., Forbindelsen mellen det europaeiske og asiatiske Kobbermarked, *Scandia*, 12 (1939), pp. 151-80.

FUETER, E., *Storia del sistema degli Stati Europei dal 1492 al 1559*. Firenze, 1932.

FULLER, J. F. C., *Armament and History*. New York, 1945.

FUNG YOU-LAN, Why China has no science, in *The International Journal of Ethics*, 32 (1922), pp. 237-63.

GENTILINI, E., *Il perfetto bombardiere*. Venice, 1626. (The first edition was published in Venice in 1592, slightly different in the form, but not in the substance.)

GIBBON, E., *The History of the Decline and Fall of the Roman Empire*. Boston, 1856.

GILLE, B., *Les origines de la grande industrie métallurgique en France*. Paris, 1947.

GILLE, B., Les Développements technologiques en Europe de 1100 à 1400 in *Cahiers d'Histoire Mondiale*, 3, 1956.

GLAMANN, K., The Dutch East India Company's Trade in Japanese Copper, in *The Scandinavian Economic History Review*, 2 (1953), pp. 41-103.

GLAMANN, K., *Dutch-Asiatic Trade 1620-1740*. Copenhagen-The Hague, 1958.

GODINHO, V. M., *A Expansão Quatrocentista Portuguesa*. Lisbon, 1945.

GODINHO, V. M., *Les Grandes Découvertes*. Coimbra, 1953.

GODINHO, V. M., Le repli vénitien et égyptien et la route du Cap, in *Eventail de l'Histoire Vivante—Hommage à Lucien Febvre*. Paris, 1953, vol. 2, pp. 283-300.

GODINHO, V. M., *A economia dos descobrimentos Henriquinos*. Lisbon, 1962.

GOETZ, H., Das Aufkommen der Feuerwaffen in Indien, in *Ostasiatische Zeitschrift*, 12 (1925), pp. 226-9.

GOHLKE, W., Das älteste datierte Gewehr, in *Zeitschrift für Historische Waffenkunde*, 7 (1915-17), pp. 205-6.

GOODRICH, L. C., Note on a few early Chinese Bombards, in *Isis*, 35 (1944), p. 211.

GOODRICH, L. C. & CHIA-SHENG FÊNG, The early development of firearms in China, in *Isis*, 36 (1946), pp. 114-23.

GOODRICH, L. C., *A Short History of the Chinese People*. New York, 1951.

GRANDBERG, O., *Allart van Everdingen och hans " norska "Landskap det gamla Julita och Wurmbrandts Kanoner*. Stockholm, 1902.

GRILL, E., *Jacob de la Gardie, affärsmannen och politikern 1608-1636*. Göteborg, 1949.

GUIARD Y LARRAURI, T., *La industria naval vizcaina*. Bilbao, 1917.

GUGLIELMOTTI, A., *Storia della marina pontificia nel Medio Evo.* Firenze, 1871.

GUICCIARDINI, F., *Storia d'Italia,* ed. by C. Panigada. Bari, 1929.

GUICCIARDINI, F., Relazione di Spagna (1512-13), in *Scritti autobiografici e rari,* ed. by R. Palmarocchi. Bari, 1936.

GUPTA, B. K., *Sirajudaullah and the East India Company 1756-1757. Background to the Foundation of British Power in India.* Leyden, 1962.


HAEBLER, R. G., *Wie unsere Waffen Wurden.* Leipzig, 1940.

HAGEDORN, B., *Die Entwicklung der wichtigsten Schiffstypen bis in 19 Jahrhundert.* Berlin, 1914.

HAHR, G., *Åkers styckebruk.* Stockholm, 1959.

HALE, J., War and public opinion in the fifteenth and sixteenth centuries, in *Past and Present,* 21 (1962), pp. 18-33.

HALL, A. R., *Ballistics in the Seventeenth Century.* Cambridge, 1952.

HAMMER, J., *Geschichte des Osmanischen Reiches.* Pest, 1827.

*Hankuk Haeyang Sa,* (ed. by the Korean Naval Office, Heakun Benbu), Seoul, Danki 4288 (A.D. 1955).

HARDY, E., *Origines de la tactique française.* Paris, 1879-81.

HASSENSTEIN, W., Über die Feuerwaffen in der Seeschlacht von Lepanto, in *Zeitschrift für Historische Waffenund Kostümkunde,* New Series 7 (1940), pp. 1-10.

HECKSCHER, E. F., *Sveriges Ekonomiska Historia.* Stockholm, 1935-49.

HEIJKENSKJÖLD, C., Svensk styckegjutning och lodstöpning av järn under perioden 1540-1840, in *Artilleri Tidskrift,* 64 (1935), pp. 57-79.

HENRARD, P., Documents pour servir à l'histoire de l'artillerie en Belgique. Les fondeurs d'artillerie, in *Annales de l'Academie d'Archeologie de Belgique,* 45 (1889), pp. 237-81.

HILDEBRAND, K. G., *Fagerstabrukens Historia: Sexton-och Sjuttonhundratalen.* Uppsala, 1957.

HIME, H. W. L., Who invented the leather guns, in *Proceedings of the Royal Artillery Institution,* 25 (1898).

HIME, H. W. L., *The Origin of Artillery.* London, 1945.

HO PING-TI, *The ladder of success in Imperial China,* New York, 1964.

HU TSUNG-HSIEN, *Ch'ou hai t'u pien* (preface dated 1624); (Two copies of this work are available at the Asiatic Library, of the University of California, Berkeley).

HUDSON, G. F., *Europe and China*. London, 1961.

HULTBERG, G., Om Åkers styckebruks äldre historia, in *Bidrag till Södermanlands äldre Kulturhistoria,* 27 (1934), pp. 27-42.

HUMMEL, A. V., (ed.), *Eminent Chinese of the Ch'ing Period*. Washington, 1944.

HYMA, A., *The Dutch in the Far East*. Ann Arbour, 1953.


IBN BUHTUR SALIH IBN YAHYA, *Ta'rikh Bairūt*, ed. by P. L. Chiekho, Beyrouth, 1898-1902.

IBN KHALDUN, *Kitab al-ibar wa- Dīwān al Mubtada wal Khabr fī - ayyām al - 'arab*. Cairo, 1867.

IOVIUS, P., *Historia sui temporis*. Paris, 1558.

IRVINE, W., *The Army of the Indian Moghuls*. London, 1903.


JAKOBSSON, T., *Beväpning och Beklädnad* (vol. 2 of *Sveriges Krig 1611-1632*). Stockholm, 1938.

JAKOBSSON, T., En vapenhistorisk dyrgrip i Armémuseum, in *Armémusei vänners meddelande*, 5, Stockholm, 1942.

JAKOBSSON, T., *Artilleriet under Karl XII: s tiden*. Stockholm. 1943.

JANIÇON, F. M., *État présent de la Republique des Provinces-Unies*. The Hague, 1729.

JANSSON, A., *Bergsbruken i det forna Gripsholms län*. Uppsala, 1952.

JANSSON, S. O., *Måttordbok*. Stockholm, 1950.

JAPIKSE, N., *Resolutien der Staten Generaal*. Rijks Geschiedkundige Publicatien, 85, The Hague, 1941.

JENKINS, R., The Rise and Fall of the Sussex Iron Industry, in *Transactions of the Newcomen Society*, 1 (1920), pp. 16-33.

JENKINS, R., *Collected Papers*. Cambridge, 1936.

JOHANNSEN, O., Die Quellen zur Geschichte des Eisengusses im Mittelalter und in der neuren Zeit bis zum Jahre 1530, in *Archiv für die Geschichte der Naturwissenschaften und der Teknik*, 3 (1912), pp. 365-94.

JONES, J. W. & G. P. BADGER (ed.), *The Travels of Ludovico di Varthema*. London, 1863.

JUAN DE LA CONCEPCION, *Historia general de Philipinas*. Manila, 1788-1792.

KAEPPELIN, P., *La Compagnie des Indes Orientales*. Paris, 1908.

KAHLE, P., *Das Turkische Segelandbuch für das Mittelländische Meer vom Jahre 1521*. Berlin und Leipzig, 1926.

KAMMERER, A., La Découverte de la Chine par les Portugais au XVI siècle et la cartographie des portulans, in *T'oung Pao*, suppl. to vol. 39 (1944).

KEBLE CHATTERTON, E., *Ship-models*. London, 1923.

KILBURGER, J. P., Kurzer Unterricht von dem russischen Handel, in *Büschings Magazin für die neuere Historie und Geographie*, 3 (1769), pp. 245-386.

KÖHLER, G., *Die Entwickelung des Kriegswesens und der Kriegsführung in der Ritterzeit*. Breslau, 1887.

KURTS, B. S., *Socinenie Kilburgera O Russkoj torgovle*. Kiev, 1915.


LANE, F. C., *Venetian Ships and Shipbuilders of the Renaissance*. Baltimore, 1934.

LANE, F. C., The economic meaning of the invention of the compass, in *The American Historical Review*, 68 (1963), pp. 605-17.

LAPEYRE, H., *Une famille de Marchands, les Ruiz*. Paris, 1955.

LE COMTE, L., *Empire of China*. London, 1737.

LEE UNSANG, *Lee Chungmu Kong Il Dae Ki Kwangin*, Danki 4279 (A.D. 1946)

LE GENTIL, G., *Fernão Mendes Pinto*, Paris, 1947.

LEJUENE, J., *La formation du capitalisme moderne dans la Principauté de Liège au XVI siècle*. Liège-Paris, 1939.

LEVENSON, J. R., *Confucian China and its Modern Fate*. Berkeley, 1958.

LEWIS, B., *The Arabs in History*. New York, 1960.

LEWIS, M., *The Spanish Armada*. New York, 1960.

LIN YIAN TSOUAN, *Essai sur le P. Du Halde et sa description de la Chine*, Fribourg, 1937.

LINSCHOTEN, VAN, J. H., *Voyage to the East Indies*, ed. by A. C. Burnell and P. A. Tiele. London, 1885.

LOMBA, F. SOYO Y, *Lierganes*. Madrid, 1936.

LOPES DE MENDONÇA, H., *Estudos sobre navios portugueses nos seculos XV e XVI*. Lisbon, 1892.

LOT, F., *L'art militaire et les armées au Moyen Age*. Paris, 1946.

LOT, F., *Recherches sur les effectifs des armées françaises des guerres d'Italie aux guerres de religion*. Paris, 1962.

[174]

LYTH, S. G. E., *The Economy of Scotland in its European setting.* Edinburgh and London, 1960.

MAFFEI, G. P., *Le Historie dell'Indie.* Bergamo, 1749.

MALMBERG, A., *Seklernas Finspång.* Stockholm, 1963.

MANKOV, A. G., *Le mouvement des prix dans l'État Russe du XVI siècle.* Paris, 1957.

MAO YÜAN-I, *Wu-pei-chih,* 1628 (A copy of this work is preserved at the Asian Library of the University of California, Berkeley).

MARDER, A. J., From Jimmu Tenno to Perry: sea power in early Japanese history, in *American Historical Review,* 51 (1945), pp. 1-34.

MARSIGLI, F. L., *l'État militaire de l'Empire Ottoman,* The Hague-Amsterdam, 1732.

MATTINGLY, G., *The Armada.* New York, 1962.

MAURO, F., *Le Portugal et l'Atlantique au XVII siècle 1570-1670.* Paris, 1960.

MAVOR, J., *An Economic History of Russia.* London-Toronto, 1925.

MAYERS, W. F., On the Introduction and use of Gunpowder and Firearms among the Chinese, in *Journal of North China Branch of the Royal Asiatic Society,* (1869-70), pp. 73-104.

MEILINK-ROLLOFSZ, M. A. P., *Asian Trade and European Influence.* The Hague, 1962.

MELIS, F., La situazione della marina mercantile all'inizio dell'età enrichina, in *Actas do Congresso Internacional de Historia dos Descubrimentos,* vol. 5. Lisbon, 1961.

MEYERSSON, Å *Läderkanonen från Tidö.* Stockholm, 1938.

MONTECUCCOLI, R., Aforismi applicati alla guerra possibile col Turco in Ungheria, in *Opere* (ed. by U. Foscolo and G. Grassi). Torino, 1852.

MONTU', C., *Storia della artiglieria italiana.* Rome, 1933.

MORSE, H. B., *The Chronicles of the East India Company Trading to China.* Cambridge, (Mass.), 1926.

MORYSON, F., *Itinerary,* ed. by Ch. Hughes. London, 1903.

MORYSON, F., *An Itinerary.* Glasgow, 1908.

MU, FU SHENG, *The Wilting of the Hundred Flowers.* New York, 1963.

MUNDY, P., *Travels in Europe and Asia,* ed. by R. C. Temple. London, 1907-9.

NADVI, S. A. Z., The use of cannon in Muslim India, in *Islamic Culture* 12 (1938), pp. 405-18.

NANI MOCENIGO, M., *L'arsenale di Venezia*. Venice, 1927.

NEEDHAM, J., *Science and Civilization in China*. Cambridge, 1954-.62

NEEDHAM, J., Poverties and Triumphs of the Chinese Scientific tradition, in A. C. Crombie (ed.), *Scientific Change, Historical Studies in the Intellectual, Social and Technical conditions for Scientific Discovery and Technical Invention*. London, 1963 pp. 117-53.

NEF, J. U., *Industry and Government in France and England*. Ithaca, 1957.

NEF, J. U., *La guerre et le progrès humaine*. Paris, 1950.

NEF, J. U., *The Rise of the British Coal Industry*. London, 1932.

NICOLAS, N. L., *History of the Navy to the French Revolution*, (2 vols.). London, 1847

NIEUHOFF, J., *An Embassy to China*. London, 1669.

NIXON, J. A., Health and Sickness, in C. N. Parkinson, *The Trade Winds*, London, 1948, pp. 121-138.

NYSTRÖM, P., Mercatura Ruthenica, in *Scandia*, 10 (1936), pp. 239-96.


OAKESHOTT, M., *Political Education*. Cambridge, 1951.

ODÉN, B., A Netherland Merchant in Stockholm in the Reign of Erik XIV, in *The Scandinavian Economic History Review*, 10 (1962), pp. 3-37.

OETTINGEN, W., *A Filarete's Tractat über die Baukunst*. Vienna, 1890.

OLECHNOWITZ, K. F., *Der Schiffbau der Hansischen Spätzeit*. Weimar, 1960.

OMAN, CH., *A History of the Art of War in the Middle Ages*. Boston and New York, 1924.

OMAN, CH., *A History of the Art of War in the Sixteenth Century*. New York, 1937.


PAGEL, R., *Die Hanse*. Oldenburg, 1943.

PANIKKAR, K. M., *Asia and Western Dominance*. London, 1961.

PAUMGARTNER, H., *Welthandelsbräuche*, ed. by K. O. Müller. Stuttgart-Berlin, 1934.

PEGOLOTTI, F. BALDUCCI, *La pratica della mercatura*. Ed. A. Evans. Cambridge (Mass.), 1936.

PEHRSSON, P., *De till Sverige invandrade vallonernas religiösa förhållanden*. Uppsala, 1905.

PELLIOT, P., Le Hōja et le Sayyid Husain de l'Histoire des Ming, in *T'oung Pao*, 38 (1948), pp. 81-292.

PENROSE, B., *Travel and Discovery in the Renaissance*. New York, 1962.

PFISTER, L., *Notices Biographiques et Bibliographiques sur les Jésuites de l'ancienne mission de Chine, 1552-1773*. Shanghai, 1932-4.

PHELPS BROWN, E. H. & S. W. HOPKINS, Seven centuries of the prices of consumables compared with builders' wage rates, in *Essays in Economic History* (ed. by M. Carus-Wilson), vol. 2, London, 1962, pp. 179-96.

PIERIS, P. E., *Ceylon*. Colombo, 1913.

PIERIS, P. E. & M. A. FITZLER, *Ceylon and Portugal*. Leipzig, 1927.

PIRENNE, H., *Histoire de la Belgique*. Bruxelles, 1911.

PIRI R'EIS, *Bahrije (Das Türkische Segelhandbuch für das Mitteländische Meer vom Jahre 1521* (ed. and translated by P. Kahle). Berlin-Leipzig, 1926-7.

PORTAL, R., *L'Oural au XVIII siècle*. Paris, 1950.

POSTHUMUS, N. W., *Nederlandsche Prijsgeschiedenis*. Leiden, 1943.

POSTHUMUS, N. W., *Inquiry into the History of Prices in Holland*. Leyden, 1946.


QUARENGHI, C., *Le fonderie di cannoni bresciane ai tempi della Repubblica Veneta*. Brescia, 1870.


RADA, DE M., Relation of the Things of China, in *South China in the Sixteenth Century*, ed. by C. R. Boxer. London, 1953.

RATHGEN, B., Feuer und Fernwaffen des 14 Jahrhunderts in Flandern, in *Zeitschrift für Historische Waffenkunde*, 7 (1915-17), pp. 275-306.

RATHGEN, B., Die Pulverwaffe in Indien, in *Ostasiatische Zeitschrift*, 12 (1925), pp. 11-30 and 196-228.

RATHGEN, B., *Das Geschütz im Mittelalter*. Berlin, 1928.

RAU, V., A Embaixada de Tristão de Mendonça Furtado e os Arquivos Notariais Holandeses, in *Anais de la Academia Portuguesa da História*, ser. 2, vol. 8 (1958), pp. 95-160.

RAYCHAUDHURI, T., *Jan Company in Coromandel 1605-1690*. The Hague, 1962.

RAZIN, E. A., Istoriia voennogo isskusstva, vol. 3: *Voennoe iskusstvo manufaktornogo perioda voiny*, Moscow, 1961.

REY-PASTOR, J., *La Ciencia y la tecnica en el descubriemento de America*. Buenos Aires, 1945.

ROBERTSON, F. L., *The evolution of naval armament*. London, 1921.

ROGERS, J. E., *A History of Agriculture and prices in England*. Oxford, 1866.

ROSENBLAT, A., *La Población indigéna de América desde 1492 hasta la actualidad*. Buenos Aires, 1945.

ROTMISTROV, P. A. (ed), *Istoriia voennogo iskusstva*, vol. 1, Moscow, 1963.

RUDDOCK, A. A., *Italian Merchants and Shipping in Southampton 1270-1600*. Southampton, 1951.

RUSSELL, P. E., *Introduction* to O'Neil, B. H. St.J., *Castles and Cannon*. Oxford, 1960.


SACERDOTI, A., Note sulle galere da mercato veneziane nel sec. XV, in *Bollettino dell'Istituto di Storia della Società e dello Stato Veneziano*, 6 (1962), pp. 80-105.

SANSOM, G., *The Western World and Japan*, London, 1950.

SARTON, G., *Introduction to the History of Science*. Baltimore, 1927-47.

SASSI, F., La politica navale veneziana dopo Lepanto, in *Archivio Veneto*, ser. 5, vols. 38-41 (1946-7), pp. 99-200.

SATOW, E. M., Notes on the intercourse between Japan and Siam in the seventeenth century, in *Transactions of the Asiatic Society of Japan*, 13 (1885), pp. 139-210.

SCHELTEMA, J., *Rusland en de Nederlanden*. Amsterdam, 1817.

SCHICK, L., *Un grand homme d'affaires au debut du XVI siècle, Jacob Fugger*. Paris, 1957.

SCHLEGEL, G., On the invention and use of fire-arms and gun-powder in China prior to the arrival of Europeans, in *T'oung Pao*, series 2, vol. 3 (1902), pp. 1-11.

SCHUBERT, H. R., The first cast iron cannon made in England, in *The Journal of the Iron and Steel Institute*, 146 (1942), p. 131 P. -140 P.

SCHUBERT, H. R., The Northern Extension of the Wealden Iron Industry, in *Journal of the Iron and Steel Institute*, 160 (1948), pp. 245-6.

SCHUBERT, H. R., The superiority of English cast-iron cannon at the close of the sixteenth century, in *Journal of the Iron and Steel Institute*, 161 (1949), pp. 85-6.

SCHUBERT, H. R., *History of the British Iron and Steel Industry*. London, 1957.

SCHULTE, A., *Geschichte der Grossen Ravensburger Handelsgesellschaft, 1380-1530*. Stuttgart-Berlin, 1923.

SCHURZ, W. L., *The Manila Galleon*. New York, 1959.

SCOVILLE, W. C., *The persecution of Huguenots and French Economic Development, 1680-1720*. Berkeley-Los Angeles, 1960.

SCRIVENOR, H., *History of the Iron Trade*. London, 1854.

SEMEDO, A., *Histoire Universelle de la Chine*. Lyon, 1667.

SERJEANT, R. B., *The Portuguese off the South Arabian Coast*. Oxford, 1963.

SERRANO, L., *La Liga de Lepanto entre España, Venecia y la Santa Sede*. Madrid, 1918-20.

SIMPSON, L, B., *The Encomienda in New Spain*. Berkeley, 1950.

SIMPSON, L. B., *Many Mexicos*. Berkeley, 1957.

SINGER, CH. & ass., *A History of Technology*. Oxford, 1957.

SINOR, D., Les relations entre les Mongols et l'Europe jusqu'á la mort d'Arghoun et de Bela IV, in *Cahiers d'histoire mondiale*, 3 (1956), pp. 39-62.

SOMBART, W., Studien zur Entwiklung des modern Kapitalismus, in *Krieg und Kapitalismus*, vol. 2, München und Leipzig, 1913.

SPRANDEL, R., Die Ausbreitung des deutschen, Handwerks im Mittelalterlichen Frankreich, in *Vierteljahrschrift für Sozial und Wirtschaftsgeschichte*, 51, (1964), pp. 66-100.

STAUNTON, G. T., *Miscellaneous notices relating to China and our commercial intercourse with that country*. London, 1882.

STENEBERG, K. E., *Kristinatidens måleri*. Malmö, 1955.

STRAKER, E., *Wealden Iron*. London, 1931.

STRUMILIN, S. G., *Istoriia chernoi metallurgii v SSSR*. Moscow, 1954.

*Svenskt Biografiskt Lexikon*. Stockholm, 1918.

SVENSSON, S. A., *Svenska Flottans Historia*. Malmö, 1942.

SVÄRDSTRÖM, S., Julitatavlan, in *Svenska Kulturbilder* (S. Erixon & S. Walein eds.), vol. 5, Stockholm, 1937, pp. 169-200.

TAVERNIER, J. B., *Travels in India*. Ed. by V. Ball. London, 1889.

TAWNEY, R. H. & E. POWER, (eds.), *Tudor Economic Documents*. London-New York-Toronto, 1953.

TAWNEY, R. H., *Business and Politics under James I.* Cambridge, 1958.

TAYLOR, E. G. R., Camden's England, in *An Historical Geography of England before A.D. 1800*, ed. by H. C. Darby. Cambridge, 1951.

TEIXEIRA, M., Os Bocarros, in *Actas do Congresso International de Historia dos Descobrimentos*, Lisbon 1961, vol. I, pp. 359-86.

TEIXEIRA BOTHELO, J. J., *Novos subsidios para a Historia da Artilheria Portuguesa.* Lisbon, s.d.

TEIXEIRA DA MOTA, A., L'art de naviguer en Méditerranée du XIII au XVII siècle et la création de la navigation astronomique dans les Oceans, in *Le navire et l'économie maritime du Moyen Age au XVIII siècle* (ed. M. Mollat and ass.), Paris, 1958, pp. 127-48.

TEMPLE, R. C., (ed.), *Travels (of P. Mundy) in Europe and Asia.* London, 1907-9.

TENENTI, A., *Venezia e i corsari.* Bari, 1961.

TENENTI, A., *Cristoforo da Canal. La Marine Vénitienne avant Lépante.* Paris, 1962.

TENG SSÜ-YU & J. K. FAIRBANKS, *China's Response to the West* Cambridge, (Mass.), 1961.

TENNENT, J. E., *Ceylon.* London, 1860.

THOMAS, P. J., *Mercantilism and the East India Trade.* London, 1963.

TOSI, C., *Dell'India Orientale.* Rome, 1669.

TOUT, T. F., Firearms in England in the fourteenth century, in *The English Historical Review*, 26 (1911), pp. 666-702.

TOWNSEND, M. E., *European colonial expansion since 1871.* Chicago, 1941.

TOYNBEE, A., *Civilization on Trial and The World and the West.* Cleveland-New York, 1962.

TRIGAULT, M., *China in the Sixteenth Century, the Journals of Matthew Ricci*, (ed. L. J., Gallagher). New York, 1953.

TRIP, H. J., *De Familie Trip.* Groningen, 1883.

TUCCI, U., Sur la pratique vénitienne de la navigation au XVI siècle, in *Annales: Economies, Societés, Civilisations*, 13 (1958), pp. 72-86.

UNDERWOOD, H. H., Korean boats and ships, in *Transactions of the Korea Branch of the Royal Asiatic Society*, 23, part. 1 (1934) pp. 1-99.

UNGER, W. S., *Bronnen tot de Geschiedenis van Middelburg*. Rijsk Geschiedekundige Publicatien, The Hague, 1931.

URLANIS, T. S. *Rost naselenija v Evropi: opyt ischisleniya*. Moscow, 1941.

USHER, A. P., Spanish ships and shipping in the sixteenth and seventeenth century, in *Facts and Factors in Economic History, presented to E. F. Gay*. Cambridge, (Mass.), 1932, pp. 189-213.

VAN DER WEE, H., *The Growth of the Antwerp Market and the European Economy*. The Hague, 1963.

VAN DILLEN, J. G. (ed.), *Bronnen tot de Geschiedenis van het Bedrijsleven en het Gildewezen van Amsterdam*. Rijsk Geschiedkundige Publicatien, *n.*69, The Hague, 1929; *n.* 78, The Hague, 1933.

VAN HOUTTE, J. A., Anvers aux XI et XVI siècle. Expansion et Apogée, in *Annales: Economies, Societés, Civilisations*, 16, (1961) pp. 248-78.

VAN KAMPEN, S. C., *De Rotterdamse particuliere Scheepsbouw in de tijd van de Republiek*. Assen, 1953.

VARTHEMA, L., See di Varthema.

VÄTH, A., *Johann Adam Schall von Bell S.J., Missionar in China*. Cologne 1933.

VIGON, J., *Historia de la Artilleria Española*. Madrid, 1947.

VINCENZO MARIA DI SANTA CATERINA, *Il viaggio all' India Orientale*. Venice, 1678.

VITERBO, F., *Fundidores de Artilharia*, Lisbon, 1901.

VOGEL, W., Zur Grosse der Europäischen Handelsflotten im 15, 16 und 17 Jahrhundert, in *Festschrift Dietrich Schäfer*, Jena, 1915, pp. 268-334.

WALTERS, H. B., *Church Bells of England*. London, 1917.

WANG LING, On the invention and use of gunpowder and firearms in China, in *Isis*, 37 (1947), pp. 160-78.

WEBER, H., *La Compagnie Française des Indes*. Paris, 1904.

WERTIME, TH., *The Coming of the Age of Steel*. Leiden, 1961.

WHITE, L., *Medieval Technology and Social Change*. Oxford, 1962.

WHITEWAY, R. S., *The Rise of Portuguese Power in India*. Westminster, 1899.

WIBERG, K. F., Louis de Geer et la colonisation Wallonne en Suede, in *Bulletin de l'Institut d'Archéologie Liégeois*, 12 (1876).

WILSON, C. R., *The early annals of the English in Bengal*, Calcutta, 1895-1900.

WOLFF, PH., *Commerce et marchands de Toulouse*. Paris, 1954.

WOLONTIS, J., *Kopparmyntningen i Sverige 1624-1714*. Helsingfors, 1936.

WORCESTER, G. R., *The Junks and Sampans of the Yangtze; a study in Chinese Nautical Research*, Shanghai, 1947-8.

WRIGHT, TH., & J. O. HALLIWELL (eds.), *Reliquiae Antiquae*. London 1843.


YERNAUX, J., Les von Trier, fondeurs de cloches et d'artillerie à Liége au XVIe siècle, *Chronique Archéologique du Pays de Liége*, 1937, pp. 6-13.

YERNAUX, J., *La métallurgie Liégeoise*. Liége, 1939.

YU SUNG-YONG, *Su-A-mun Jip*, Seoul, Danki 4291 (A.D. 1958).

# INDEX

Luzon Islands, 133 *n*.
Lyon, 26, 27 *n*.
Lyonnais, iron manufactures in, 69

Macao, 32 *n*., 89 *n*., 114, 115, 119, 124, 139, 159
Madagascar, 142 *n*.
Maestricht, 49
"Mahometta," Turkish gun, 94, 98
Malabar, 114
Malacca, 105 *n*., 107, 132
Male, Louis de, Flemish commander, 75
Malines, Spanish gun foundry at, 30, 34 *n*., 38, 47
Malta, Knights of, 79, 80 *n*., 102
Mamluke, 90, 91, 92, 93, 103, 130
Manchester, 146
Mankov, A. G., *quoted*, 155
Manoel I, King of Portugal, 31 *n*., 132, 135
Marathas, 140, 146
Marienburg, 30
Mariotte, Jean, iron manufacturer at Liége, 59, 158, 159
Marsberg (Westphalia), Dutch iron works at, 50, 59
Marseilles, 79 *n*.
Marselis, Gabriel, gun merchant, 158
Marselis, Peter, gun merchant, 59 *n*.
Mathew, Edmund, ordnance manufacturer, 46
Maximilian, Emperor, 25 *n*., 26, 38 *n*., 82
Mazarin, Cardinal Giulio, French statesman, 67
Medina del Campo, Spanish gun foundry at, 33
Medina Sidonia (Alonso Perez de Cuzman), Duke of, 85 *n*.
Mei-Weng Tin, Chinese scholar official, *quoted*, 119 *n*.
Metz, early use of cannon at, 22 *n*.
Mexico, 27 *n*., 133 *n*., 142

Milan, 29, 30, 112
Millimete manuscript, 21
Minamoto Iyeyosu, Japanese lord, 110 *n*.
Mir Hussain, Egyptian admiral, 101
Moghuls, 128, 129 *n*., 140
Mohammed II, Sultan of Turkey, 93, 94, 96 *n*, 98
Mohammed IV, King of Granada, 90
Mongols, 16, 105 *n*., 119
Moniot, Guillaume, gun manufacturer, 50 *n*.
Mons, 30
"Mons Meg," English gun, 22-23
Montecuccoli, Raimondo, Imperial general, *quoted*, 98-99
Mookurrib Khan, 105
Moors, 80 *n*., 87 *n*., 90, 103
Moryson, Fynes, English traveller, *quoted*, 49-50, 87 *n*.
Moslems, *see* Turks
Mu Fu-Sheng, Chinese writer, *quoted*, 120
Mundy, Peter, English traveller, 87 *n*., 111 *n*.
Muscat, 102

Nagasaki, Dutch factory at, 112
Namur, 30, 50 *n*.
Naples, 30, 79 *n*.
Narva, 56 *n*.
Nåvekvarn, Swedish gun factory at, 72 *n*., 154
navigation, difference between Atlantic (Northern) and Mediterranean, 76-81, 84-85, 136-137
Nef, J. U., *quoted*, 151
Negroponte, The, 17, 140, 162
Nelson, Horatio, Earl, British admiral, 77
Newbridge, iron works at, 39
Newton, Sir Isaac, English astronomer, 146
Ning-yuän, defence of, 121
Nieuhoff, Johannes, Dutch traveller, *quoted*, 118 *n*.